DEAREST JANE . . .

DEAREST JANE . . .

Jane Torday and Roger Mortimer

Constable • London

Constable & Robinson Ltd
55–56 Russell Square
London WC1B 4HP
www.constablerobinson.com

First published in the UK by Constable,
an imprint of Constable & Robinson, 2014

ISBN 978-1-47210-591-2 (hardback)
ISBN 978-1-47210-593-6 (ebook)

1 3 5 7 9 10 8 6 4 2

Printed and bound by CPI Group (UK) Ltd, Croydon, CR0 4YY

For Tommy, with my love

CONTENTS

CONTENTS

Thanks and Acknowledgements

So many thanks are due – not least for the interest, support and encouragement of wonderful friends. Thanks go to those loyal members of my family and step-family for their demonstrations of kindness and understanding. Foremost among them is my son Piers who, as a writer himself, has given me editorial guidance, encouragement, creative suggestions and crucial criticism, always delivered with tact, humour, patience and kindness. Alongside him, the further uplifting cheer of Piers's partner, Will. Warm hospitality and recreation has been provided by my kind son and daughter-in-law, Nick and Clare, on my regular visits to them in Somerset. The love, fun and frolics of my three small grandchildren are the best of tonics.

I must applaud my brother Lupin for launching what has turned out to be a roller coaster of amusement – our father's letters. My thanks to Andreas Campomar at Constable & Robinson for appreciating the potential of the Roger Mortimer letters and publishing them. Perceptive and helpful editing measures have been provided by Charlotte Macdonald and

Howard Watson. From the beginning, my agent and long-time friend, Andrew Hewson of Johnson and Alcock, has steered me along and kept me steady with his wisdom, experience and abiding good humour. That Andrew's predecessor, John Johnson, was my father's literary agent has added further meaning and pleasure to our connection.

My husband, Tommy Bates – whose family's involvement in racing dates back for nearly a century – was a dedicated fan of my father's racing writing long before we met. For his love and his tolerance of my long hours incarcerated in my study, and for his faith in this book, I dedicate it to him.

Jane Torday

Introduction

My Dear Child,
Please temper your hilarity with a modicum of decorum.

Roger Mortimer

My father, Roger Mortimer, was a compulsive correspondent. He wrote to me often – 450 letters plus postcards and notes, yet I was only one of the many recipients of letters from a journalist and writer fully occupied in making a living. In 2008, I advanced on the job of archiving this great store of letters – secreted away for years in drawers, boxes and bags, they surfaced in no particular order. As I reread them for the first time since I had received them back in the last century, I speculated on how I could compile them into an entertaining book for others. I crept gently along with my project, in fits and starts, never losing sight of it but not having it in full view, either.

As readers, our responses to any story will change in the way that we ourselves do, as the years roll by. My reactions to my father's letters as they arrived when I was a girl, young woman and then approaching middle age, were entirely different to the overview I have now, from rereading them through the filter of being a parent and grandmother – and step-parent/grandmother. To this must be added the powerful impact of digesting the letters in such a concentrated form, en masse. I found myself forming a new relationship, a different understanding, with my late father – on paper.

In the background was my brother Lupin, champing at the bit to tell his own story of my father. We had already agreed to disagree on how we would present our letters from this great comic figure who happened to be our father. We were, however, unanimous in our belief that our father's extraordinary letters to his children deserved to be shared with a wider readership. I did not plan to reproduce my personal letters hook, line and stinker. In common with my father, biography and history fascinate me so it was a more rounded memoir that I had in mind, based on some sterling extracts from his letters.

Time was not on my side. Although I have been writing, one small way or another, all my life, I needed help to get me going in this case. I found it on a week's Creative Non Fiction course with the Arvon Foundation in Devon.

I was happily knuckling down to my task when, suddenly, a streak of greased lightening whizzed past – it was my brother Lupin. His book, entitled *Dear Lupin . . . Letters to a Wayward Son*, was already on the stocks with this noble publisher. Holding on to the pillion behind him was sister Lumpy with her folio of letters, *Dear Lumpy . . . Letters to a Disobedient Daughter*. It was definitely time to oil my own skates.

The result is a book which by its very nature led me back into the past, compelling me to consider the best and the worst of my family life. While I have been working away in my little study at home, I have frequently laughed out loud at my father's irresistible humour. At other times, I have felt anger and sadness – and sympathy. Roger's letters glide seamlessly through an astonishing diversity of topics, reflecting his many moods from brightest to gloomiest, always with his characteristic sense of comedy – and wisdom. Honesty, courage, loyalty and a strong work ethic were qualities which informed all my father's actions. In print, his sagacity was embedded in the originality and wicked wit of his observations on members of his cast – from our cat to the prime minister – tempered by his affection for recipients of his vintage epistles.

My father's written material is sufficiently rich and varied for me to be able to identify and serve up, with confidence, some of the most tempting dishes from his long menu. If you have already enjoyed my father's comic voice through his letters, and become curious to know more about him, his wife Nidnod and their children, Lupin, Lumpy and their bossy elder sister, this book is for you. Should it be your first meeting with the Mortimer family, I wish you a most merry ride.

Jane Torday

1

Invading the Study

There is something v. nice about pigs. 'As snug as a pig in pease-straw', 'pigs in clover', 'lucky little sucking pig', 'on the pigs back', 'a regular porky boy', 'Little Pigs sleep in the sweetest of straw' etc., etc. I think I'll buy one of those mobile homes called 'Porky's cabin'.

RM

The old roll-top desk at which my father worked was never shut. Its wooden slatted top was firmly wedged back in its casing. It was a man's desk and beware the woman with the temerity to polish it. On this account my father had few worries as far as my mother was concerned; I can't recall seeing her with a duster in her hand. For our daily helps, the desk was forbidden territory.

But my father had reckoned without his elder daughter. Full of insatiable curiosity, like Rudyard Kipling's Elephant's Child, time sometimes hung heavy on my hands as a little girl. 'Use your initiative!' was a frequent suggestion. So I did – tidying, cleaning, polishing and rearranging rooms, sheds, stables, lofts and outbuildings where these activities were apparently neglected. Part of the pleasure was unearthing treasures and secrets. These were not the diversions my elders and betters had in mind. Like the Elephant's Child I was sometimes spanked for my pains.

Should I appear in the study on some pretext when my father was working, I was dispatched with 'Make a noise like a bee and buzz off' or 'Make a noise like a hoop and roll away'. The study, always an upstairs room, was his sanctuary – though not a silent one. The landing echoed to the repetitive clatter of typewriter keys as my father vigorously tapped out his thoughts for books, articles and letters. His typewriter was perched, somehow securely, on an unstable leather inlaid panel with a hinge missing at the centre of the roll-top desk.

My father and his typewriter were so inseparable a team that it sometimes seemed as if this machine might be one of his limbs, like an arm or a leg. Black, metallic, inky and cumbersome, his first typewriter was, I think, a Remington. I was still of tender age when he discarded this magic monster and handed it over to me as he settled down with his new model, an Olivetti. I was overjoyed with the sudden power this machine bestowed upon me. By tapping one small finger over those lettered keys I could produce PRINTED words on paper.

In each of our family homes, my father's study was arranged identically: the desk positioned alongside a window framed by curtains invariably featuring the colour maroon. Extending from a wall would be a single bed, for his study also served as his bedroom. When weary, he had no hesitation in lying down with a book and drifting off into 'a good zizz'. He might announce, 'I'm off to my zimmer for a bit of Egyptian PT on my bracket [bed]', or sigh as he mounted the stairs, 'I'm off to let demon doss embrace me in his hairy arms.'

'The Miller's House
[1980s]

My bed here is only just preferable to a Bengali fakir's bed of nails and I intend to jump on it to alter the contours. Because of the lumps and chasms, I have been a bit short of Egyptian PT. It's odd how elderly individuals, who cannot be all that far off death, fuss about insomnia. After all they are going to get plenty of the other thing before long.'

His study shelves were packed with bloodstock catalogues and racing reference books. A bedside table would support a radio and lamp, around which novels, biographies and works in progress would be piled at random, nearly concealing ring marks from uncountable sticky coffee mugs which had rested on its surface. Sporting and military prints hung on the walls and among the framed black-and-white photographs was one of Roger on horseback, soaring over a fence at a 1930s point-to-point. We could never believe it was him.

Animal mascots being a big thing in our family, a special position was reserved in the study for the most successful present I ever chose for my father. I had purchased it in the early 1960s with my pocket money francs in Mortain, a little provincial town in France. 'Droopy' was a small, squidgy rubber dog with a lugubrious expression.

'The Miller's House
1 June 1990

Life has not been all crumpets and honey but I look back on some happy days at the seaside, particularly when we

shared out the loot on the final day. Shopping at Mortain and St Lo!
Best Love
xx D'

My father and my mother, Cynthia, shared a personal emblem in the shape of a pig – should my parents have been honoured with a coat of arms, two prancing pigs, arm in arm, would have fitted the bill.

A gingham fabric pig hung behind my father's bed, an easier expression of his love for my mother than her conjugal presence. Their silver wedding in 1972 was celebrated by a little pair of silver pigs who sat on the sitting-room mantelpiece. Marriages have been based on stranger pleasures. One birthday, my father was given a huge notepad of pink pig-shaped paper – he slid its pages into the typewriter to bang out letters to his children, economically using both sides. Letters on his porcine paper did not necessarily grunt with good cheer: the growls of a grizzly bear were as likely.

At the beginning of each school holidays, the study assumed a dark, Dickensian demeanour, when we were summoned there individually to apply our attention to paternal admonishments. Gravely, school report in hand, the catalogue of criticisms would be recited. Our father reminded us, rightly, of the 'hard-earned cash' with which he parted for our benefit. Soberly, we left the room promising to do better, our heads bowed. The holidays would pass and, all too often, good resolutions would pass with them.

Over time, a writer's room can emanate a very particular atmosphere, reflecting the essence of its occupant. Orderly and meticulous with his paperwork, my father made regular clearances of documents and memorabilia, and discarded incoming correspondence – including all his children's letters.

He was proud of his claim that all letters from the breakfast delivery would be answered by the midday postal collection.

'Budds Farm
[1973]

I have been going through old family papers, destroying much. Would you like this cutting from *The Times*? The next time I get a mention in that publication will be when I appear in the 'Death' column. Unless I forget myself one day and you see a paragraph headed "Well-known journalist faces serious charge. Alleged incident in Reading Cinema."'

A decade later, he wrote, 'As you are the keeper of the family archives and mementoes, I enclose some odds and ends. I have been tearing up and burning things all morning.' Fortunately, his folder of wartime letters was not destined for the incinerator. He entrusted it to me five years prior to his death. 'You can do what you like with these after I've gone,' he instructed.

When my father's final hour came, his roll-top desk was found nearly empty bar the odd paper clip in a dusty cubby hole. But his typewriter – by then electric – still held a few paragraphs of a half completed racing article between its rollers. He was eighty-two years old.

There is no record of what his correspondents had to say to him – their letters were long ago crumpled into wastepaper baskets – but we know a good deal of how he responded. How astonished he would be now to know that the litany of thoughts, gossip, jokes, chastisements, advice and love that he had dispensed to his children in the last century would have a second life in the twenty-first century.

Less surprisingly, the real, living presence of such a characterful, entertaining father etched as many memories on the heart as he endowed on paper. My father's impromptu performance of the dying swan from *Swan Lake*, as he twirled his fifty-year-old self lightly but with tragic demeanour around the drawing room of our childhood home, was an unforgettable tour de force. I ended up as a heap of uncontrollable laughter on the floor whereas my father, throughout his silent, solo dance, retained his decorum, making it all the funnier.

Earnestness was anathema to my father, but instinctive though his humorous response was to any circumstance, there was a real depth of feeling and sensitivity at the core of his nature. There were emotions to be dealt with, values to be adhered to and a code of conduct to be respected, as his letters – never heavy no matter what the content – increasingly revealed as both he and I grew older.

As an impressionable child, there was one occasion which shines out for me as the seminal moment when first I became aware of the profounder aspects of my father and how history had shaped the man he had become – as you will discover.

2

A Beach for Heroes

One late summer's day in 1960, on a family holiday in France, my father decided that we should make an expedition to a big beach that was of particular interest to him. On arrival, my parents, brother, sister and I, aged ten, carried our beach bags down from the car and selected a nice picnic spot for ourselves. The beach was enormous, stretching out from east to west on either side of us. In front of us, as far as the eye could see, curled and frothed a deep band of sea, the English Channel.

My mother and I were soon in our bathing suits and as we set off towards the sea, my father quipped, 'Buzzing Bee and Fiddling Flea went down to the sea to bathe.' His version of 'Adam and Eve and Pinch-me went down to the sea to bathe, Adam and Eve were drowned, but who do you think was saved?' Buzzing Bee, generally abbreviated to 'The Buzzer', was my mother's nickname at the time – one of many bestowed upon her. Fiddling Flea was my nickname, mercifully only on the beach.

Everyone was hungry after our swim and once we were dry and dressed, the picnic hamper was opened and hunks of crusty baguette were shared out, along with butter, pâté, slices of *saucisson*, sardines, Camembert and peaches – all fresh, French and quite delicious. I had little inclination to run around and play games halfway through lunch, unlike my younger brother and sister. Food interested me much more. My mother had promised to explore the beach with the younger ones if they would sit still and eat lunch, and as soon as the picnic had been devoured the three of them set off together.

My father and I remained at our little encampment near the sand dunes. Between us on the rumpled tartan rug was the empty picnic hamper. My father looked at me. 'Well, little Jane,' he said. 'Do you realise that we are in a very remarkable place?'

I cast my gaze around and saw that the beach was not merely an expanse of sand that stretched into infinity but that if you looked to left or right, it was punctuated by curious, irregular shapes. 'Not so very long ago, this was possibly one of the most important beaches in the whole of France,' continued my father.

This was intriguing information. My father always enjoyed sharing his knowledge and this was clearly a prelude to further facts concerning the beach. Whatever it was, it wouldn't be boring. He did not bother to say things unless they made you think or laugh. Preferably both. I looked at him expectantly as he lay there on his side, propped on one elbow, his long legs crossed over. This was a habitual position for my father on a beach, one which he found comfortable for reading, his preferred activity. Above his faded aertex shirt, a jaunty red and white spotted kerchief round his neck blew gently in the sea breeze. Unusually, on this occasion he seemed to have neither book nor newspaper to hand.

'How long do you think this beach is?' he asked, before answering the question himself. 'Five miles long – which is one of the factors which made it ideal as a beach for an invading force to land on. It is why it became one of what are known as the Normandy Landing beaches.' Not wishing to appear dim, always a concern in conversations with my father, I responded cautiously to this information.

'It's probably impossible to imagine now but this beach – Omaha beach it is called – was where, on a bloody awful day in June 1944, in appalling weather, American forces landed to launch the last big push against Hitler. If they teach you anything at school, you will come to learn that this was the D-Day invasion of France. It was a gigantic undertaking. Of course, our own troops played a major role, staging their invasion on other landing beaches here in Normandy. If D-Day had not succeeded, things would have turned out very differently for all of us,' he pronounced with grim satisfaction.

Amazed, I sat in silent wonder. My father, on the other hand, was warming to his theme and starting to expand upon it. As he spoke, I gradually began to take in the surrounding scene from a different perspective. It was not just a beach for gentle holiday pastimes. If you looked hard enough, remnants of the multiple rows of defences installed by the Germans were still in place, now softened and veiled by the shifting sands. As the child I was, it was not an easy thing to envisage that only sixteen years earlier, this beautiful beach had been a bloody and brutal battleground, the site of one of the most dramatic chapters of our recent history. Now, people in bright and cheerful colours seemed to be enjoying their holiday pursuits all around us; there were no bombs exploding, no tanks weighing through the sands, no guns firing; there were no soldiers fighting for their lives, encumbered by battledress sodden by the sea from which they had waded on to the beach; there were no moans and cries from wounded or dying men.

My father's emotional and eloquent description of D-Day was gathering pace, weighted with a history that could not lightly be dismissed. With his keen sense of the meaning of place and of the past, I could start to grasp why this Omaha

Beach might move him to memories of the world war in which, after all, he had played his own part.

In 1939 my father was a regular, professional soldier. He had been in the Army since leaving school – a classic progression of Eton, Sandhurst and the Coldstream Guards. At the outbreak of war, he was Captain Roger Mortimer, thirty years old. As I listened to him describing the military action in Normandy, following D-Day, it became clear that he had not played a part in this crucial allied invasion or in the subsequent Battle of Normandy. I inevitably started to wonder where he had been in the war, which battles he might have fought in. Now full of curiosity, this question rapidly became pressing. I may even have asked that classic question: 'What did you do in the war, Daddy?' However I phrased it, the answer I received was comprehensive and devastating.

My father spoke gravely: 'I had the misfortune, possibly the ineptitude even, to be wounded in action in Belgium in May 1940. I was knocked out and when I came round, I found I had been taken prisoner by the Germans.'

I can remember the sound of the sea resonating with my father's voice as he unfolded too much his personal story from his capture in 1940 until his liberation in 1945 – how he spent five whole years in prison. To him, it had been a seemingly interminable period of time. To me, it was unimaginable – nearly half my own lifetime at that point.

His revelation had a powerful impact on me. This was my father's own real story which started before the one I knew, the one in which he had met, fallen in love and married my mother, become a writer, had children, bought a house in the country, made a garden, enjoyed friends and told jokes.

It was an awakening for me in my little, self-absorbed world. I had never felt true hunger, serious cold, discomfort or fear. My life was just about perfect. I would never complain again.

As he talked, I would chance a question when I could, anxious not to break the spell and bring my father back to the present, when he might get up, shake himself down and make his customary parting shot – 'Well, there we are, my dear child' – before wandering off to find the rest of the family. Warmed by a new and intensely loving admiration for my father, it struck me that he too was someone's child, the only son of his parents. What worry they must have endured in the war, fearing that they might never see him again.

'What was it like when you came home again?' I ventured.

Frowning, my father said, 'Well, it was all very difficult.'

I had already conjured up a heart-warming picture of his homecoming, scenes of the welcome and joy which would embrace the long absent and exhausted son, who though over six foot had weighed well under eight stone on his return. How thrilled my grandparents must have been to have him home again.

'I'm afraid being thrilled to see me wasn't really my mother's style. Rather the reverse, in fact. I was made to feel like a major inconvenience because I had not given her enough advance warning of my arrival and it put the servants out. Food was rationed and there was something about shortages of soap!'

I was incredulous.

'There was not all that much pleasure in being at home. I was fond of my father and we got on well. He spent the greater part of his leisure hours at his club or on the golf course.'

He added, 'I can remember in one of the worst winters of the war, getting letters in prison from my mother full of emotion about one of her pet poodles being ill. There we were, prisoners – hungry, cold, with very few parcels of provisions getting through at that point – with no knowledge of what the future held.' A silence fell upon us both.

As the air grew cooler and the tide pulled out into the further distance, my father's memories were still in full flow. How proud I felt of his endurance – and yet how angry and how sad. Where had people found the strength and courage to stand up to Hitler's tyranny? I knew that people called out to God in terrible circumstances, that praying to him might help. I also knew that my father was not remotely religious. Perhaps in wartime though, God might have had a meaning for my father?

'No,' he laughed, without amusement. 'God was not important to me, neither then nor now. What mattered most of all in prison was comradeship – the friendships with your fellow prisoners. That is what saw me through.' Finally, he smiled.

The hurly-burly of family life soon resumed its usual patten and we were happy enough to see my mother, brother and little sister reappear, damp, sandy and a little weary. The sun had gone in and the Mortimer family gathered up their things and set off to the car.

But I ended my day looking at the world rather differently from how I had seen it on arrival at Omaha Beach. In the years to come, I would sometimes think back to that afternoon, recapturing the scene in my mind, sitting with my father and listening to his dear, familiar voice, his turns of phrase. As a child I often infuriated my father and as a teenager I concerned him constantly, but that afternoon we had initiated a quality of communication together, father and daughter, that would often renew itself as I grew up.

That father of mine went on to teach me a great deal more about life in all its aspects over the coming thirty years, often through his letters. In that autumn of my eleventh year, I was sent off to boarding school. From that moment, and for the rest of his life, my father wrote to me regularly – some 450 letters, unique and extraordinary in content, fizzing with his bon mots.

Before Roger became a parent at thirty-nine, he had already lived nearly half his life and had the experiences which shaped the man he became: Roger the racing writer; Roger the husband; Roger the father; Roger the friend. And throughout, Roger the wit.

Let's go back now and meet the young, bachelor Roger as a soldier abroad – latterly as a prisoner of war. From the late 1930s, my father's letters home to his own parents and others illuminate this key period of his story.

In July 1937, Roger was a twenty-seven year-old officer in the Coldstream Guards, embarking on his first overseas assignment.

He set sail in 'a small white vessel' of the British India Line. In his earliest existing letter home, he describes the ship passing smoothly through the Bay of Biscay, a beautiful dawn as they sailed into Gibraltar and how, in Malta, he was captivated by the island and its people. His final destination was Alexandria in Egypt.

His battalion had been dispatched to the Middle East on a peace mission to curb and contain the civil unrest and terrorism, rife in what was then the British Mandate of Palestine. At the core of the conflict was the resentment and anger of resident Arabs at the waves of Jewish immigrants arriving as they fled persecution in Europe.

Roger was English by birth and in taste and habit. Committed to the life of a professional soldier – a career initiated by his father who regarded him as a somewhat shambolic character who could only benefit from military discipline – Roger did not have the instincts or outlook of an adventurer. He responded with great pleasure to the charms of civilized watering holes in Europe, but ultimately he was at his happiest and most at ease in his own country. I will not say 'at home' as that was a place of only intermittent enjoyment for him, controlled as it was by a mother for whom warmth meant something generated from a heater.

His letters home from this period introduce us to some of the qualities that Roger later distilled into his epistles to his children. Restless and bored in the company of anyone who took themselves too seriously, he yawns at the tedium he is subject to: the Royal Egyptian Yacht club, dreary guests at formal social occasions, pompous and inefficient Army officers, aggressive nationalists, political fanatics . . . dictators. All could be laughed at – along with himself – sometimes lightly, at other times with a sharp twist of the lemon.

Roger's easy capacity for friendship was always coupled with a need for regular retreat into solitude. Company was all well and good, but he relished quiet periods in which to read, reflect and enjoy his own thoughts. Sometimes, though, it is not the solace of solitude but loneliness which percolates through those letters. There is no mention of a girlfriend, significant or otherwise. Maybe he just chose not to permit any girls to dance across the pages of letters to his parents.

Roger was not constrained by the stiff upper lip of his generation. He was not inhibited in expressing his feelings about unpleasant, uncomfortable or fearful experiences; and the period he served in Egypt and Palestine provided its share of them. Finding himself in a region of terrorist attacks, bombs, shoot-outs, assassinations and road ambushes, there was more than a chance that Roger might not have survived to tell these tales. Addressing the downside of things, sympathetically, mischievously or caustically, added further spice to his letters to his mother, father and other relations.

Alexandria
Winter 1937

The weather here is perfect – very hot and sunny with a pleasant sea breeze and not too cool at night either. I have left off my vests and never wear a waistcoat before dusk.

The chief trouble is the mass attack by flies and bugs; every Wednesday is a day set apart for de-bugging every conceivable article of furniture and apparel and even so they continue to thrive.

At present Alexandria is rather like Le Touquet in mid-winter – all the amusing places closed till the spring – but the locals are very hospitable and entertain a good deal. Never have I seen people drink more; apparently the climate is suitable for soaking and you can certainly put down a packet here without any ill-effect.

Would you like some Jaffa oranges? Do let me know and I'll send you some after the Christmas rush. I've sent off some Turkish Delight but God knows if it will ever get there, they're so hopelessly inefficient here.

Social and recreational life in Alexandria occupied the time whilst awaiting orders, as Roger told his father, Pop, in a number of letters:

We've been pretty tense and anxious lately but on the whole life is quite enjoyable. I sail most afternoons in the harbour, being a very nautical and seamanlike member of the Royal Egyptian Yacht Club – extremely smart and exclusive (I don't think). We usually go out in a boat which holds four or five people (it's called a 'Fairy' I believe) and cruise round the harbour watching the boats come in and out and meeting the Imperial Airways Seaplanes. It's usually rather rough outside the harbour so I find I enjoy myself more if I exercise a certain discretion and refrain from committing myself to the mercy of the waves and my own very limited nautical abilities. There are races in the harbour three days a week and although I sometimes take an extremely minor part as portion of the crew in these events, I find them rather a strain owing to the intense seriousness with which they are taken by the local yachtsmen.

My social outings have been severely limited – I'm afraid I'm not a popular success with the local 'gens chics'. However, I toiled off to a very stiff lunch party the other day (invitation card 6" × 4") and paid for my temerity by undergoing a three-hour ordeal sandwiched between two of the dreariest bores I've ever met. One of them would lean across to talk to me and perspired most liberally on to my plate. I nearly covered my food with my handkerchief whenever I thought he was going to address me.

Best love,
Roger

I went up to Cairo this week to do some work there; it's far worse than here, very much hotter and terribly dry and dusty. The Nile has reached a record height and people are beginning to get nervous of a flood. This is really an extraordinary country: even at the main bookstall at Cairo Central Station it is quite impossible to buy anything but literature of a highly pornographic description!

Best love,
Roger

I'm just off to motor down to Moascar (military garrison) about two hundred and twenty miles away in the desert. I'm not taking the Vauxhall as I know it would never make it on the ghastly roads out here, and it is far too valuable to me for running about town. I leave at midday in an Austin 7 (military) and drive from the Canal road to the Pyramids (about 120 miles) and I'll spend the night out there in the open. The next day, I leave the road and drive cross country over the desert, my only guide being a compass whose accuracy has been more than questionable since a cow stood on it at Sandhurst! I expect the last 100 miles will have to be done at about 10 mph and I shall be lucky if I don't stick in the soft sand. The country is hideous the whole way except for occasional bursts of wild flowers.

I went for a picnic with some pretty tiresome girls at Aboukir Bay, a most lovely place for bathing and sailing, and prawns the size of small lobsters. I very rapidly tired of the party and spent the day with some native fishermen who were far more amusing and rather better mannered. I think I shall have to hire a very small boat next summer and just cruise quietly about in it.

Best love,
Roger

An awful dinner party last week – 34 people and I sat next to a fabulously wealthy and exceedingly vulgar old bitch who was in the back row of the chorus of a Greek cabaret before marrying the richest man in Egypt. I told her a lot of shocking lies and asked her to come on a cruise on my 100-ton yacht to the Aegean Islands; she has accepted and is I think looking forward to it.

Best love,
Roger

There is not much to do in the evenings here – but there are good places where you can eat yourself silly on excellent food for about half a crown; the cinemas are indifferent and all the films are cut and they adhere to the odious French habit of having a long interval in the middle of the big film. Thank God for Penguin Books!'

Best love,
Roger

Then Roger found himself caught up in a modern Battle of Jericho. There were plenty of military challenges in the area. When my father later described his days in Palestine to me, it was clear that over and above the conflict, he personally liked both Jews and Arabs for their different qualities, not least in the Arabs' readiness to always laugh at a joke.

Dear Pop,

I have just returned from a short trip to Jericho where we were dispatched to restore order and re-establish the police who have been turned out by the rebels over the last three months.

We had another of those bloody night drives – a convoy a mile long, leaving billets at 2.45 a.m. and getting to Jericho at 9 a.m. I thoroughly enjoyed it: You go down a twisting, precipitous road with the hills rising sharply up on either side. The whole 25 miles can have changed very little since biblical times and the only signs of modern civilisation were the ashes of burnt out Jew lorries, driven up without escort from the Dead Sea Potash Company and meeting with the inevitable fate on what must be the world's best road for ambushes.

Bethany is a charming place, without any of the unfortunate

traces of tourist-catching vulgarity that mars so many places in Jerusalem.

After 20 miles or so downhill, we reached the Dead Sea, with Jericho in the distance. It's a very small town, appalling hot and stuffy in summer and full of mosquitoes – with plenty of trees and surrounded by banana groves. The inhabitants are mainly of Sudanese extraction but periodically the place gets overrun by the gangs who come down from the hills and raise hell.

We met with very little opposition but a few natives were shot trying to break the cordon. British HQ was established at the Jordan Hotel, kept by a club-footed Greek whose trade has been ruined by lack of tourists and non-paying gangsters. I enjoyed my stay there as I had my first night in a bed since we left Alexandria. The bugs were rather more annoying than usual and all had to swallow quinine every day to avoid malaria.

One afternoon there, an old Arab rode into our HQ on his donkey and asked if we could spare him some iodine for a couple of scratches. On examination, we found six bullet holes right through him, all stinking and gangrenous; apparently the poor old boy had been shot up about two days before by an aeroplane which also polished off about fifty of his goats.

God knows how long we shall be out here – I should imagine about another six months. I don't mind living in mild discomfort but its rather boring, never getting out of uniform, having no books to read, and never seeing anyone at all except soldiers.

The more I see of the Palestine Police, the more I realise how incredibly idle and indisciplined they are. They cause us endless trouble by letting all their rifles get stolen, spreading secret information and getting pissed and shooting up harmless people.

The more I see of the Army on semi-active service, the more hopelessly inefficient they seem to be: thank God there wasn't a war! Some of the British regiments out here are absolute jokes, like the Ws who have lost five trucks, several Lewis guns, shot up their own patrols and run like Hell whenever they meet an armed gang of more than one. Then there are the KO who are nothing more than an armed gang themselves and the RS who are absolute savages. The Buffs and Black Watch, though, are both first class as are the 11th Hussars.

Best love,
Roger

'Thank God there wasn't a war'! Oh my dearest father, don't hold your breath.

This letter to his sister Joan indulges in one or two more gentle pleasures beyond the debris and squalor of poverty and strife in Palestine.

I rather enjoyed Jerusalem, firstly because it was mildly exciting, secondly because the Old City is a most intriguing place, partly fascinating and beautiful, partly squalid and repellent. Some of the Arab hovels I went into were deep in excreta, with human beings, goats, donkeys and chickens all squatting silently and miserably in the same room; once or twice I've had to light my pipe to avoid being sick. On the other hand, some of the convents and hospices are beautifully clean and very attractive indeed and run by the most delightful people. I lived in a very high building on the edge of the city wall and at five o'clock in the morning, with the sun rising beyond it, it was a very beautiful sight, especially as there was complete quiet owing to the curfew. Most of the city has altered but little since Our Lord's time; Pontius Pilate's house can still be seen.

I am at billets in Ramleh at present and would be very comfortable if the electric light hadn't been cut off and if either the bath or the lavatory worked. There is a lovely view across the plain to the hills which seem to change colour every hour of the day.

I caught a big chameleon here and kept it for a day or two. They are very tame and settle down in no time. I let this one go when I went off to Jaffa for four days work.

It's rather dull when one's not working here as you can't leave camp at all or you are likely to get kidnapped or shot.

The following letters bring up all kinds of intriguing points: the state of my father's wardrobe, terrorist attacks, British officers misbehaving . . . the deteriorating world situation.

Life continues its uneventful round out here: I haven't been outside the city traffic checks for nine weeks and my work doesn't seem to get any less. We're all waiting anxiously for the Government policy to be outlined and that may give us some idea of the duration of our visit here. As we were originally prepared for a two-month visit, I only brought very few clothes here and I am attending social functions among the Jerusalem elite in grey flannel trousers with a patched seat and a coat that was donned with pride for the first occasion in my Sandhurst days.

Forty Arabs were blown up just down the road last week by Jews who had placed a bomb in the Arab market, skilfully concealed in a basket of carrots. One unfortunate gentleman was squatting on the basket when the bomb blew up and was completely disintegrated except for his legs

21

which were paraded up and down the street all that day by his female relatives, accompanied by piercing and incessant lamentations. The same night, an infernal machine, which would have almost destroyed Jerusalem, was discovered on a roof by a British policeman who luckily heard the machine ticking. Most of the Arab assassinations are now done by boys under fourteen who are handed the weapon and shown the quarry by a terrorist.

I'm glad I'm not in England at present, there seems to be so much squabbling, wind and national hysteria about. It may be dull here but we don't worry much about Europe and there are worse conditions to be in than mine – a nice, dull, peaceful groove.

Manoeuvres in Egypt have been very severe this year – very strenuous and in dreadful weather. The new mechanised brigade – pride of the Near East forces – returned to its base in sad ignominy on the train, all the mechanism having been rendered useless by two days in a sandstorm!

I hope to take four days leave to Egypt next month or in May, which I feel I am now entitled to.

Best love,

Roger

The Conference has provided no solution to this squabble over here, so I suppose we're stuck here T.F.O. [till further orders]. We're all beginning to get rather browned off as we're given no clue as to our future except the knowledge that there's no leave going this year. However, an ugly world crisis seems to be brewing up so there's a chance we may get shoved off to Egypt to keep the Italians quiet. What a truly bloody world it is at present and not the remotest sign of any improvement in the future. And to think I'm doing it all for about the same wages as my grandmother gives her 2nd or 3rd gardener.

Quite a lot of murders outside the hotel this week, one of which was seen by Guardsman Newash who pursued and captured the assassin. The popular method now is to hand the gun to a boy of about ten or eleven, who actually does the dirty deed, knowing full well that his youth precludes him from the gallows.

The flowers out here are lovely and the hill country has been miraculously transformed into a vast rock garden. At one place I saw about two acres of the most magnificent lupins I've ever seen, and even the Jerusalem suburbs are less nauseatingly hideous than usual.

I have employed a tutor for the evening hours and learn Arabic from him with almost humiliating difficulty. I think I'm beginning to improve and can now occasionally startle some particularly annoying yokel with some acid remarks in his native tongue.

Some regiments have been having trouble with the officers and I'm rather glad to hear the Buffs, who I think are rather priggish, are having to court-martial one of their officers. He was in command of a platoon post on the railway and unfortunately his sex urge was stronger than his sense of duty. Tiring of the boredom of isolation, he used to sneak off at night and bed down with some alluring Rachel in a Jewish colony. Unfortunately he used to make his journey in the wireless lorry so that when his post was attacked in his absence, no SOS could be given to HQ and a disaster was only just averted. An RAMC [Royal Army Medical Corps] Major is also durance vile [restraining order] for calling the CO of the 5th Fusiliers an old bastard to his face! Well I hope this finds you less browned off than it leaves me.

Best love,

Roger

Christmas in Palestine, 1938: Roger was as near to the birthplace of the Messiah as he would ever be, but not on a pleasant Christmas break to the sound of the merry organ and sweet singing of the choir. He was not away in a manger, but often caught up night-time alarms and excursions.

The situation here remains static: even if we get back to Egypt, the European situation rules out any hope of leave to the UK. These bloody dictators never let up on one for a second; they have almost entirely ruined soldiering as a pleasurable profession and in spite of rumours, I do not believe their power shows any sign of being on the wane.

Very busy here lately: only one night in bed out of the last ten, owing to these windy generals being scared stiff of being thought inactive ('lacking in drive' or 'not a live wire' is the usual term used). Consequently we are shoved out at midnight every day to go and inflict moderate hardship on some perfectly peaceful village.

We did however have a good raid on Hebron: it was two days of hell, very cold, very arduous and well carried out. With the help of informers we picked out several hundred terrorists, having rounded up and questioned 800 men in 36 hours. Then, if you please, the bloody staff, having urged us on, makes us release all but a hundred as 'they hadn't expected so many and don't quite know what to do with them'. The big bunch of cloth-headed saps! No wonder we all get browned off.

We've moved after nine weeks in the open to real comfort at this excellent German hotel in Jerusalem. The comfort of a bed, carpet, electric light and other kindred amenities that I was beginning to forget are more than welcome. Well, a Merry Christmas to you all, and a peaceful new year.

With the instability in Europe and increasing threat posed by Hitler, my father's next destination turned out to be in the cooler climes of Birkenhead, in preparation for war. He described this period years later.

The Miller's House
Kintbury
21 July [1980s]

Dearest Jane

As you know I was on leave from Egypt when the Hore-Belisha expansion of the Army took place. I was a junior captain and found myself suddenly in command of a Searchlight Militia Battery, RA, in Arrow Park, Birkenhead. My junior officers tended to be moth-eaten old dug-outs from World War I. The other ranks were Merseyside teenagers. We had no searchlights, no rifles, no NCO instructors, no parade ground, no snacking irons, no kitchen utensils, no clerks, no cooks, no uniforms. We were riding on the rims. Belisha thought that as long as he assembled individuals there was no need to fuss about organisation, training, standard of living. He was a flat-catching shit backed by the *Daily Mirror* and the radical press. The Merseyside teenagers were basically OK and I grew to like them, and vice versa I think. I was very moved by the send-off they gave me when I left to rejoin the Coldstream at Pirbright. A lot of them had no religion and when I filled in their particulars they gave as their religion 'The Prudential' or 'The same as you sir, if you don't mind'. I eventually got a Battery Clerk from the labour exchange. A cynic, highly efficient, he had been quite a nob in the local communist party. We got on very well. My BSM was a very smooth riding instructor from the RHA. By far the best young officer I had was John Garnett, Marlborough and Royal Welsh Fusiliers, killed in 1940 as soon as the fighting started.

Best love

xx D

Roger didn't have much time for Leslie Hore-Belisha, the Secretary of State for War better known today for pedestrian road safety due to his 'Belisha beacons' at road crossings. His appointment was not a popular one with Parliament or the top ranks of the Army. Hore-Belisha gave some highly regarded generals the sack, a downgrading he himself received in the early months of 1940.

I'm delighted that Hore-Belisha was sacked. In my opinion he was a self-advertising careerist, a liar, not over-scrupulous, and a sucker up to the vulgar press.

Between the declaration of war in September 1939 and Hitler's invasion of Belgium and the Netherlands in May 1940, British forces were engaged in constant military manoeuvres, training exercises and preparation for action. It was a time of unsettling hiatus – the Phoney War. As part of the British Expeditionary Force (BEF), Roger was sent to northern France with his Coldstream battalion in early 1940.

I was detailed to come up here at four hours notice from the Base: I was rather relieved in a way at not going to the 2nd Bn where my memories are not of the happiest; moreover, the Commanding Officer used to be Riley's right-hand man and I'm afraid I never treated him with the respect due to his seniority and spent a good deal of time and ingenuity in making him 'the butt': the fact that we have not had to meet in the tenser atmosphere of war is a matter of mutual relief and if I'd been in his place I should have been very loathe to receive me into his fold!

I'm a fairly junior captain in this Bn and I am doing duty as 2nd in command to Jerry Feilden which suits me well especially as I have a hell of a lot to learn about this sort of soldiering. Jack Whittaker is our Brigadier, I'm glad to say, as no one could be nicer. Arnold Cazenove is almost unknown to me; he is very serious, painstaking and industrious and demands (rightly, I think) a very high standard indeed. I bet there isn't a better Battalion in the BEF as regards turnout; we work like blacks, digging every day from dawn till dusk with occasional variations in the shape of 15-mile marches. I find myself very tired when my last duty is done and more inclined to sleep than anything else. I had a bloody journey up, taking 48 hours with two minor train accidents. I arrived at 4 p.m., very tired and dirty and with the worst cold I've ever had and shivering in a tremendous blizzard. At 8 p.m. we did a night drive, yours truly sitting in an open lorry with no windscreen, and then proceeded to walk back some 16 miles, getting in at dawn. I felt like death when I started but 100 per cent better at the end. Could you please send another issue of kippers and a cake from Mrs Tanner would be welcome. Our billets are easily the best in the BEF: we have a very good company mess, central heating, good WC etc: sleep in the next door house in a very classy mansion owned by a rich industrialist. I have a delightful bedroom and get ragged a good deal by the seven children, who I frequently see sitting in a long row on jerrys.

Best love to Mummy and I'll write when I get time. Am unlikely to get leave before the end of June.

Roger would not get leave in June. The Germans had other plans for him. In the meantime, February 1940 found him lulled into tranquillity, living in a French arcadia.

Fine warm weather here with very sharp frosts every night. I wish there was a golf course near, as it's just the right time of year for that sort of thing. I only wish I could hop down to the NZ on Sunday and play a round and a half, no doubt exceedingly badly, with a large lunch in between.

I had arranged to go to Paris last Sunday with Rupert Gerrard and Tommy Gore Browne, but at the very last moment on Saturday morning, just as we were setting off, some dim old bore of a general announced his intention of inspecting us at 11 a.m. on Sunday. This was equally tiresome for the guardsmen, as on Saturday afternoons we hire three buses and take a trip to the nearest town. Consequently they had no time left to get cleaned up and everything swabbed for this singularly ill-timed visit. We duly paraded on Sunday, but after a tedious wait a message came through to say we would be an hour and a half late; I suppose we should have expected this but nevertheless, our feelings towards the general were scarcely improved by this announcement. However, I felt it my duty to give him a civil reception, so I posted some drummers with French 'Cors de Chasses' on the balcony of the turret and when he emerged from his staff car, they blew a loud and highly original fanfare – the sort of thing that precedes the entry of Prince Charming in a provincial pantomime. The general was visibly shaken so I seized the initiative and had him well under control the whole time. He proved to be a dim, pleasant sort of Belisha general: he inspected the men 'standing easy' if you please, and asked them all well-meant but fairly silly questions, such as 'Does your family write to you often enough?' I think he was pleased with his visit and he was very complimentary afterwards.

We have a padre living with us which is a pretty fair bore as he is obtuse and foolish, even for his station in life, which is saying a good deal. He's not a shit in any way, rather to the contrary, but he's appallingly ignorant and out of touch with reality to such an extent that he really shocks me. Also he is apt to make rather sly, smutty remarks to show what a jolly, broad-minded sport he really is!

Deep in the winter of early 1940, he wrote to his uncle.

1st Reinforcement, 2nd Battalion Coldstream Guards
1st Infantry Base Depot
BEF
9 February 1940

Very many thanks for your most welcome letter. I should be most grateful if you would be kind enough to send me some 'mental nourishment'. I am quite content to rely on your selection and any preference I have would be between David Cecil's 'The Young Melbourne' and Franklin Luckington's 'Portrait of a Young Man'.

My life here continues to be distinguished solely by the completeness of its rural quietude: my former companion has moved on and though I miss the conversation, the joint attack on *The Times* crossword and the general knowledge papers we set each other every night, I am very happy in complete solitude as long as the post arrives occasionally and I have something to read. By good fortune I managed to get hold of Tolstoy's 'War and Peace', which I had always shied away from formerly: I enjoyed it more than anything I've read for years and it kept me quiet for almost a week.

The best of this sort of existence is that one is able to do all sorts of things that in more normal times one never think of doing – at any rate, I wouldn't. I have become rather a keen naturalist in a primitive sort of way and spend a good many afternoons watching birds and I think I shall shortly be able to publish a small brochure dealing with the life and habits of the little owl in this part of France! Now that the thaw has set in, I'm going to buy a rod and do a little coarse fishing in the canal.

Little owls, thoughts of fishing and not a hint of conflict in that early spring air – how removed that little corner of France seems from a time of war. In a letter to me in the 1980s, he recalled that halcyon interlude.

I have seldom been happier. There was no other officer there, it was too cold to work, and I had a snug room with a huge stove and piles of books sent from kind friends in England. In those days books cost 7/6d, not £10.

I still find the following letter about the turn of events in 1940, written to me in 1970s, to be one of the most poignant I ever received from my father.

Dampwalls
Burghclere
May [early 1970s]

Dearest Jane,

Yesterday, listening in the garden to the melancholy sound of church bells, my mind went back to a beautiful May morning in Belgium in 1940. The Germans had attacked the Low Countries and started the Blitz. My battalion moved up to Belgium from Lille and we assembled at a sort of Belgian Virginia Water, large well-kept houses with children and dogs playing on the lawns. It did not seem much like war. Suddenly a motorcyclist appeared with a message for all company commanders to meet the commanding officer at a church some miles away. Off we went – I rode a motorcycle – and as we reached the little church the locals were going into morning service in their best clothes just as they did every Sunday. They took no notice of us.

The Colonel told us that the German armour had broken through the first line of defences and we were to counterattack forthwith. The war really had started: for some of us it had ended before the day was done.

Best love to you all,
RFM

3

Roger the Prisoner

Roger Mortimer supplied a lot of the laughter, for which
many of us are eternally grateful.

Francis Reed, POW

The Nazis invaded Belgium on 10 May 1940. The fierce Battle
of Belgium – or Flanders as it is sometimes known – lasted
for two-and-a-half weeks before the evacuation of British
troops across the Channel back to England. In the meantime,
Captain Roger Mortimer carried out his orders to defend a
rearguard position beside a canal in Louvain, central Belgium,
against the oncoming Germans. During the ensuing action, he
was knocked unconscious. When he regained consciousness,
it was to discover that he was now a prisoner of the Germans.
According to the Coldstream Guards records, it was 17 May
1940.

His captivity commenced in an unusual manner. Within
the first twenty-four hours, my father found himself wearing
clean clothes and having an excellent and enjoyable dinner
with a general. A civilized occasion with a hospitable host.
Except that the general in question was German and his guest
was a British prisoner.

The General von Reichenaw and Roger were not strangers

to each other. Both were racing enthusiasts and they had met at Ascot on a few occasions before the war. On the evening following my father's capture, the General was running though the list of British prisoners taken and spied my father's name. He gave immediate orders for a driver to collect my father from the prisoner's holding station and chauffeur him back for dinner at his commandeered residence.

On his arrival, the General greeted Roger warmly. He was shown upstairs to a bedroom with a change of clothes laid out for him. Over dinner, these two educated men enjoyed the kind of conversation that they might have held in peacetime, much of it about racing. After a good night's sleep between clean sheets in a comfortable bed, the last my father would experience for many years to come, Captain Mortimer, now POW 481, was given breakfast before once again climbing back into his dirty uniform. As the staff car drew up by the door, the General shook his hand, saying with regret, 'I'm awfully sorry about all this – I would far rather be at Ascot.'

Back in England, the information came through to my father's family that he was dead, killed in action. This alarming error was soon corrected by a report in *The Times*, of those prisoners taken in the Battle for Belgium.

Much later, in November 1940, my father was mentioned in *The Times* again, this time in an article on the role played by the 1st Battalion Coldstream Guards in the defence of Belgium. My father's bravery was commended.

> When the enemy broke through on the Belgian front and brought fire to bear on the rear, another company held their positions on the canal, thanks to the inspiring leadership of Captain Mortimer who was knocked unconscious and captured.

That my father's next destination should have been a castle –

Spangenberg in central Germany – was not to suggest further privileged treatment for himself or his fellow British officers, no matter what their social connections. The castle was the first of the five prison camps behind whose walls and fences my father was to pass the following five years.

At this chaotic point, as Britain concentrated its defences against the anticipated invasion from Hitler, there was not yet a reliable system for dispatch of parcels of clothes, food, medicines and basic necessities to prisoners of war. My father recalled having no change of clothes for quite some time and being compelled to tear off the tail of his shirt as a handkerchief. A fellow POW had a copy of *Gone with the Wind* – every one of its many pages were torn out for use as lavatory paper. There are no letters from Roger in those first months in existence – if indeed he had been in a position to write any.

Innovative measures for survival – or equally, to raise morale – occupied prisoners' waking hours, as described here by Freddy Corfield who was to become one of Roger's closest friends in prison. It was early autumn at Spangenberg Castle.

> Roger and I grew beards, which, despite the expert attention of a bearded naval officer, we both found uncomfortable and later abandoned. We also endeavoured to produce a passable smoke from the rapidly fading leaves of Virginia creeper which covered the castle walls. It was not a success.

A photo of a bearded, beaming, big-jumpered Roger is a handsome one – if one didn't know better, one might think he was enjoying a sailing holiday. That beard came in for comment from John Surtees, one of a new autumn intake of prisoners, on his arrival at Spangenberg. John had met Roger once before in discouraging circumstances. Their second meeting was no more auspicious:

My first sight of Roger was at Corps Camp at Tweseldown in July 1935, when we young Etonian cadets struggled onto Parade in front of the tall, fair-haired moustached and immaculate Guards Officer Mortimer, under whose temporary command fell the Eton College Training Corps contingent. We were not smart, and it was not long before we became aware of it. Those who collapsed in the sweltering heat, some of them suffering from hangovers, had their names taken without delay. No one was seriously penalised, but we regarded this officer with a certain amount of opprobrium, or at least, disfavour.

Five years later, in the autumn of 1940, on my arrival at the prison camp at Schloss Spangenberg, there was the fall, fair-haired, luxuriantly bearded and now far from immaculate figure, dressed in a pale sweater and battledress trousers. He was dispensing a plate of lettuce sandwiches to members of our two-dozen party. It was my bad luck not to be awarded a sandwich – an oversight which Roger was not allowed to forget for the next fifty years.

It was the last sight of a lettuce I had until 1945. We had been travelling by barge and cattle truck for 14 days and we were famished.

These were the opening shots between John Surtees and Roger. It was the beginning of a friendship – unswerving in its loyalty – consolidated in prison and lasting for the next half a century.

When, after the war, John and Roger wrote to each other, they addressed the other by their prison number, i.e. 'Dear 481'. A prison number is not a typical term of endearment but nicknames of any kind were a little hobby of my father's – they bubble to the surface of his later letters, long after he had absented the notorious nickname territory of public school and the Army. Roger got off very lightly himself in the nickname game. He was known as 'Paul' in his earlier years as a Guards officer, a name inspired by the dry fizz of Pol Roger champagne. A compliment. Now, in prison, he was initially called Gort – possibly because 'Mort' happened to rhyme with the name of the erstwhile Commander of the BEF in France, Lord Field Marshal Gort, under whose command Roger had fallen in the Battle of Belgium.

As 'Gort', my father enjoyed a week of solitary confinement in August 1940, according to John Mansell, POW:

> Gort had back chat with a sentry yesterday when gardening. The sentry had said to him – 'London will be entered in eight days.' Gort had bet him something or other that it wouldn't be and was arrested for bribing the sentries. The sentry, gesticulating, said that in six days Winston Churchill would be so high – bending down to illustrate the height. Gort pointed out that Hitler would be so high – bending even lower. The charge for this offence is 'Insulting the Fuhrer'. Gort was given eight days confinement for his bribery and insults.

Roger's new POW friend Fred Corfield turned out to have an agricultural background and was soon christened 'Dungy Fred' by Roger. On Fred's request, Roger gave him some lessons in German. 'But Roger's sense of humour always got the better of him, and I only learnt the rudest words and expressions, which, being quite unrepeatable, I consequently found of rather limited use.' Dungy Fred later became better known as a Conservative minister, Sir Frederick Corfield.

At the outset, Roger spoke a smattering of German. He took his studies further in prison, remarkably even taking advanced exams in the language while incarcerated. Later in life he was prone to season his speech with the odd bit of Deutsch. He liked its crispness. *Zimmer* (room), appealed to him, describing his own room as his Zimmer Z. Feigning annoyance he might bark at you – or his dog – '*Du bist ein Schweinhund!*'

Whether for study or pleasure, books offered a retreat into a private refuge from the enforced, unrelenting intimacy of community living. For POWs, reading was one legitimate route of escape. Parcels of books somehow managed, some of the time, to make safe passages around the world without being bombed into smithereens or torpedoed and sunk. Roger was a voracious reader so gifts of books – novels, biographies, military history and books on racing – were an absolute lifeline, as well as a talking point in his letters home.

The meaning of leisure was somewhat different in prison. There was rather an excess of it, filled by conversations, cards, music, artistic endeavours, shows, sport, gardening, knitting and sewing. It might nearly sound an idyll. It wasn't. The German commandants of the Offizierlager or Oflags – camps for officers – were not permitted to inflict extremes of brutality as they were constrained by the Geneva Convention, but the line was a fine one. Conditions were devoid of physical comfort, often unpleasantly cold and wet, with hunger a regular companion. Any activity could be summarily interrupted by impromptu roll calls at any hour of the day or night, with POWS sometimes standing outside for long periods; there were frequent inspections and searches where any possessions might be confiscated or destroyed. There was no lack of Nazi ingenuity in devising humiliations – countered by plenty of inventive British humour.

In these camps, fellow prisoners became close friends and groups in a hut became like a family, but of course one half of the human race was completely absent – women. My father's letters home and the memories of his fellow POWs explain a little of the camaraderie, humour, highs and lows they shared over those long years:

18 September 1941

I'm afraid I must be a dreadful nuisance to you but all your efforts are certainly appreciated at this end. The Red X too is settling down and we get one parcel a week from them at present. The garden has rather a bedraggled look at the moment, but our roses are quite nice and sunflowers and pumpkins are also successful. I'm having a small party here tomorrow in my new room, which has a most lovely view and is easily the best I've had – very quiet and only two others in it, both old friends. Did I tell you that Sophie's friend Philip Moore is here? He is minus a leg and one of the nicest people you could meet anywhere. His leg is off at the thigh but has healed well. He does the most astonishing high-jumps, well over four feet. Could you send a possible book or two on racehorse breeding and if possible, also some gramophone records? We're settling down now for the winter and I feel sure that another two Christmases will see me home again. The worst of life here is its awful pettiness, lack of privacy, and the fact that captivity brings out the worst in you. I'm really delighted to have no peacetime friends with me here. One really sees so much of people that you suddenly find yourself hating people you know are really very nice. You've got to be pretty tolerant to be on terms of more than honeymoon proximity with people for fifteen months, day in, day out, and not occasionally go off the deep end.

    Love

    Roger

British Officers were obliged, by military law, to concentrate their energies on escaping from prison. In 1941 at Warburg, the third prison camp which Roger graced with his presence, two escape attempts were recorded. The motivation to escape had additional impetus at this prison. The site was almost a cliché of a Nazi prison camp, the kind seen in war movies. It was a mud heap on which sat prison huts stretching far into the distance across a high, exposed plain. The desolation was completed in the traditional manner – twelve-foot high fences with the area between the inner and outer fence packed with rolls of barbed wire. Every hundred yards or so was a watchtower with searchlights and armed guards. The good news for Roger was that he shared the pleasures of Warburg with many of his new friends – including John Surtees and Desmond Parkinson – with whom he embarked on what might accurately be described as escapades. John describes one foiled attempt that he and Roger planned.

[We substituted] ourselves for members of a working party who went outside the camp to collect stores, coal, parcels and so on. Our haversacks, which had been taken out and concealed in bushes by the cooperating men a day or so before, were discovered. We were threatened with reprisals to the whole camp if we didn't declare our identities. That earned us fourteen days each of solitary confinement; Roger regarded it as rather a peaceful alternative to camp routine, but his cell had a better light for reading than mine did.

Desmond Parkinson, then in his early twenties, recollected another escape plan involving a team and a lot more effort.

Shortly after arrival at Warburg, Roger started a tunnel from the bath house and I was one of his slaves on the project. Others included John Surtees, Fitz Fletcher, Freddie Burnaby-Atkins, Michael Price. In those days tunnelling techniques were very primitive and, as we had to dig a shaft sixteen feet deep before starting on the tunnel proper, fresh air at the working end was nonexistent and I still remember the terrible headaches we all had after doing our stint at the face. But, as you can imagine, with Roger as our tunnel master, there were many light moments. But I don't think any of us had much faith that we would eventually emerge on the other side of the wire. This lack of faith was not misplaced, since after a heavy rainstorm, a senior major decided that this was the moment to dig his little vegetable patch outside the bath house. This led, in short order, to the collapse and flooding of the tunnel and then the subsidence of the bath house itself . . . This did not deter our intrepid tunnel master, Roger, and we were soon at it again, starting from a room in one of the huts, but our efforts were discovered by the Germans after a very short time indeed.

When Roger wrote in caustic tones to his father from Warburg in February 1942, he had been incarcerated for nearly two years:

I'm afraid my letters are the last word in dullness but I am up against the same difficulties as yourself. I have had to give up skating as my knees wouldn't stand it and I could only progress rather unsteadily like a rabbit with a broken leg. Time fairly flies in prison and I can't believe it is over two years since I was last in England. One's occupations are very varied here today; I'm room orderly and have many menial duties to perform: in addition I've had a German lesson and darned a three-inch hole in my socks. I think I only have two ambitions in life left: to possess a water closet and to be able to hire someone to darn my socks. I hope you won't entirely give up golf as I intend to stage my first comeback against you at the New Zealand Club. With any luck I may have forgotten my previous style and will launch out with something new and hard enough to achieve any measure of success. I wonder which of us two will age most: if you keep your head and don't overdo things, you'll probably find yourself taken for my younger brother. I suppose there will be a lot of nice, young, rich widows knocking about after the war. I only hope they won't all be sold out before I get back. Well, Best Love to you all. I am confident I shall be home within two more years.

Roger

Roger was allowed just the statutory two letters per month on narrow, prison-issue paper with twenty-five cramped lines to fill. Roger's handwriting shrank to the smallest legible size. I suspect that the style of his later paternal letters, often devoid of paragraph breaks, was developed in prison when space on the page was limited. To pass the censors, POW letters home permitted only innocuous content – the topic of war was verboten *– but irony and satire tended to escape attention. War or not, Roger's consistent concern was not to bore others. Writing from Warburg in July 1942, he shares the pleasures of his current modus vivendi with his father.*

The weather here is perfect and I just lie about in the sun without any clothes on and let my mind go completely blank. The time passes admirably and I only emerge from a state of semi-coma at mealtimes. I played my first game of prison tennis last week – half an hour on a mud court, two balls both wet and black, no stop netting at all. Prison life has several advantages. For the first time for twenty years I'm free from financial embarrassment; however many letters arrive, it's long odds against a bill. Secondly, even if I have to live at a very humble scale after the war, it can hardly fail to be a slight rise on my present condition. Also it's marvellous having no dreary routine: if I feel like it, I just go back to bed after breakfast and stay there all evening until appel. Thank God I've always been bone idle and never felt the restless urge to do something.

In fact Roger was doing something. He was engaged in subterfuge on a nearly daily basis for four years at different camps. The penalty, should his high security risk activities have been discovered, would have been severe. He could have been shot.

The subterfuge began one snowy February evening at Spangenberg when the guards neglected to search a batch of new prisoners prior to their entry into the camp. The new arrivals who were shepherded through the gates included some doctors who, on seeing a gathering of prisoners nearby, discretely tried to attract their attention, pointing to a medical case which one of them carried. The opportunity was seized at once. A POW who spoke fluent German distracted the guards in conversation, allowing just enough time for the medical case to be spirited away by some other prisoners, who included Roger and Fred. They hurried their plunder up to their room, a hayloft over the stables just inside the main gate.

On opening the medical case, they found a small mahogany box containing an object of immense value – a radio. After nine months deprived of news from the outside world they now had the possibility of connecting to the BBC. The mahogany casing was quickly destroyed to reduce the radio, powered by four valves, to the smallest possible size. Dungy Fred recalled:

> By the grace of God it worked off German voltage, and its flex was fitted with the necessary adaptor to fit in a light socket. Immensely excited, we tuned into the BBC and I shall never forget that first reception.

This life-transforming connection might so easily have been short lived if a safe hiding place had not been found. The loft floorboards were lifted and the radio secreted snugly between the joists. Roger and Fred were not just responsible for the security of the radio: they became the news broadcasters on a nightly basis. Notes on the news were taken down before summoning representatives from each prison barracks to a news conference. The deputy newscasters were sworn to secrecy and the notes had to be returned to Roger and Fred to be burnt.

Spangenberg was the first receiving station for the radio, christened 'The Canary Bird', but it was to journey to several destinations before its time was done. After three weeks the Nazis announced that the entire camp was to be moved to Poland, and the POWs' accommodation was now about to take a dramatic turn for the worse. It was essential that the Canary Bird made the journey too, and it was carefully hidden in a restitched medicine ball by a former saddler. On arrival in Poland, Roger and Fred and their comrades were marched to their new centre of confinement, a hideous fort at Thorn. They were led down cold stone corridors dripping with water to a stone barracks of equal dampness. When other senior officers reported that their room was actually under several inches of water, the responding laughter of the British contingent at the sheer bloody awfulness of it all confounded their Nazi guards.

Roger wrote to his cousin Tom Blackwell from Thorn.

31 March 1941

I think you'd laugh yourself sick if you saw my new home. Dartmoor Castle simply isn't in it. I've never lived below ground level before, but you soon get used to it. The weather is the worst part – bloody cold and still snowing. My winter clothing parcel has never arrived and I've had no news from my family for over three months as they won't write by Air Mail. Have opened the cricket season and find I'm really rather good with a rubber ball.

Roger

16 April 1941

My Dear Tom,

This letter may be a trifle incoherent as I'm feeling rather sleepy after a truly delightful lunch of turnip stew – you can imagine how pleased I am to get so much of my favourite vegetable. Most of all I miss a comfortable WC, the *Sporting Life*, women and music. I've been trying to learn Russian but my enthusiasm is dwindling and I think I prefer lying on my bed reading of past years' racing and thinking of bygone, happier days. I still do PT every morning, as then my conscience permits me to do damn all for the rest of the day.

Roger and Fred continued to issue daily news bulletins. They learnt from the BBC that the Hitler/Stalin non-aggression pact was coming under strain. At Thorn, prisoners saw for themselves, from their mean fortress windows, that there were German troop movements in the area. The Germans did not want the inconvenience of a load of British POWs to deal with in a zone where conflict might increase and accelerate.

This was good news for Thorn's current guests who were sent packing back to Spangenberg at very short notice. This relatively pleasant interlude was brought to an end when, before Christmas 1941, Roger and his comrades were moved to the camp referred to earlier, the muddy dump of Warburg. The Canary Bird travelled once more, tucked into its medicine ball. A new camp meant a new hiding place. In

Warburg, the little radio spent the larger part of its existence literally hiding in a shithole. The POWs kept their washing things in Red Cross boxes, and the radio was secreted in one. Fred described the process:

> The box hung beneath the seats covering the latrines which were situated over a particularly noxious pit, in a hut four or five yards from one of the doors to our hut. Every morning and evening I marched to the wash house clutching my Red Cross box; in the evening I returned via the latrines and exchanged my washing box for the one containing the radio: in the mornings I repeated the action in reverse order.

In 1942 Roger and his comrades were moved yet again – this time to Eichstätt. There is little doubt that the Germans knew, by now, of the existence of a radio. Searches were continuously carried out and, as John Surtees said, 'It was astonishing they never found it.' At Eichstätt, an attic in one of the prison blocks was supported by roof beams so badly riddled with woodworm that it was no problem to carve out a niche for the radio.

By the time Roger wrote to his father on 19 September 1942, it was obvious that his close friendships had become central to his survival of prison life. The deep bond of tolerance and understanding established between these imprisoned men was not going to be discarded once the war was over. The longer they had endured captivity, the deeper the damage, but there would be solace in these long-term friendships.

I'm afraid you may not have heard from me for some time owing to us all moving camp. Most of us came on here but one of my oldest prison friends went off to a smaller camp, I think owing to the severity of his war wounds. The journey here was easily the most comfortable I have had in this country and we passed a very comfortable night in second-class carriages. The surroundings of the new camp and adjacent town are remarkably pleasant and a striking contrast to the last place. The camp itself is also rather better and will probably be alright once we have organised it efficiently. Unfortunately, I am separated from several old friends as I'm living in a special block for those with a 'prison past'. However, I'm in a room with seventeen extremely nice people most of whom I know well and with whom I've been messing for the past twenty-seven months. Still, these partings and breakings-up of old messes are rather sad things in prison, where one's whole existence and happiness depend on comradeship and living with people whose views and habits are roughly similar to one's own.

Preparing for the joys of Christmas 1942, Roger's tone was one of reflective resignation.

We are spending Christmas quietly – a large breakfast and then lying in bed until supper-time. Very many thanks for 360 Players cigarettes. I have lots of Sept and Oct letters from you and Mummy. I'm reading as much history as I can and have just plugged gamely through 2,000 pages of Garven's 'Life of Joe Chamberlain' and am now cleaning up on 'Palmerston' with Morley's 'Life of Gladstone' as a little treat in store. The great thing about reading history is that it confirms my impression that human nature is not only nasty, but what is far worse, foolish too. Prison is an amazingly good eye-opener on human nature, especially in the early days when things were not too good. I'm playing in a knockout bridge competition. The only fun is the amazing people you find yourself playing against.

In January 1943, to ring the changes, Roger and a friend, Hector Christie, swap roles, each writing to the other's parents. 'Thank God 1942 is over. A drearier year I've never known', wrote Roger as he introduced Hector, whose bulletin on Roger was upbeat.

I thought perhaps you'd like to know that the old job is really well, in terrific form and confident, like me, that it will be any day now. We manage to laugh a lot and Roger has brought the art of living to a very fine point. I wish I could take things quite as easily and smoothly, although I find the good example of a morning in bed a most excellent one which suits me well. I really feel you will be seeing him this year, and you won't find, I think, that this dreary time has done any harm whatsoever to a quite irrepressible person.

Home soon? There were another two-and-a-half years to go.
At Eichstätt, a new craze was sweeping through the camp: gambling. Roger, along with role as newscaster and an additional responsibility on the camp security team, was appointed one of the chief stewards overseeing the gaming tables, along with Jack Poole, who had the particular distinction of surviving imprisonment in both world wars. In February 1943 Roger described Jack to his father.

Jack Poole really is a splendid person, always even tempered and usually extremely amusing. He brings a welcome breath of White's into the place. We are also partners in a humbler sphere every day, i.e. at either end of a long saw on the wood dump.

White's is the prestigious London club.

Roger, Jack and the committee had to blacklist a few cheaters from the gaming tables. Amongst those who played fair were quite a few 'swells' who played by rules of 'settlement after the war'. On another level, an honest, middle-aged schoolmaster found himself in debt to the tune of £80 which he was quite unable to pay. He found a way of honouring his debt – mending worn-out socks of fellow POWs at five shillings a hole. Keeping their scant wardrobes in repair was a continuous process. My father became an accomplished knitter during that time and for many post-war years his tweedy gardening jumper with deliciously lurid cuffs in lime-green and pink was an enduring example.

Eichstätt was an improvement on Thorn but the Germans continued to think up ingenious little ways to aggrieve the POWs. When my father first received a precious pair of warm corduroy trousers in a clothing parcel, the Germans chopped them off at the knee. Later, at another camp, a fresh pair of corduroy trousers got through to Roger, unmolested, and at some point an American friend of Roger's sister sent him a thick, duck shooting coat from the US. He attributed his physical survival in no small part to the insulation of that coat. April 1943 brought snow, not springtime, to Eichstätt. Roger was being dispatched for regular spells of solitary confinement, or what he called 'rest and solitude' and 'silence and meditation'. In a letter to his father, he wrote:

I must say I always give a fairly hollow laugh when I get letters saying I will be home soon. It is greatly to your credit that you have never indulged in nonsense like that.

In this letter of 30 June 1943, Roger was extremely low, with very understandable reason.

This has been a wretched month. Today, to crown everything, most of my room have been moved to another camp, including Freddy Corfield whom I've lived with for over three years in quiet content and a considerable amount of laughter. What sanity I still possess is largely due to him. I feel very lonely and adrift now. Friendship is the only anchor one has in prison, and now after three years I feel just as if I was starting all over again. I suppose my resistance to the bleakness of things is decreasing, but at present I feel like attaching my old school braces to the lamp bracket, fitting a snug knot behind my ears and jumping off the table. I expect things will seem better soon and perhaps I'll be home one day soon. Anyway, it might so easily be worse.

Roger

My father had lost the comradeship of a close friend and co-operator of the Canary Bird. Despite it all, the letter ends in brave filial style. Later that summer, in August, he recounts:

Two inmates made unsuccessful attempts to commit suicide last week – presumably from sheer boredom and despondency. I must say though, to fail even at suicide shows a deplorable lack of skill and determination. For myself, I'm bored but by no means despondent.

Two weeks later, deeply frustrated, Roger's letter home is a sardonic response to his parents' domestic preoccupations and grievances at home. Wartime was hard for them, too, but how their views must have grated.

I wish you hadn't suggested my learning chartered accountancy this winter: it may be useful but it is hideously dull. I'm still hankering after law, especially as I can get a competent tutor. I hear you've been looking for a home in the country – how very exciting for you. I only wish I could be there too. Mummy writes very despondently as if she had already assumed the onerous duties of sole cook and housemaid – I take that to be merely an instance of that astonishing capacity for looking on the bleakest side of everything which is such a feature of our family life and which I myself share to the full. Ever since I can remember we've always been hovering on the edge of a bed sitting room in the Cromwell Road, but by tremendous good fortune we never seem to get there. I am quite prepared to be told that you are going up to the city in clogs, as you are unable to stump up for a new pair of prinkers. Never mind, with the money I've saved the last three years I'm quite a capitalist and will doubtless be able to assist in hiring a girl to come in once or twice a week to help with the heavy work. Of course I should like to stay in the Army if possible, but if that isn't on, I should like something to do with the executive side of racing, or the police. How about the racecourse police? I'm also prepared for a small fee to succeed Bob Lyle on *The Times*.

Best love,
Roger

Here is the first recorded suggestion by my father that he might make something of his racing interests, perhaps even finding himself a job in some capacity. If prison life had a silver lining, it was the time my father had been able to spend on enlightening himself through extensive reading on the bloodstock breeding of racehorses. For those who have rarely if ever set foot on a racecourse, that pursuit may sound as fascinating as gaining expertise in railway timetables. Yet reclining on his slatted prison bunk, lost in volumes of race form, Roger was transported to another world – the rolling green racecourses of England in peacetime.

Roger produced his first article on that esoteric subject whilst in prison, in a little POW magazine. A surviving copy of this publication was sent to me by a former POW comrade in Canada. I was thrilled to receive this little fragment of my father's history. In his inaugural piece, though, his typical turn of phrase was yet to find its place in print and his article was delivered with respectful earnestness.

By the autumn of 1943, Roger's tone was much lighter again – his life seemed to have settled into a more tolerable mode. He had achieved a first-class result in some Royal Society of Arts exams and the autumn sunshine had enabled him to enjoy plenty of cricket: 'Some of it really high class considering the conditions – matting wicket, bumpy outfield etc.' Later in September he sent home 'A Day in the Life of a POW'.

I'll endeavour to describe my routine at present. I usually get up with extreme reluctance at 8.30, shave, have a cold shower, make my bed and clean my shoes by 9 o'clock, when we have morning appel. At 9.15 we have breakfast in our room – a cup of tea without sugar, and two slices of bread with butter on one and jam and margarine on the other. After breakfast the room orderly, assisted by whoever is on duty for the room – sweeps and washes up. I usually work in the silence room at the other end of the camp and squat on a wooden stool peering vaguely at my German primer till 12 noon. Lunch is a plate of vegetable soup followed by biscuits and cheese. In the afternoon, I sit and read outside if it's fine, or on my bed if it's wet. Actually I invariably do more talking and mobbing than reading. Tea at 4 p.m., the same as breakfast. Afterwards I usually walk, have a net or take some form of exercise and a cold shower at 6 p.m. followed by appel at 6.30. Dinner at 8, the big meal of the day, meat (supplied by Red +) and potatoes followed by stewed fruit or a savoury (all Red +) and a cup of cocoa. 8.30–10 everyone talks their heads off and 10.30 lights out. One's room is one's castle. Other prisoners don't ever come in unless asked, and after a year you probably don't know half the people in the next room by name.

Roger

It was a day reminiscent of the better form of prep school. Francis Reed, a good POW friend, recalled my father as a raconteur regularly welcomed in his room during that period.

I was in a room of sixteen (eight of whom were Etonian, which the rest of us managed to survive) . . . Roger was in a room of six in the same building and was a very frequent visitor to 'The Nursery' as our room was known. He was about ten years older than most of us. He had done a stint in Palestine and had considerable experience of high, and sometimes low, life in London, altogether a man of the world. How we delighted in hearing his stories.

If I seem to be making Roger out to be rather a Wodehousian character, he certainly wasn't. He was very well read and with a personal memory which must have stood him in very good stead as the famous racing journalist he became. It was said that of the 100 boys at his prep school in his final year, he could still reel off the names of 98 of them.

Francis Reed demonstrated his appreciation by knitting my father 'a rather nice heather mixture tie out of an old sock'.

Additional stimuli for Roger could be found in some of the camp lectures and debates. Of universal interest was a proposal that was to revolutionize Britain after the war – the

Beveridge Plan which initiated the welfare state, establishing the National Health Service and state pensions. My father's response was a heartening one.

We've been having a number of lectures and debates on social reform and the Beveridge Plan: most people here are pretty progressive except one or two hide-bound landowners and a few RCs. I think many of the reforms are long overdue and to oppose them would be short-sighted and ungenerous, and perhaps a cause of serious trouble. Certainly the Conservative party will almost cease to exist if it continues to show such half-hearted enthusiasm for what is a general or reasonable demand. Whether our economic position will be able to stand it is a very different matter.

By September 1944, Roger derived some satisfaction from his new found domestic skills.

Well, I'm settling down for the fifth winter in gaol, not with any noticeable degree of pleasure, but with as good a grace as is permitted by my surly and melancholic nature. Many thanks to all kind persons who wrote and assured me 'Home by Christmas' (same for the third or even fourth year running). May they not have to do it many times more. I've taken on the job of chief of the woodpile again and am looking forward to smashing about 200 tons of gnarled old roots. My policy is to centralise as far as possible – in fact to do all the talking and very little of the work – a typical jack-in-the-office. In the evenings I half cook for the room. I'm beginning to get a sort of touch or flair after weeks of painful experimenting and I'm capable of dishing out really good stuff. There is very, very little that cannot be improvised from a basis of biscuit crumbs and a lump of margarine. At present my specialities are fishcakes, fried currant pudding and I'm coming on at 'Shapes' trifle, bubble and squeak and mock macaroni cheese. In the spare time left over I shall knit feverishly.

Best love to you all,

Roger

But the inevitable arrival of winter could always be depended upon to lower the most robust spirits.

10 November 1944

A very dreary day with sleet and snow driving across from the west. It's hard work on the woodpile these days as my clothes never seem to get dry and we can't afford a fire in the evening yet. A lot of clothing parcels have come in recently, mostly sent off in June, July or August, but so far my luck is out. I'm getting very ragged in the trouser line but I've still got Tony Rolt's Sandhurst knickers which are standing the strain well. Underclothes are truly hideous and I'm continually putting my feet through the wrong hole. However, by knitting, sewing and swopping I get along alright and it's wonderful how the poor help each other. Cooking is rather dull on half a parcel a week and I try to save on that, as they've completely ceased to come through and we're out on Dec 15th. Altogether this winter is rather bleak but we all remain cheerful and try to get over shortages by ingenuity.

A main course might still be 'meat' at this stage – typically, half a tin of bully beef between six men, mashed up with some low-grade turnips and potatoes, which were prison camp issue by the Germans. This would be followed by bread pudding – old crusts soaked in water and gingered up with a smattering of dried fruit, and baked. A month later, in his Christmas greetings to family and many named friends, Roger is rightly proud of his plum pudding – I'm told it also contained chopped bootlaces for currants . . .

10 December 1944

After three months of saving, I hoarded enough to make a pretty big Christmas pudding – breadcrumbs, margarine, raisins, apricots, prunes, sugar, beer, marmalade, egg powder, a tinned apple pudding and biscuit crumbs. I wrapped it in greased lavatory paper, tied it up in Everard's towel and steamed it madly for 7 hours. It is now hanging from a hook on the wall. The flat sounds nice, but I pity you moving. I know something about moves and they're hell.

Roger means the trauma of being moved from one prison to another.

No sign of any clothes or food parcels, or I fear, those cigars you kindly sent. I had a record week on the woodpile last week and we cut up about 9 tons with three saws and 3 axes in spite of stinking weather. It doesn't seem like five years since I saw you all, and as far as I'm concerned, absence only makes the heart grow fonder and I don't mean that in the ironical sense.
    Roger

The New Year did indeed have a move in store. His weary, resigned and cynical tone shows that my father knew little of the extent of the momentous changes which lay ahead, as the war ground horribly through its closing stages.

1 January 1945

Well, here we are at the beginning of another dreary year of prison life; it is increasingly hard to visualise liberty. Prison has ceased to be an episode and has become one's normal life. One's pre-war friends are vague memories and one's friends are those of your fellow convicts that you can still tolerate after living at close quarters with them for four-and-a-half years. Naturally, we get duller and more useless year by year and I think our worst feature is that we are all very great bores indeed, self-centred, critical and altogether dim. One's existence in the winter is entirely based on food and fuel and it certainly hasn't been a gala winter for either. Books never arrive, or at any rate, very rarely, and one's correspondents dwindle away year by year. If anyone writes to me this year and assures me I shall be home for Christmas, I shall regard it as a very bad omen indeed. I hope prison life will become more normal during the coming year and books, clothes and cigarettes will start filtering though again.

In those final months of the war, the atmosphere at Eichstätt oscillated between hope and elation, fear and despair. As new prisoners were continuously being brought into the camp, they were full of news – often conflicting and confusing information – on military movements and manoeuvres on all sides. Germany was now a country in a state of collapse. There was intense speculation amongst the POWs as to when and by whom they might be liberated and what their fate was likely to be. Roger, in true acidic form, opined that 'If you ask me, we'll all be carved up like a bank holiday ham.' However, his mordant wit was generally welcomed for its cheering effects, as Desmond Parkinson recorded in his diary.

> Wed 24 January 1945: Morty came in for a brew and was in colossal form. He talked most amusingly of his experiences at Sandhurst and as a Subaltern.
> Mon 29 January 1945: In the evening Morty came to visit us and was given stick by one and all.

Desmond's account in his diary culminates in a dramatic day in April 1945, a brutal experience which had a most terrifying effect on himself, my father and their close friends. The heading in Desmond's diary on 14 April 1945 speaks volumes:

> BLACK SATURDAY. The most tragic, terrifying and emotional day of my life as a prisoner.

My father was beside Desmond on that fateful day. This is a summary of that day's events, based on Desmond's diary: the Nazi authorities ordered that POWs must be evacuated from Eichstätt and moved to another camp, Moosberg, where conditions were said to be dire. There was no transport – prisoners were to march the full distance, each with their entire possessions on their back. Leaving early in the morning, our POWs had been tramping on their road for barely an hour when a solitary US plane appeared in the sky. Immediately a great cheer was raised by the men and morale soared. Twenty minutes later, a formation of eight US Thunderbolt bombers appeared overhead. These planes commenced a bombing attack – not on our POWs – but on a convey of German lorries on a parallel road nearby. Alarming though this scenario was, it seemed clear that the pilots were taking pains to avoid the onward column of prisoners. That did not turn out to be the case. As soon as the lorries had been destroyed, the planes swooped over again and, dipping very low, opened a sustained attack of gunfire on the POWs, their allies. No amount of signalling and waving of handkerchiefs succeeded in halting the attack.

Again and again the planes swept down and strafed us from practically road level. Mercifully they must have used up their bombs on the lorries. By this time, Freddie, John, Morty and I were trying to make ourselves as small and inconspicuous as possible in a little hollow some ten yards off the road. We felt horribly exposed and very frightened. My instincts were of self-preservation, but this soon gave way to complete fatalism, punctuated by prayers and thoughts of my family.

It was only when someone had the presence of mind amongst the mayhem to unfurl a Union Jack and lay it in the across the road that the bombers ceased their attack and withdrew. By which time, eight comrades had been killed and forty-two wounded.

At last, we were told that we could make our way back to the camp. We set off carrying our absurdly heavy kit. I have never been so thankful to get back anywhere as I was to reach the comparative sanctuary of our camp at Eichstätt.

I must admit that this whole adventure has shaken me badly, like most other people too. The fact is that after five years of this unreal life , one's powers of resistance to any shock are practically nil and all the terror and tragedy of the morning has hit me deeply. Luckily we are to spend the night here and march off at dusk tomorrow evening, only moving at night. This will give us all a chance to regain our balance. I thank God that all my own friends are safe and sound . . . It is depressing to think that, before the day of our liberation, the line of battle will have to pass over us and that today's horrors may only be a foretaste of things to come.

There would be further darkness before the dawn. Their final camp, Moosberg, was a living hell to be endured before Roger and his surviving comrades would become free men. Their next destination was home – at last.

Years later, my father would reflect back on his life. On 5 May, the anniversary of VE Day, he wrote to me describing his own situation on the day that Europe was liberated.

The Gloomings
5 May [1970s]

Dearest Jane

VE Day. I spent it in 1945 on an airfield in Bavaria waiting for a Dakota to take me part of the way home. Having been in robust health for the entire time in prison, I now contracted diarrhoea. The US Dakota pilots were as drunk as an Irish priest on St Patrick's Day and flew the whole way at just above ground level. Every Frenchman with a gun fired at us. We had been released some days before by General Patton's Army. Patton was a howling cad but a dashing soldier. He hated the English. We were in Moosburg which really was anus mundi. There were 50,000 half-starved Russians in the camp. When these individuals got at the booze and began rounding up German women between the ages of six and ninety-six, there were some very unpleasant scenes I have done my best to forget. We were all confined to the camp by the Yanks but

I took no notice of that and went for a walk with Charlie Rome and Peter Black, my first stroll as a free man since May 1940. It was not very romantic as the Russkis and others crapped everywhere! A lot of the Yanks were unattractive and seemed to regard spitting as normal behaviour. I made friends at merry Moosburg with Peregrine Worsthorne's brother, a jolly little fellow who taught medieval music at Worcester College, Oxford. We are quite chummy to this day though he is an RC. His stepfather Montagu Norman was a v. bad Governor of the Bank of England.

Love to all,

xx D

Another letter is a reminder that my father was old enough to recall the impact of the First World War on his schooldays. As a younger boy, he had wondered at half the women in London appearing in black mourning dress, notably during the Battle of the Somme. After the waste and loss of life on such a scale, it was unimaginable that similar sacrifice could be demanded just twenty years later. His anger is palpable; his memories of German war criminals fascinating.

Hypothermia House
11 November [1980s]

My Dearest Jane

Armistice Day. When I was a boy, Armistice Day was taken very seriously. To make the faintest squeak of noise during the two minutes of silence rated a crime only slightly less deserving of dire punishment than murder. At Eton the whole school assembled in School Yard for the Two Minutes Silence and when the big clock finished striking eleven, silence was absolute. A fair number of my contemporaries had lost a father or a brother in the war. Some of the older masters were visibly moved, remembering the many boys of high promise they had taught and who had given their lives. Over 1,300 Etonians were killed in World War I (we then called it 'The Great War'). My own house had won the football cup in 1914. The photograph in the dining room showed that six out of the eleven members of the team had been killed. The possibility of another European war would at that time (1922) have been considered too improbable for serious consideration. It was not, I think, until 1936 that I fully appreciated that we were doomed. When I think of some really splendid friends who were killed in the last war, I wonder if they would reckon they had been swindled if they could see England as it is today. Incompetent politicians, corrupt trade unions, punks, muggers – charming. The only good result of the last war was getting rid of that dangerous lunatic Hitler. For a short time I looked after some odious war criminals in a house in Kensington Palace Gardens. One, a general, was almost illiterate and simply had no idea of how to spell quite easy German words. He was just a crude thug. Far worse was a former Bavarian priest who gave me a feeling of acute nausea whenever I saw him. He was really cruel in an oily, odious way. Cruel war criminals were seldom Prussian; nearly always Bavarian or Austrian. The nicest man we had in London was Field Marshal von Runstedt, far more agreeable and amusing than many English senior officers, certainly more so than American top-ranking officers. I used to take him in a drink in the evening and we had a good gossip together. No one ever pinned any war crimes on him. A man turned up there, Hauptmann Ebse, who had punished one of his own sentries for failing to shoot me dead when he had the opportunity to do so in 1943. I soon had him scrubbing the cookhouse floor and peeling potatoes with a blunt knife.

I also had to look after a lot of English officers awaiting trial by court martial for various offences. They were quite a jolly lot and I got up a successful little bridge tournament among them to help them pass the time.

Best love,

xx D

As an avid reader of twentieth-century military history, he was perpetually re-examining the events of the two wars that reshaped our world.

The Crumblings
4 August [1970s]

My Dearest Jane,

The date, August 4th, always makes my blood run chilly. I can hardly bear to think of the appalling slaughter, all to no purpose. In the first few months of the war the French suffered more casualties than this country did in 4 years. They had been trained to attack come what may, and wearing blue coats and red trousers (the officers in white gloves) they advanced shoulder to shoulder with standards flying and trumpets blaring. The Germans sat tight and mowed them down with little loss to themselves. Gestures, like the dying French officer who called to his men 'Debout les morts!' were not much use. By Christmas the officer class had been destroyed. Even now I cannot read the staid official account of the Battle of the Somme without tears coming to my eyes. The British Army that attacked the Germans that day was an army of volunteers, the flower of the nation (the regular Army was wiped out at Ypres in 1914). At the Somme, the infantry, half trained, attacked Germans in deep shelters protected by uncut wire. They lost 55,000 killed on the first day, few of them ever setting eyes on a German. Some divisions were completely obliterated. Most battalions went into action with about 24 officers; few emerged with even half a dozen. That is why the left-wing actors in 'Oh! What a Lovely War' were so despicable, the whole attitude being that the officers shirked their duty and left everything to the other ranks. The average lifespan of the 2nd/Lt in the front line was about three weeks. Richard Attenborough's malice in 'A Bridge Too Far' against certain senior officers (dead, conveniently for him) was contemptible. Less serious is that really there has not been much 'douceur de vivre' for the middle classes since 1914. World War II destroyed it all together.

Love,

xx D

This chapter is dedicated to my father and his trusted friends and comrades, both those who died and those to whom he remained close for many more years.

As ever, I give the last word to my father:

The Olde Nuthouse
20 March 1982 [on his pink pig paper]

A good lunch party given by Desmond P. for ex POW chums. All healthy (bar me) and materially successful (except me). Two with dubiously earned knighthoods. One guest had a sexual slip up (male masseur) but has made a million in Thames Valley newsagents' shops.

xx D

4

First and Worst

[1960s]

My Dear Child,
Thank you for your twittering letter. Parts of it were legible
and almost coherent.

> Yours ever,
> D

[1970s]

Dear Little Jane,
I trust you are in your customary robust health, eating like a
starving hippopotamus as usual, and managing to keep out of
the more hideous forms of trouble.

> Love,
> xx D

[1980s]

Dearest Jane,
Thank you so much for your letter; the pleasure of receiving
it was enhanced by its scarcity value.

> Best love,
> xx D

The doorbell rang and dressed up in my best, starched summer frock, I rushed to open it. My parents were having a party. As the arriving guest stepped over the threshold, my father loomed into view. 'This is Jane,' he said cheerily. 'My first and worst.' Tears smarted my eyes, and I turned tail and rushed away.

The role of the eldest child is a double-sided coin. Enjoying exclusive attention for a while, they will also receive the full focus of their parents' anxieties in their first effort in that universal experiment – bringing up a child.

As the eldest, I received the largest quota of letters from my father, a bonus of his determination to launch me into the world to make my own way, as soon as I was able. Unlike Mr Bennet in *Pride and Prejudice*, my father saw more options for his daughter's future security than marriage; I don't think he could foresee any man who might commit himself to my small range of charms. My voice was too loud, my interests too trivial, my nose too large and my dress-sense too curious: I was destined to work. In this aspiration on my behalf, my father was rewarded – intermittently, as consistency of purpose was not a conspicuous virtue in the Mortimer children.

In my earlier years, between the ages of eleven to twenty-two, my father's letters – usually funny, deeply understanding and affectionate – were often also sharp with criticism.

'Sending a child away to school is merely a middle-class abdication of parental responsibility,' my father would pronounce in grave tones. Nevertheless, the children of this responsible father were sent away to school. As his children's trunks were loaded into the car for school, he found it irresistible to chant:

> Going to school, Father Goodbye,
> Take care of Mother and don't let her cry.

My small Hampshire boarding school, Daneshill near Basingstoke, had a friendly, family atmosphere. Our youthful headmistress could be depended upon for her humour and fairness as she steered her 'little toads' towards their O levels, assisted by a sample of sterling teachers along with others whose lessons increased a sense of the world's mysteries but not our knowledge of them. By the time I was fifteen my father commented, 'I've been paying for your education for ten years and you're still as ignorant as a piece of lavatory paper.' He once wrote to me:

'Dear Wafer Head,

You left those nice buttons I gave you on the mantelpiece. I think your head is full of eggshells, old socks and a copy of the *Woman's Magazine* for 20 October 1937.'

I attribute any mental deficiencies to the 1960s bedtime custom for females to wind their hair over great prickly curlers – 'rollers' – and pass their nights, apparently asleep, with these vicious porcupines anchored with pins all over their craniums.

My father enjoyed stimulating his children's idle brains with board games, cards, dominoes, quizzes and general knowledge tests designed by him. Our least educational game was played in the middle of Sunday lunch, between the roast and the pudding: 'The Spinning of the Knife'. My father would take an ivory handled 'best' knife and spin it round on his tablemat. 'Now, whoever this points at will win a gigantic prize next week!' Cries of glee! 'Whoever this points to will find a huge splinter in their left toe tomorrow!' Cries of woe! The game often got completely out of hand, concluding only with my mother's customary protest, 'Oh really, Roger – I do wish you would back me up with the children!'

That we were confident in the love of our parents did not alter, as far as I was concerned, the sense of confusion that they were inadvertently adroit at creating. They each expressed colourful opinions but there was little consensus between them. Having no original thoughts of my own, I soaked up my parents' commentaries and exchanges like a sponge, storing them away for my own use. When, in naive ignorance, I reiterated their views, they sounded at best precocious, at worst pretentious and, to my own peer group, somewhat weird.

My parents' differences could only be exacerbated by their children's progression – if it can be called that – into adolescence.

For teenage Jane, shrouded in cigarette smoke, on went lashings of eye make-up under a curtain of hair hanging over skinny ribbed jumpers and miniskirts or skimpy purple dresses from Biba. As my parents pointed out with castigating candour, I looked ridiculous in such fripperies – common and tarty. One day my father drove me to the station to catch a train to London. He glowered at the feather boa round my neck, the donkey jacket beneath it and the plum, bell-bottom trousers from which peeped my white Courrèges patent leather boots: 'I just hope you are not going to see any of *my* friends in London,' he growled. 'I hope I won't either,' I replied, smiling sweetly.

As far as appearances were concerned – not only my own but that of my mother and sister – there were 'teases' ever at the ready, making us feel invisibility would be infinitely desirable. It is a wonder we ever left the house unconcealed.

By now I was at a sixth-form college in Oxford, broadening my experience but not scaling any heights in exam results. There had been some hope as I had passed my O levels at fifteen-and-a-half.

The most important status symbol was a boyfriend, ideally

a young man who would enjoyably assist a young woman in dispensing with her virginity. It was an easily achievable ambition in a town teaming with fascinating undergraduates with similar missions in mind. 'She was as pure as snow until she drifted,' mused my father with a warning glint in his eye. Many a crisp paternal letter arrived in my college pigeonhole.

After my year-and-a-half at Oxford came the next stage. 'Coming out' was not about your sexuality, but becoming a 'deb' and 'doing the season'. My father's relief was as great as my mother's disappointment at my indifference to this ritual – although with extraordinary graciousness, I conceded to go to what now would be called 'awesome' parties, thrown by my existing friends. Insufficient funds played a significant role in my father's attitude to launching his daughter as a deb – and in my own. Both cash and confidence were thin. On that front and with a shared wariness of 'the meat market', my father and I were united.

My mother longed for this bolshie daughter to get caught up in a whirlwind of upper-crust boyfriends with healthy tastes. 'People from *my* world, Jane. It was all *such fun*. I mean the word "boyfriend" meant something quite different in my day – you had lots of them and they were just *boys* who were *friends*. I don't know why you want to sit around having *psychological* conversations with all those bloody intellectuals [anyone who went to university]. I really wish you wouldn't be so analytical, Jane.'

'Cocktails and laughter, but what comes after, nobody knows,' murmured my father from his armchair.

But my father was proved wrong about my prospects of marriage. After half a handful of significant boyfriends, and a number of others who were not, at the tender age of twenty-two I had the very good fortune to marry a very nice, amusing and intelligent man, Paul Torday, the father of my two sons. We were to remain together for the next eighteen years.

Marriage marked a great sea-change in the tone of my father's letters to me. There was relief – delight even – that his daughter had won the heart of a really good man to take charge of her. From then on, my father confided many more of his personal thoughts to me, ranging widely over his reflections on our family and his life and times.

'Via Dolorosa
Burghclere
6 February [1970s]

Of course this perpetual letter-writing is sheer self indulgence. In fact it is a vice, egotism bordering on narcissism. Perhaps I ought to go and see a really good man about it before the whole thing goes too far and lands me in serious trouble.'

We did not always agree – how dull that would have been. I debated with my father on his racist views, right-wing politics, anti-feminism, anti-religion, how to bring up my children, how to bring up his children, how to pacify my mother, vegetarian food and why I did not have enough red flowers in my garden. Two emotional events in my life caused my father great worry and distress. During these troubling phases, he demonstrated immense sensitivity and kindness, untainted by criticism or reproach. Inevitably one of these events was my divorce from my first husband, Paul, which occurred in my father's final years. I can now empathize with his devastation in far greater depth than I could at the time. Apart from one brief meeting, sadly he never knew my second husband, Tommy Bates, a long-time fan of Roger's writing, whose life I have happily shared for two-and-a-half decades. Meanwhile, Paul married Penelope, his second wife, in the early 1990s.

As the oldest child, I was blessed with the longest period in which to enjoy my father's unique company. From 'first and worst', I now appreciate that I was the 'first and most fortunate'.

My Dearest Jane . . .

Barclay House
25 October [early 1960s]

Thank you for your affectionate and interesting letter this week . . . or am I thinking of someone else?

Horserace Totalisator Board
Monday, summer 1964

You and your mother are entirely different in character and it behoves both of you to be tactful and tolerant. Remember this little quotation: 'Intolerance is the compliment paid by second-rate people to those whose views happen to differ from their own.' In the meantime, 'Aequam Memento rebus in arduis sevare mentem' ('Remember when life's path is steep to keep your mind even'). And always remember things are seldom as bad as they seem except when they're worse.

In the predictably volatile climate of my adolescence, after leaving school I was speedily dispatched to France to polish my French chez the formidable Contesse de Bernard de la Fosse in her chateau in the Loire. Her daughter, Madame Watson, was my tutor. My subsequent destination was sixth form college in Oxford. I was not quite sixteen.

Barclay House
4 September 1964

I hope you had a good flight. I shall look forward to hearing your first impressions of life at Blois. Barclay House seems very quiet without you and peculiar as it may seem, I really think your mother misses you very much. It certainly seems strange to have no one to ask me 45 times a day 'How are you?' as if I was a perpetual invalid! Charley B has given me a very nice present of a cigar and two bars of chocolate. Well, enjoy yourself and work hard; keep in touch and let me know if there is anything you want (except money).

Barclay House
16 November 1964

I have had a letter about you from Madame Watson and doubtless to your intense surprise she speaks quite well of you! Would you believe it?

Barclay House
25 November 1964

I hope we have fixed up for you to go to Oxford. It will give you a chance to learn a few things in the broader sense; the more you learn the more interesting life becomes and the more interesting you yourself become to other people. The trouble with so much of the female education in this country is that it stops too soon and girls are launched into the world knowing damn all except the top twenty and the latest fashions. That is tedious for them and more so for those with whom they have to associate. After all, you can't live on teenage charm forever!

Love,

xx D

Barclay House
17 January 1965

You will soon be grown up and presumably will then be regarding pop music with the same bored nausea as other adults. Try not to get into debt or into any other sort of foolish trouble (one false step, if you don't think twice, bang goes your motto and mother's advice). If you do, let me know and I will help; that is what parents are for. Well, behave yourself and go easy on the mascara.

Horserace Totalisator Board
4 October 1965

I hear you have moved into a new house; no doubt you will add to its general tidiness and sense of quiet decorum. On the whole you were very helpful last holidays and it was good of you to cope with Louise so much, thereby enabling your poor mother to have a brief rest. A fatigue party is hard at work trying to tidy up your room. Try getting rid of a lot of your things; it is surprising how little you will miss them. Try and read a few books. I'm sorry you did not tackle 'Decline and Fall'; I think it is one of the funniest books ever written. I particularly like the bit about Oxford. Captain Grimes is one of the great comic characters in English history. I enclose a small present for some of the peculiar meals you cooked in the holidays; I will give you another when you stop putting all that stuff on your eyes that makes you look as if you were in a No. 3 touring company of the Black and White Minstrels.

Yours ever,

RM

I was not yet sufficiently sophisticated to appreciate Evelyn Waugh.

The Sunday Times
25 January 1966

I'm glad you enjoyed your Geburtstag and it was nice of you to write. I very much enjoyed the lunch and have fallen in a big way for Sally. I wish I was 43 years younger. It was natural of your friend to assume I am a don: in fact I am one, and have been leading a double life for years, being Regius Professor of Islamic Studies at Reading University. Keep it to yourself, though, or your mother might ask for more housekeeping money.

Sally Ann Roberts was a close friend I made at Oxford – a raven-haired beauty, intelligent, ambitious, of memorable integrity and wonderful company. Tragically, her potential was never fully realised. She died after an accident on her twenty-first birthday.

Barclay House
5 November 1965

Guy Fawkes Night and all around I hear bangs and explosions. How the English adore standing out in the cold watching their children burn themselves quite badly with highly unpredictable squibs and rockets. I enjoyed seeing you last week but I would rather you did not wear a long discarded jersey, clearly from a male wardrobe. I trust you are working hard and not looking too farouche. If there is one type of adolescent that gives me quite a severe pain it is the male or female to whom the label of 'student' is unmistakably attached. Undergraduate, OK, but 'student', never. It makes me think of spotty young socialists at the London School of Economics. Avoid, therefore, if you can the cult of ugliness so distressingly fashionable with the young.

Barclay House
22 November [mid 1960s]

Thank you very much indeed for sending me a charming and well-chosen card and a most interesting pair of scarlet braces manufactured from what appears to be genuine elastic. Thank you, too, for that odd looking stopper. Into what am intended to insert it? (Don't bother to answer that question.) I received a bottle of liqueurs from your brother; he originally intended to give me a table for my lavatory, but unfortunately, due to a miscalculation in planning, the table was so big that when it was introduced, not without difficulty, into the lavatory, I was unable to get within three-and-a-half feet of the seat. By the way, Louise gave me two bars of chocolate.
Best love,
D

Barclay House
24 January 1966

I expect you to have fun but at the same time you have reached
the age when you have got to come to terms with reality.
I wish I could detect in you some signs of wanting to plan
your life; drivelling on about clothes and parties is perfectly
permissible and natural at your age, provided it is not the
main theme of your life but just a gay background to some
more serious purpose.

If you can decide what you want to do and how you intend
to do it, I will try and help you, but the tiresome fact that you
have to digest is that I have spent my earnings on education
for you all; once your education is over you've had your lot
as far as money is concerned; I have not even anything saved
up for my old age or for your mother when I give the bucket
a resounding kick. Please take this in and start planning your
life accordingly.

I must now get some gin out for Mrs Hislop who is coming
for a drink.

Yours ever,
RM

Barclay House
[1966]

I have just had a letter from St Clare's complaining that you
are extremely casual over your work, that you are missing
classes, and that you are obviously not giving sufficient time
and thought to your homework. I expect you to enjoy yourself
at Oxford, but I also expect you to have sufficient common
sense and strength of mind to work properly.

As regards the future, I suggest you pull yourself together

and try to get into your foolish little mind that in just over a year's time you will be completely self-supporting, and I emphasise the word 'completely'. Your standard of living will depend on your own industry and intelligence, not mine. At present you are too scatty and disorganised to hold down the job of waitress in a Camberley coffee bar.

It is really up to you. I don't mind spending all the cash the tax collector permits me to keep on children's education provided the children respond and make the most of their opportunities. It infuriates me to be told that you are chucking those opportunities away. Hard work is almost entirely a matter of self-discipline and moral courage; I trust you are not devoid of those qualities.

Just get that finger of yours out and at the risk of spraining your brain, just THINK.

Your affectionate and exasperated father.

Barclay House
[Mid 1960s, postcard]

Good News for You! I will let you off that £1 you borrowed from me and were just about to send off.

Love,

D

Barclay House
18 May 1966

I have just read your letter with some concern. Most of life is a compromise, and until you are 21 and completely independent there will probably have to be a compromise between your ideas and wishes and those of your parents. I don't claim to know what is right for you; I can only offer advice based on experience. In an imperfect world, money is of considerable importance and you are not, in my opinion, the sort of person that would be really happy in poverty. Therefore I want to prepare you to earn your living. If I had the means I would be only too willing to support you financially until I become a pillar of greasy smoke at Woking Crematorium. But unfortunately I am getting on for sixty, which is horribly old for a journalist as at that age one loses any facility for new ideas or originality of expression. At any time now I may be given a kindly reminder that I have out-served any useful purpose that once I had.

I do not seek to control your life, only to equip you to cope with the modern world. I wish I felt certain I knew what was best for you in the long run. As the old Field Marshal observed: 'It is easy to do your duty; the difficulty is in deciding where your duty lies.'

Best of British luck and much love,

x D

Barclay House
3 August 1966

I really am sorry you are having such a rough time but try and realise that for all their faults and follies, your parents are on your side and will do all they can to help. That's what parents are for! Let me know at once if there is anything I can do for you. I love you very much and will do anything I can to help you solve any difficult problems satisfactorily.

Best love from your occasionally well-meaning father,

xx

Barclay House
3 April 1967

Could you please, by 10 April if possible, let me know your
plans for the future? Much as I like having you at home
where you do much useful work, I feel that the time has
come for you to earn your living. I do not think I am being
particularly unreasonable in suggesting you get down to
work, as except for a spell at Miss Wilson's Secretarial
Academy, you have been unemployed (bar some Christmas
work) since you came home from Oxford last July. In the
words of the old song:
   'We don't want to lose you,
   But we think you ought to go.'
   It would be kind of you, therefore, to let me know your
plans; not just dithering generalities, but firm intentions.
   Yours ever,
   D

Barclay House.
27 April 1967

I miss you very much here and the house is deplorably quiet
without you and Charles. I expect you may feel a bit lonely
and homesick for a day or two but I think you will find Eton
quite a friendly place and you will meet plenty of people of
your own age.

*A colony (household) of bachelor beaks (masters) at Eton,
desperate to secure a cook for a term, handed me the job.
How kindly and indulgently they treated me; I was fascinated
by them. The youngest, now Sir Jeremy Greenstock, rose to*

become a high-profile ambassador at the United Nations;
Mark Phillips became a housemaster – as did Howard Moseley
and dear, splendid Michael Meredith (Eton Librarian) – to my
future sons. Michael Kidson was legendary for lavishing his
affable brand of derisory wit upon his pupils, other masters
and myself. Always on the side of the boys, he bailed out
my brother more than once. Fifteen-year-old Charlie, aka
Lupin, visited me regularly for tea, snacks and surreptitious
cigarettes.

Barclay House
April 1967

Charles is really very pleased to have you there; inspire him
to work if you can. He made a typical remark after we left
you last night: I asked him who the masters were and his
only comment was 'The one that hadn't shaved is rather
nice.' Your room looks quite pleasing; let me know if there
is anything you want. I will bring back some sausages from
Newmarket next week and drop them at the Corner House
for you. Don't smoke too much or try to be bright and chatty
at breakfast.
    Best love,
    xx D

Barclay House
30 April 1967

I thought it might cheer you up as you toil at the stove
cooking for the beaks at the Corner House to receive a

letter. I hope you will establish a new standard of food at Eton and banish forever boiled cod and caper sauce followed by cornflower shape. Now the warm weather is here, an imaginative hors d'oeuvres is delectable, followed by lamb cutlets and new potatoes. If your clients show signs of losing weight, block them up with a tremendous suet roll, washed down with a tin of golden syrup. Boiled beef, dumplings and young carrots form an excellent stopper too, particularly if preceded by a bowl of thick pea soup nourished with cream. Keep an eye on that irresponsible but not entirely detestable brother of yours and ensure that even if he declines to work, he occasionally washes and changes his socks.

If you fall in love with a beak, choose a rich one. Preferably not a scientist of leftist views. I suggest a classical scholar with a nice place in Wiltshire and a villa in the South of France.

Budds Farm
Autumn 1967

So glad you have landed yourself a nice job in London entirely on your own initiative. You will soon be able to employ your brother (or me) as butler – chauffeur – social secretary!

Best love,
xx D

If only I could remember which job was being applauded!

Budds Farm
28 April 1968

I hope you are behaving with suitable decorum now you are living alone in your super-luxury flat in the heart of fashionable, exotic Notting Hill Gate. Today the de Mauleys are coming to lunch so no doubt we are in for a feast of lively, intelligent conversation ('Does Jane see lots of nice people in London and go to lots of lovely parties?'). I think I shall say you are walking out with Tariq Ali.

Lady de Mauley could be relied upon to promote the necessity of meeting the right people.

Budds Farm
Tuesday [1969]

I hope you are conducting yourself with bourgeois decorum and are giving no practical demonstrations of your approval of the permissive society.

Budds
6 May [late 1960s]

I trust you are well and are living up to the exacting social standards of darkest Islington. Your dear mother of course fears the worst and seems to think you would be better off with a nice chaperone somewhere near Pont Street.

Sois sage,
xx D

183 The Turf Club
Monday [January 1970]

It is very kind of you to ask me to dinner on the 23rd bearing
in mind the long-established fact that parents tend to be
odious with their children, and children only slightly less
so with their parents. What costume shall I wear? My old
blue three-piece, betraying to one and dreary all my middle-
class background, or a bottle-green wig, spangled pyjama
suit (displaying emerald in navel). I trust your various 21st
birthday parties go off well and I personally see no difficulties,
but from your poor mother's point of view it is as complicated
as the Versailles Peace Treaty and probably as unsatisfactory,
too.

The 'Au Revoir' Home for Distressed Gentlefolk
Barbara Castle Crescent
Brookwood
Surrey
22 July 1970

My Poor Improvident Child, not entirely to my surprise you
seem to be thoroughly disorganised and in grave financial
difficulties. I have therefore instructed Mr Featherbole of
Lloyds Bank to cable you £30 forthwith at your current poste
restante address. It ought to arrive tomorrow. Your brother
set off at 9 p.m. today; at 9.45 he was back, having forgotten
his luggage. At 10.15 he was back again having forgotten his
razor (an item which will probably not be over-employed). He
is a very likeable moron. Louise, who has had a bad school
report, sends her love. Thank you for the photograph. Can it
have been you in a herringbone suit and slight beard?

I had left my job as an advertising copywriter for a summer on a Greek island, travelling with Paul who had taken his typewriter to do some writing. A writer at heart, his first bestselling novel was published in 2007 – Salmon Fishing in the Yemen – one of many. Lupin drove out to join us for a spell. He arrived four days after we had left. Back in London, I became distracted by different people and activities.

Le Petit Bidet
Burghclere Les Deux Eglises
Sunday [November 1970]

How is your curious existence progressing? What are the latest episodes in this heart-gripping serial that plumbs the depths of human emotions and strikes a new note? Have you succeeded in busting open that terrifying monopoly in the creation of bizarre shoulder bags that was threatening western culture, nay even civilisation itself? Are you still in the throes of a meaningful relationship with the trendy, avant-garde critic of wet and dry groceries whose name continues to elude me? What pulsating dramas are being steamily worked out behind those prim Georgian facades of groovy Gibson Square? No one tells me anything and I'd like to be told – though not at any great length.

My phase of making beautiful handbags was of little appeal to my father. The trendy avant-garde critic was funny, clever and sanguine Scot, Colin Adamson – still a true friend.

Ward No 27
Mortimer Home for the Mentally Under-Privileged
Nuthampstead
Herts
[Late 1970]

I enjoyed seeing you last week and thank you for helping. I thought you looked well despite efforts, worthy of a nobler cause, to maintain members of the tobacco trade in full employment. I'm sorry if your own life is giving you trouble. I wish you would get another job. I think you are squandering your talents. The fact that most of your relations are mad, egocentric, irresponsible, unreliable, financially incompetent and hysterical – in fact a truly lamentable collection of middle-class dropouts – is no excuse for you to make a morose hash of your own life.

    Best love,
    xx D

My father was right. However, things took a happy and decisive turn in April 1971 when I became engaged to Paul.

Budds Farm
May 1971

We are meeting Dr and Mrs Torday this week. I expect from what they've heard of us they'll nervously be awaiting two total lunatics; I don't think they'll be disappointed. To promote a merry family atmosphere for your nuptials, I have decided to dismiss my worries about Charles from my mind and to wash away my resentment in a copious flow of stimulating alcoholic beverages, with the East Woodhay Silver

Band playing 'Here's to the next time' in the background.
Your affectionate father,
xx

*In July, we married in St Mary's Church, Islington, with a
reception in Chelsea.*

The Sunday Times
1 October 1972

I am delighted to hear from your dear mother that you have
moved to a very attractive house. Stet Fortuna Domus!
Harrogate is (or used to be) a sort of poor man's Baden
Baden. I once stayed there for the St Leger (1937) and was
permanently sloshed in the Majestic Hotel. The waters at
Harrogate are good for the liver but somewhat unpredictable
in their immediate results. When I was a boy an old admiral
warned me never to trust a Harrogate fart. Coarse counsel
but wise.

*After a year we left London when Paul was offered a job
with a company near Leeds. We bought a cottage close to
Harrogate.*

The Sunday Times
The Editor in Chief's Office
Midnight [1972]

I am content that you seem happy in Yorkshire but of course
wish you were not so far away. However, I intend to motor to

Harrogate before long to take the waters since my liver and kidneys are howling out for treatment. I shall look forward to taking a number of delicious meals chez Torday.

Budds Farm
31 January 1973

Just a brief note to wish you and your ever-loving husband a successful New Year and what the prayer book calls a happy issue out of all your afflictions; which includes your driving test.

The Sunday Times
2 April 1973

It really was nice seeing you – and the esteemed P. Torday, too, this weekend and your visit gave Cynthia and myself a lot of pleasure. Of course I'm sorry you are off to live in Northumberland – I must look it up on the map one day – but one cannot expect one's children to spend their lives within an hour's drive of the old soaks at home. The best way to keep in touch will be by correspondence; I will endeavour to write to you once a week and I hope you will try and do roughly the same.

Change was on the way again. Following the tragedy of the death of my mother-in-law in a car accident in Kenya, Paul brought forward his long-term plan to go and support his father in the family engineering business near Newcastle upon Tyne.

Budds Farm
[1970s]

I'm sorry I was short with you on the telephone. I ought
not to have answered it as I was doing something I thought
(mistakenly) was important. Your mother is entertaining 4
men in the kitchen including a postman press-ganged into
moving a swarm of bees. Your mother has monopolised the
conversation and not even a bee has managed to get in a
buzz. Am now off to do a vase for the flower show.

  xx D

*The 'important' activity that I had disturbed was the boiling
of his breakfast egg. He hated the telephone.*

HM Office for the Deciphering of Ancient Documents
19 Sludge Street
London WC1
[1970s]

I sent a page of your last letter to a local handwriting expert,
Mrs Eunice Thribbs. I did not reveal your identity and she
drew the following conclusions: 'Your Pakistani friend is
a victim of recurrent malaria and his consequently shaky
hold of a cut price biro has led to malformation in much
of the script. A modest knowledge of the English language,
in particular the spelling of words containing more than
one syllable, adds to the problems of even a pertinacious
reader. I conclude that the writer is male, over seventy
years of age, several times married, has suffered from
trench feet, is willing to please but is handicapped by scanty
education and an unfavourable environment. His religion is

Primitive Methodist, his favourite dish curried rabbit and his colour shocking pink. Lucky day – the martyrdom of St Vitus.'

xx RM

Budds Farm
15 June 1974

I wish you and the highly esteemed Paul Torday were here as it is very hot and conditions are ideal for croquet and jugs of Muscadet with the unexpended portion of yesterday's fruit salad floating around on top.

Budds Farm
28 August [mid 1970s]

It is very kind of you to invite the Budds Farm mob up for Christmas; personally I would as soon have the Kray gang. I will certainly give your generous invitation most serious attention. Why, you may ask, does the old dodderer not accept at once? The reasons are as follows. While in full appreciation of your comfortable house, bounteous hospitality and stimulating company, I rather dread in midwinter two car drives of inordinate length particularly with the car loaded to the roof. Also, as one gets more and more senile and decrepit, one is reluctant to leave one's one own home and is happier amid the old familiar lares et penates. However comfortable the beds, I never sleep well away from my own bracket, although sometimes the non-stop drone of your dear mother's voice induces a form of coma not totally un-reminiscent of blissful unconsciousness. I am sure all the other members of my family are looking forward to coming to Hexham and would be bitterly disappointed if they were prevented from doing so. My present inclination, therefore, is to send them with my blessing and some money for petrol and to hold the fort here with the dogs. I think your mother will be in far better form without me and will find ample compensation for my physical absence in the knowledge that she can make the wildest and most inaccurate statements with rather less fear of contradiction.

This didn't prevent my parents from spending Christmas with us in Hexham and, two years later, at our next home, a rented farmhouse near Corbridge – Brocksbushes.

Budds Farm
27 December [late 1970s]

It really was kind of you to shelter the Budds Farm Oldsters under your wings and to take such unremitting trouble to give them a very happy Christmas. I don't often get champagne for elevenses! (Unfortunately.) I like Brocksbushes very much indeed. I very much enjoyed occupying the 'Senex suite' which greatly reduces the danger of grave injury when falling out of bed.

The 'Senex suite' involved a double mattress on the floor of a bright yellow bedroom.

The Olde House with No Loo Paper
29 December [early 1980s]

Thank you both so much for giving us such a happy Christmas which I assure you was greatly appreciated by Cynthia and myself. Your charming house was beautifully warm and the browsing and sluicing were of a high order. The 'groaning board' reminded me of two lines by F.J.B. Snelgrove (The Byron of Upper Norwood):

> 'Where grapes and grouse commingle gaily,
> And capers mix with capercailye.'

I think your particular brand of hospitality, based on a judicious mixture of solicitude and laissez faire has everything to recommend it. Thanks for all your presents. I am wearing the red socks and drank tepid Nescafé out of the pig-mug. Give my love to the scholar and the athlete.

With Love and gratitude
xx D

The scholar and the athlete were my sons. Yes – we had moved again. Our landlords needed Brocksbushes for themselves, so we bought enchanting Matfen High House when property prices were peaking.

The Old Damp Ruin
Burghclere-under-Water
3 January [early 1980s]

Paul still stands impeccably high in Cynthia's estimation (a bit annoying for me) and she leads acquaintances to believe that he is a cross between Sir Winston Churchill and St Francis of Assisi.

My mother Cynthia is now irretrievably known by her nickname – Nidnod.

Loud Screechings
Burghclere
2 March 1981

It was a great pleasure having you to stay and your brief visit made me regret all the more that you live away up north with the Eskimos. It was most agreeable, too, having the highly esteemed Paul Torday to stay, and both of you were not only extremely helpful but very tactful with Nidnod who has the lowest combustion point of any adult resident in this country: or in Europe for that matter. Paul was probably the success of your mother's birthday party. More seriously, watch your husband carefully and try to ensure that he does not work too hard. It is quite an easy thing to do, to work too hard, and then the penalty is very severe. I once had a commanding officer who was dead keen on what he termed 'rest discipline'. In his own case, his particular form of self-denial included two large glasses of gin and French before lunch, two large glasses of vintage port after a snack of steak and kidney pudding, marmalade roll and stilton cheese, this frugal diet being followed by deep sleep on a sofa till 4.30 p.m. when the waiter aroused him with Indian tea and muffins, sometimes a generous slice of plum cake as well.

Mind you look after your health and as far as possible lay off that dried up camel crap which is commonly referred to as tobacco. You have a lot of nervous energy. Do not be too prodigal in its expenditure.

Love to you all,

xx D

The Old Ice Box
Monday, January 1979

Of course being 30 years of age is a rather depressing landmark though nothing like as bad as 40 when many members of your sex enter the dreaded realm of Old Bagdom, never to return. I was 30 the year the Second World War started! I have had a fairish ration of life since then, some of it rather awful, some not unamusing. I long ago realised that happiness was an unattainable target and settled for contentment: which sounds stodgy and probably is. I cannot compare the lives of your generation with those of my contemporaries since circumstances are so entirely different. In my day members of the middle and upper classes (both sexes) did not marry as young as they do now. Men in particular had years of comparative freedom from domestic responsibility and if they possessed any enterprise at all they had a very good time one way or another. A young man married at 21 was reckoned odd or boring: of course, girls who marry young nowadays are sentenced more or less for life to an existence of nanny, cook, housekeeper, dog-doser, part-time chauffeur, hospital nurse and entertainer of her husband's friends. My mother never changed a nappy, sat up with a sick child and felt quite exhausted after ordering meals (one sort for the family, another for the servants). Probably most of your existence will be lived after 30 and at times you will feel frustrated and depressed, but as long as you can keep on speaking terms with your family and have a few loved and loving friends, life will produce many compensations. Of course as you grow older you do not make friends in quite the same way as you did when you were younger: you are not so close and you do not exchange confidences in the old uninhibited way. Friends too are apt to move on to a different level when they marry or you yourself do.

I am now nudging 70, and like it or not, the end of the road cannot be far off and one has to accept it. One merely hopes that the last furlong will not be unutterably sordid. Of course, I have many regrets, but none over my major sins (except that I did not commit more of them). I do, however, deeply regret glaring cases of unkindness, ingratitude, insensitivity, ill-manners, moral cowardice and snobbishness; particularly ingratitude to those who have loved me, or at least learnt to tolerate me. I expect I shall be asked some awkward questions on Judgement Day but I must say that I have got one or two little points I intend to put to God. Did you hear of the trendy schoolmaster who died suddenly and went to Heaven? On arrival the first person he saw was the Devil. He expressed mild surprise to St Peter who replied, 'Didn't they tell you we had gone Comprehensive?' I expect that with your lively mind you must at times feel stifled by Northumberland. Even in Berkshire life is pretty turgid. If we go out to dinner the conversation seldom rises above the price of restaurants in London, the shortage of domestic help and the eccentricities of Mr Wedgwood Benn. The fact is that unless you go to London a fair amount you become a turnip. I am a complete bumpkin: as James Forsyte used to complain, 'no one ever tells me anything'. Marriage often results in having to live in areas one would hardly have chosen oneself. Look at all those gallant women who, in the days when we had an Empire and were not ashamed of it, 'followed the drum' into some really ghastly holes.

Osbert Sitwell as a young man was stationed at Aldershot. A ballet fan, he had to cut short parties after the ballet, explaining he had to get back to Aldershot. 'Qu'est que c'est cet Aldershot?' asked Diaghilev, 'C'est une femme?'

Best love,

xx D

My dear father was pretty dismissive about 'The North' – but then that was his take on the provinces in general. Feudal though it felt then, conservative though it may still be, there are plenty of livewires in the beautiful county of Northumberland!

The Drippings
Dampwalls
15 January [early 1980s]

I expect you are too busy to work seriously on a book. The trouble with writing a book is that it absorbs too much time and energy: it becomes the centre of your existence and is likely to make you a very great bore indeed to one and all, particularly to one's ever-loving family. I think you are fully capable of writing a readable book, but it will be terribly hard work while you are looking after children. However, persevere, and like the late Miss Barbara Pym you will very likely win through in the end. Only women can really write about women and very often their books appeal particularly to other women (and I'm not just thinking of that awful old ratbag Barbara Cartland).

My father unfailingly encouraged me in any writing project. Ideas sometimes crystallized into published features, articles or small books for niche markets. On my study shelf sits a card from my father in 1981:

Congratulations! I'm glad we appeared in the *Sunday Times* together, a fairly rare journalistic combination I imagine.
  xx D

Budds Farm
19 February [early 1980s]

Thank you for your letter which I enjoyed although it appeared to have been written with the sharp end of a shooting stick dipped into soot. The photographs were interesting rather than flattering: don't let any sociologist get hold of them or else we'll all be on TV as a typical problem family. It is cold enough here to make an Eskimo turn up the central heating; unfortunately I am unable to do so due to the prohibitive cost of oil. Moreover, damp logs do little but disprove the theory that there can be no smoke without fire. I have been bullied into buying something called a 'duvet' and I must admit I like it: so does my dog whose breath at present would drive a tractor.

Budds Farm
[Mid 1980s]

Probably in many ways you would be happier in NW1 but . . . Have you thought of writing a serious book? Some episode in history, something requiring not just slapdash pen-and-ink diarrhoea, but patient research. How about the Bywaters-Thompson murder case. Mrs Thompson was a remarkable woman who was really hanged for adultery rather than murder, her case being 'worse' as she was so much older than Bywaters. How much did the attitude of the judge help to condemn her? Were the appalling rumours about her execution really true? I don't want to give you advice which is always unwelcome unless it accords with the notions of the recipient. I do though suggest that you do not dabble in too many things but decide on a target and stick to it. You have imagination and ability but somehow you have not directed them to a truly suitable target. I personally think you have a good book lurking in you somewhere provided you can add patience to your other talents and virtues.

P.S. I was not a total failure in the seedy world of journalism but did not write a word till I was 37. My first book came out at 46.

In my bottom drawer I have that book – two years research, not into a murder case but the history of boys' prep schools. I needed to understand why British parents, including ourselves, sent our sons to boarding school at such a tender age. My father loved the book, an endorsement insufficiently echoed by publishers.

Budds Farm
[Mid 1980s]

I am delighted to hear you are making your mark with the RHS. Perhaps you will eventually go down to history as the Gertrude Jekyll of Appletree Bank. Have you got the right type of boots? A sunken garden sounds a good idea as long as it does not sink with all hands during a long spell of hostile weather. Above all, don't try and do too much. No one of your age thinks they are mortal but there is a limit to strength and energy. If you go flat out at both writing and horticulture you may spring a leak. Try and develop the habit of intermittent indolence. Any BF can overwork: I did it myself once and paid dearly for it. When a book is going well, it is all too easy to put in too many hours a day. If you start losing your zest for steak and kidney puddings, are assailed by demon insomnia and wake up with throbbing headaches, take a week off and revise your routine. It is healthier to work before breakfast than after 6 p.m.

Very hot today. Whenever I look at *The Times* to see what the temperature in Newcastle is, it is always 57!

Best love,

xx D

We were now in our sixth home, Lanehead, near Allendale. Downsizing, we bought a ruined shell plus four acres of land in a beautiful, remote setting. As overseer of building works, I was not of the calibre seen on TV's Grand Designs, *sporting a safety helmet whilst anchoring roof slates in howling gale. I preferred to wield my spade to make a garden, simultaneously writing a book,* An Idiot's Introduction to Gardening, *which sold at the Royal Horticultural Society bookshop. Gardening – its pleasures and pains – were another bond between my father and I.*

The Miller's House
7 June [1980s]

We are very fortunate in Kintbury in that among the inhabitants is Professor J. H. Forklifter who has done some impressive work on ancient inscriptions in little known Indian dialects found in a temple in one of the remoter parts of Bengal. I gave him your letter and he kindly got to work on it. He made sense of about 75 per cent of it but is puzzled by your reference to the cricket match on Christmas Day in Nova Scotia. Anyway, thank you very much for writing; your industry was greatly appreciated.

Woodlings Burghclere
Tuesday [early 1980s]

I don't often complain about my offspring but I have a complaint to make against you. Namely, that I see you so seldom. If I live to be 75 (not a good bet the way things are going at present) the meetings left to us barely reach double figures. The solution is not easy: perhaps we could split the distance and have a piss up at the Majestic at Harrogate?

Best love,
xx D

Budds Farm
22 January 1980

I hope you'll have a very happy birthday, remembering to temper your hilarity with a modicum of reserve. I expect you feel fairly ancient at 31, but the thirties are a pretty good epoch on one's life. One is some way from being a dodderer but old enough to realise what a BF one often was in one's twenties. You ought to have a good time with the children during the next nine years or so, after which the birds will start spreading their wings. Your brother was wonderful value up to the age of 13. Too many birthdays just at present. Mabel is 88 tomorrow and still very on the ball. John Surtees is 61 on Saturday and I am sending him a tasteful card. You are fortunate at having your 31st birthday at home in the bosom of your near and dears.

I had quite a run of birthdays away from the old homestead, as follows:

Alexandria

Jerusalem

La Guirche

Spannenberg (a small but repellent prison camp)

Warburg (a large and even more repellent ditto)

Eichstätt (slightly better)

Ditto

Ditto

Trieste

Senior Officers School

Your mother is at her art class and is threatening to take up painting in oil. We had a very successful lunch party on Sunday, Emma E. being the cook. I think a reasonably good time was had by all. I have just had a belated card from Basil Madjoucoff, who is now the Very Reverend Basil Madjoucoff, Pastor and Dean! Thinks: was it my finest hour when I beat him in the final of YMCA table tennis tournament in Jerusalem?

To make your guests nice and talkative, I think the easiest drink is an old-fashioned Bronx: 1/3 Lemon juice 1/3 Any old brandy even something brewed up behind the Corbridge Gas works 1/3 Cointreau. Anyway, my dear child, have a good time and try and forget the country is on the brink of national bankruptcy and World War III.

Best love,

xx R

The Old Lazar House
Burghclere
27 August [early 1980s]

Dear Little Miss Voluble,
    It was very nice seeing you again and your lively conversation added a new facet to breakfast.

The Miller's House
14 January [1980s]

Thank you for your letter which I greatly enjoyed. I am not surprised you hate rugger. It is hardly your scene. Why not offer your services as a goalpost? I had a nice Christmas present yesterday – a bottle of champagne. Whenever you feel unwell, have two glasses of champagne. If that does not cure you, you are very seriously ill.
    D xx

The Miller's House
27 December 1988

We drove home in summer weather: only saw 10 lorries in the first 100 miles. Thanks for a delicious haversack ration: the consommé was up to your best standard. I don't kid myself that a semi-moribund crumblie adds much to the traditional Christmas festivities, rather the reverse in fact, but I enjoyed myself a lot and the browsing and sluicing were beyond praise. Paul is exceptionally generous in the drinks dept. Anyway, thank you all, including those two bouncing boys, for giving me such a good time. I assure you your efforts were greatly appreciated. Thank you all very much indeed.

xx RFM

The Miller's House
26 January 1988

I enjoyed seeing you and it is difficult to believe that you are well on the way to the wrinkled forties. You certainly don't look it and you remain agreeably high spirited too. Why not have lunch with me in the early spring and I will take you to the Renoir Exhibition. A view of those fine fleshy women gives me the temporary illusion that I am still alive. We might also see 'The Shooting Party' (I enjoyed the book) at the Curzon Cinema where the seats supply adequate bum comfort. Expect a teeny Lent present from me in the not far distant future.

The Miller's House
31 August [early 1990s]

This is the last day of summer. I cannot help wondering if I shall ever see another one. I'm lucky to have seen as many as I have. It is rather sad, at least I think that it is, that we live so far apart and exist in consequence in different worlds. However, as long as you're happy!

Best love,
xx D

The mantra of loving parents: 'We only want our children to be happy.' How did that dream work out for those younger siblings of mine? Here they come.

5

Lupin and Lumpy

The Scorchings
Burghclere
12 August 1974

Dearest Jane,

I much relished having all the family here recently and in the term 'family' I include your much respected husband and the genial Sir Dennis [my baby son]. Families can be monstrous things but one of the few virtues of the Mortimer set up is that you, Charles and Louise have always got on so well with each other. If there is a family dust-up it is Chinese odds on your mother being in the thick of it, probably the instigator. Against this you must weigh the fact that she is a person of high physical and moral courage and would literally lay down her life for any member of the family if she thought the need had arisen. Her loyalty to us all causes her to expect fewer faults in us and more virtues than we actually possess.

Best love to you all,

xx D

Being the oldest may define your position in the family hierarchy, but the small significance of this primacy was diminished by one crucial detail – I was not a boy. Just as I was getting into my stride as top dog, aged three, along came my brother. If trumpets could have sounded and bells rung, they would have done. My parents were overjoyed – a boy was a proper person. Abounding in good humour from his earliest moments, he was an immediate success. There was little indication then of Charlie's future as Lupin, wildcard, renegade and occasional exhibitionist. His most extravagant act of attention-seeking as an infant was to rock his cot so hard that it moved across the room and blocked the door, which had to be removed from its hinges to gain access to the dear little fellow.

For a brief period my brother and I both attended the same private primary school. My first emotional memory of my little brother was seeing him march out of assembly with his curious gait and an untamed tuft of golden hair sticking up at the centre of his head. I was overwhelmed with a sudden rush of protective sisterly love. He was not a brother who ever beat me up, put a frog in my bed or tied me to a tree and left me to be eaten by wolves. But I was of inferior sex, and within a few years, he was reminding me daily that I was nothing but a girl, pronounced and written 'Gurrrl', a name which stuck, ultimately evolving into Miss G.

At eight years old it was time for my brother's first rite of passage: leaving home for prep school as a boarder. In his first year, his return to wind-blasted Wellesley House on the Kent coast had been delayed through illness. Later that term, I accompanied my mother on the 130-mile drive to drop him back at school. It was not a heartening experience – home was the only place where my brother wanted to be. As we drove away, I turned and watched this small lone figure waving from the school steps, absurd in his bizarre uniform of tweed plus fours, and my tears started to flow. 'It's just l-l-l-like *Oliver!*' I sobbed. I knew every song from the musical off by heart. I didn't have the reassurance of knowing that within minutes my brother would be in his dorm, ragging with his friends. And neither did my poor mother.

The floor of my brother's room at home was dense with Dinky cars and a Scalextric track which was always going wrong, a happy challenge to its owner's engineering skills, his particular talent. Later, further electronic devices were wired up over every conceivable space in his room. These gadgets were activated by clapping his hands, which he did when he awoke in the morning. Loud strains of 'You ain't nothing but a hound dog' from his icon, Elvis, throbbed through his door, a signal for his elder sister to fetch him 'a cuppa tea'. You get the picture. By twelve years old, my brother had equipped himself with a black plastic 'leather' jacket and winkle-pickers, replacing his bright blue patterned jumper – accessorized by his pink straw pork pie hat for holidays.

With his passion for cars, Charlie spent hours helping out at the local garage. Our father saw this as a harmless aberration, certainly not as a potential career path for an essentially practical boy, one devoid of academic interest and, unknown to teachers or parents, heavily hampered by a then unrecognised condition – serious dyslexia. All things being unequal, Eton was his destiny.

As for the rest, my brother has provided his own record in print. As Lupin, he became a lead player not only in my father's now legendary letters to him, but in letters to me from both my parents. At school, he was still an innocent little chap of only minor mischiefs – with the nicknames Charlie B, Tich or Twitch. Before long Lupin would gain his reputation as something of a delinquent and exhibitionist who continues to insist, even now as a 'senior citizen', that he is a 'spiv'. Always drawn to low-life scenarios dominated by every variety of unreliable nutcase, he was often highly amused by the individuals he found in the lower depths. He is fundamentally a very kind man. He has always willingly embraced those he could effectively befriend, from tragic addicts to self-deluding crooks, energetically dedicating himself to sorting stuff out for his fellow fallible human beings. In this, I include his family, to whom he demonstrated his loyalty through his consistent care of our mother in her last years and his fair and meticulous management of all her affairs on our behalf. He was a genuinely good and loving son. All these efforts have been set against a background of his personal struggle with bad health for over thirty years, undertaken with enduring courage and humour. Illness has never prevented him from tackling tasks in hand.

In 2005, he went to the Chelsea and Kensington Registry office with his partner Tim to become the first couple there to have a civil partnership ceremony. Labelled as a non-stayer, my brother as Charlie, not Lupin, has turned out to be a remarkable survivor – and that is staying power of a high order.

My first sight of my much younger sister Louise was in my mother's arms on the morning of 13 January 1958. My mother had given birth at home the day before. I had felt cheated of being excluded from such an interesting occasion, but gained a treat, being removed unexpectedly to London by my mother's friend, Lady de Mauley, to attend a pantomime along with two jolly little boys, her son, Tommy Collins, and Desmond Parkinson's son, Richard.

I was thrilled and fascinated to have a baby sister. As the youngest she was much indulged – my father doted on her, later nicknaming her Lumpy Lou or LL. But of all of our three childhoods, Louise's was the one spent in the greatest isolation with little sibling support on tap as she witnessed increasing ructions between her parents. When she was three years old, my brother and I went off to boarding school. By the time she was eleven, she was away at school herself, I was living in London and my parents had moved from the friendly village of Yateley to live at Budds Farm, Burghclere, remote from all her former playmates. She rode her pony cheerfully enough, but all too often her closest available companion was the TV set. Although a serious giggler who enjoyed a good prank, and a normal child who loved playing with her friends when possible, her essential disposition was a silent one, unfathomable in its infinite reserve – perhaps a wise tactic in our family.

In the mid 1970s, while based in London, Louise fell in love, or so it seemed. The suitor who had captured her heart was Henry Carew, a vibrant young man whose verbal capacity more than filled the vacuum of my sister's silence. Both aged nineteen, they soon settled down to live together in Henry's house in London. With equal promptness they experienced parental criticism and firm opposition from both of their families – neither of whom warmed to the other – which had the foreseeable effect of cementing the bond between this very young couple. They protected themselves by popping into a registry office and getting married – in secret from us all.

'At least they didn't want to just *live* together,' said my mother when the truth came out after they had announced, aged twenty-one, their 'engagement'. Members of both families and plenty of friends attended their wedding blessing in Burghclere church.

My father accepted the situation and made as much effort as he could to be an accommodating father-in-law. He and my mother were bewildered by the hours the enamoured young couple spent in the bathroom and how often Henry was to be found brewing up energizing snacks in my mother's kitchen. Hot Hand Henry, or HHH as he became known, unquestionably had bags of energy and enthusiasm – but it just wasn't the variety to put my father at ease, let alone my mother. If their unruly dogs added little to my parents' pleasure, later their two delightful children, Becky and Benjamin, did. HHH's entry into the family was the beginning of a whole new saga.

My Dearest Jane ...

Barclay House
6 March 1964

It was a great relief to hear that Charles passed into Eton and your mother's admiration for her only son could hardly be more unbounded had he won a scholarship to Oxford and three events at the Olympic Games!

Barclay House
9 October [mid 1960s]

Louise is in good form and telling rather more untruths than usual. Charles has given up writing home – a custom I shared at his age. I am giving a lecture at Eton later this month and poor Charles is fearfully embarrassed. What unfeeling brutes parents are!

Barclay House
14 March [mid 1960s]

Louise acted the extremely important part of a tree in her school play yesterday. She remembered her part perfectly.

Barclay House
24 October [mid 1960s]

Last week I lectured at Eton and as no one actually threw anything or walked out I felt reasonably gratified. Your brother was over here on Saturday in fine form and distinctly cheeky, the young toad!

The Sunday Times
25 January 1966

Poor Charles seems rather depressed; I don't think he is the type to enjoy Eton or get the best out of it, at least not in his present frame of mind. Personally I rather detest ambitious people as a rule, but it is disconcerting when one's son resigns himself so young to a life of good-natured sloth.

The Sunday Times
[Late 1960s]

Tich seems in good form and so far likes his work. I took his friend, the ineffable GR, to Basingstoke; he annoyed me by wearing strings of beads and in general looking rather like my late governess, Miss Shaw. He is so wet that I wonder his long-suffering parents do not grow watercress on his person. Even the meanest creatures have their uses.
     Love,
     xx D

Chateau Marcuse,
Cohn-Bendit
Deauville
France
[Late 1960s]

Tich casually announced at breakfast that he had left his job and was taking a few months holiday. To make money, the old discotheque is again being circulated around middle-class homes in the Berkshire area. He is now talking of working in a racing stable. Louise is in good trim and retires to her room with a stomach-ache if the situation seems likely to develop to her disadvantage.

Wedgwood Benn House
Much Dithering
Wilts
[Early 1970s]

If anyone else says of Charlie 'Of course he's very young', I shall lie on my back and drum my heels (Lilley and Skinners mock suede recreationals) on what is left of the carpet bought in 1951 from a sale at Aldershot Co-op. He is typical of his generation of Etonians. I think they would have greeted Hitler's SS divisions with garlands of marigolds.

Budds Farm
9 March [1970s]

Charlie and I have had a very peaceful time together, but

beyond saying 'Hullo Bootface' whenever he sees me, his conversation is seriously limited. He is fed up with his new car 'the Mobile Tangerine' and is already on the lookout for a replacement. How restless and impulsive he is in matters of personal transport!

Asylum View
Much Twittering
Notts
10 July 1970

Tich is in London with that larky young Soames. I therefore expect to be rung up at 3.30 a.m. approx. from a west London police station; shall decline to provide bail but will write a cogent letter to *The Times* newspaper demanding the return of the birch.

Two of Winston Churchill's grandsons were Jeremy, the 'larky young Soames', and Nicholas, Conservative MP. At Eton, Jeremy had been a cheeky prankster along with his chum Lupin.

Windsor Castle
21 January [early 1970s]

Life here is punctuated by telephone calls from the police wishing that your brother could help them in their enquiries; or from angry men with unseemly accents to whom he has sold cars that fell apart after purchase. I shall be agreeably surprised if he is not in prison within the next three months.

The Sunday Times
[early summer 1971]

Originally Charles told me he wanted to help lunatics. That might be tough on the nuts if he took it up, but at least it would prove his sincerity of intention.

The Totterings
Little St Vitus
Wilts
Sunday [early 1970s]

Andrew Smiley is staying here, very good looking and agreeable. In respect of manners and sophistication, he is Lord Chesterfield and Charles some uncouth moujik from the Siberian Steppes! Louise has a sweet little friend here and they giggle away in corners all day, chewing Black Magic chocolates with the terrifying relish shown by those revolting proletarian children in TV advertisements.

No news of Charles's future. I went to London on his behalf and made no progress. Believe it or not, the Ministry of Defence think in view of his piddling little misdemeanour, he might represent a SECURITY RISK. Thinks: Can Twitch be the successor to Philby? Charles is being very good and patient but he is a bit anxious and naturally so. If he can't get into the Army, what next? He can't get hold of his new blue suit as his tailor has lost a trouser leg! Typical of dear Charlie's 'little disasters'.

Love

xx D

For those unfamiliar with Lupin's dramas, at the 1969

Rolling Stones concert in Hyde Park he was searched and then arrested after a policeman had queried the ownership of the valuable silver fob watch hanging from his belt. The watch had in fact been inherited from our grandfather. What Lupin had not inherited from our grandfather was the little lump of hash in a matchbox in his pocket.

My mortified parents drove to London and bailed out their son from Paddington Police Station. Today, this episode might be accepted by parents as a predictable element in their child's development. Then, had my brother set off a bomb in Hyde Park he could not have ignited my parents' rage, disappointment and embarrassment more effectively.

How proud my father was when Lupin announced his intention of joining the Army. As he now had a criminal record, he was obliged to complete a rigorous military initiation course at Tidworth before the Army could consider him as officer cadet material. Lupin threw himself into this course with creditable determination – and some success – which was soon replaced by an equal determination to abandon the Army as a route for his future. Needless to say, I was swamped with letters on this fresh catastrophe. Sympathetic to them all, I felt deeply for Lupin – 'I realise that I don't want to learn to kill people,' he said to me. My parents' sad and preoccupied faces were brightened by my wedding that same year.

Budds Farm
Thursday [mid 1970s]

Tomorrow your brother goes for an interview in London with a prospective employer. I am perturbed, though, by his attitude of extreme condescension, rather as if he was conferring a considerable benefit by his application.

Budds Farm
24 March [mid 1970s]

Possibly we have brought your brother up unwisely but he can hardly claim to be underprivileged and unloved. He is not a bad boy and his little escapades are merely the attempts to gain applause and recognition as a merry little lawbreaker by one who has signally failed to gain distinction in other respects.

'Bangla Desh'
Burghclere
4 December 1971

Louise says she can play the guitar which fills me with a dreadful despair.

The Crumblings
Cowpat Lane
31 December 1972

Louise is off tonight to see the New Year in wrapped (presumably) in the arms of Randy Andy, embryo cash-chemist and man about Banbury. I had to pick up Louise and glamorous Emma Edgedale from a Pony Club Fiesta at Bradfield last Saturday. Nowadays even dim functions of this sort end up like one of Caligula's more enterprising orgies and in ill-lit corners I perceived thirteen-year-olds writhing in postures that not so long ago were only adopted in privacy. If this goes on your offspring will probably be stripping off at his (or her) sixth birthday party. I expect we shall soon find contraceptives issued in tea-table crackers.

Best Wishes for the New Year to you and my son-in-law,
Love,
xx RM

Hotel Magnifique et du Commerce
Burghclere
31 January 1972

No news yet from Louise: I expect she will say she could not afford a stamp, thereby transforming her own indolence into an accusation of meanness levelled against her parents. I think she will get on very well in the world by and large.

Many Cowpats
Burghclere
[1972]

Your brother has just left here looking quite clean, healthy and happy. He kindly presented me with a photograph of himself with his feet on his desk and holding a copy of *The Times*. Rather saucy, I thought, from a junior salesman, but the right spirit. Your sister is here, quietly happy and totally self absorbed.

The Sunday Times
16 September [early 1970s]

Yesterday we went to Tudor Hall to see Mrs B., Louise's

Headmistress. We were ushered into a sitting room where a splendid tea was laid out. I was just moving to pick up a cucumber sandwich when Mrs B. remarked in severe tones – 'This is not for you, I'm afraid.' Rather a disenchanting start.

Le Grand Hotel de Bon Confort et de Repos (I don't think)
Burghclere
14 January 1973

Louise has passed some O levels and there is as much excitement as if she had won the Nobel Prize for reducing the incidence of liver fluke in frogs. I have no news of your brother Charles. I expected to meet him at Ascot but he did not turn up. Perhaps like Andy Capp, he has been compelled by financial stringency to pawn his overcoat. I may take Louise to Brighton for 2 nights this week. I only wish you could come, too; you might conceivably bring, after two jumbo martinis, a faint and transient smile to my raddled old features.

　　xx D

Budds Farm
[1973]

We had quite a laugh at Brighton and Nidnod was in excellent form and thoroughly enjoyed herself. Your sister was as sphinx-like as ever but I think the fact that she had a bath, radio and TV set in her bedroom afforded her pleasure. She is a true representative of the consumer society.

Schloss Burghstein
Oberblubberhausen
[1973]

Your brother Charles has got a chauffeur's ticket for the royal wedding (Princess Anne) and will drive Soames there wearing his blue suit and peaked cap.

Budds Farm
11 July 1973

Louise flies to Washington DC on Monday and the preparations for this simple expedition remind me of the general mobilisation in 1939.

La Maison des Deux Gagas
Grand Senilite
[1973]

Your sister left for America today, 24 hours late. The reason was as follows: Your dear mother insisted on doing all the preliminaries herself – bar signing a cheque for £122 in respect of the ticket – and any suggestions made by me were received with a certain frigidity. Unfortunately she had never heard of visas. Need I say more? It is fair to add that only your mother's dauntless pertinacity could have obtained a visa within six hours with all the ramrod ranks of petty officialdom lined up against her.

Budds Farm
[1973]

Louise appears to be happy in the USA. I wish I felt confident that she had spoken to her host and hostess since she arrived.

My sister – LL or Lumpy – also glorified in the nickname 'Sparky', celebrating her predominantly reserved manner. In one letter my father wrote: 'Give my love to Enigma Variations – in other words, Louise.'

Budds Farm
[Late 1970s]

We all went to Ascot on Saturday, including your brother, whose hair resembled a very old lavatory brush at one of the smaller provincial railway stations. He is, however, in good form and seems happy flogging old bits of furniture in Fulham.

Nidscovitch Nodscovitch
[Mid 1970s]

Charlie is back from Krautland. He gave evidence in some legal action and to make a good impression, he put on a blue suit and clean white shirt and had his hair cut. It was galling for him that the judge was about his own age and wore blue jeans and a T-shirt!

Budds Farm
17 September 1977

I see your brother has been in the news. I try not to get to stuffy about that sort of exhibitionism but I find amateur entertainment as a rule terribly embarrassing: your mother, though, rather fancies it and with a little encouragement would put on a similar act herself.

The Daily Mirror *reported on Lupin's £300 wager to stand on a table at Sotheby's during an auction and belt out 'Blue Suede Shoes' à la Elvis – losing most of his winnings on retrieving his car which had been clamped.*

Budds Farm
Whit Monday, 1975

Charles has spent a fortnight here covered in oil and other mechanical ordure while endeavouring to put together a peculiar little machine called a Lotus. He has at last succeeded in so doing and recently departed in a cloud of rancid fumes with Miss Lewis. The latter is rather a well-made girl and in consequence the car had a list to starboard of 45 degrees.

Budds Farm
24 April 1974

Your sister is in fine trim and quite outside your mother's control. She is chain-smoking Woodbines, has tangerine fingers and knocks back the hard stuff like a golfing stockbroker. 'Cocktails and laughter, but what comes after? Nobody knows.'

Budds Farm
2 December 1973

Your sister has returned to London. Her landlady rang me to say how much she liked Louise, not least because she never talked. She quickly added, 'I mean she does not talk when I don't want her to.' Louise now plans to have a very large cocktail party in London. I wish the Government would forbid that type of entertainment.

Budds Farm
26 January 1974

Thank God Louise's party at the Turf Club is over. I found it fatiguing. Most of the girls were alright but I did not reckon much to some of the young men with dirty shirts open to the navel. One or two complained loudly and bitterly about the excellent wine provided and demanded whisky in strident tones. However, what can you expect from a pig but a grunt? I got browned off after a bit and went and read *Country Life* downstairs. Charles and Cassandra came to dinner afterwards. Both were very agreeable and chatty but looked as if they had elected to give up washing for Lent. Louise will get into the Foreign Office only if she improves her typing. Obviously she has not got down to hard work during her year, a costly one for me, in London. She has just been fooling around and spending money; perhaps not surprising at that age.

The Foreign Office? Its credentials were pretty impeccable to an aspiring parent: 'Oh, my daughter's working in the Foreign Office', said with a quiet glow of pride. My poor father – that satisfaction was not to be his. He had once tried to set me on this path but I was not up for pinstripes and the civil service. Now it was my sister's turn, with equally negative results, as she preferred working as a sales assistant in a smart emporium off Sloane Square. Much later, when she had two children to bring up, she worked hard as a teacher at the Garden House School in Chelsea. Cassandra Hurt was Lupin's current girlfriend.

Budds Farm
2 February [mid 1970s]

Charles appeared with Cassandra. I can see he is about to spend what little money he has on an undesirable car. I reckon he has spent £6,000 on cars in four years. Louise has been on holiday for 8 weeks and now wants to go to Switzerland. I, on the other hand, am arranging for her to attend Newbury Technical College for shorthand and typing.

Budds Farm
19 March [early 1970s]

Thank you for your letter. I don't think I am too hard on Twitch. He certainly has a capacity for survival. I realise he is still young. I admit that in short spells he is energetic. Unfortunately he is, in racing parlance, a non-stayer. Also he has a bizarre capacity for making undesirable friends. I do worry about him and sometimes I think he has a lonely and unhappy life. That distresses me. I wish I could do something soothing for him.

Best love,

xx D

17b Via Dolorosa
Burghclere
August [1970s]

Your brother is in Suffolk living rough with the Rothschilds and on Monday goes to see a man at Swindon who is going to offer him a job sorting scrap metal in the North East.

Sludge Farm
Burghclere-on-the-Bog
[Early 1970s]

No news of Charles; I feel his next job will probably be an auxiliary fireman in the Chamber of Horrors at Madame Tussauds or salesman in the cake department at Harrods.

The Sunday Times
23 October 1972

No news of late of your brother: I shall not be surprised to hear he has a new job being shot out of a cannon at Billy Smart's Christmas Circus. By the way, Charles's new alias is 'Melville Miniwad'.

Schloss Blubberstein
Montag [early 1970s]

I have just received a complicated apparatus for inducing moles to expire by gassing them; sometimes I am tempted to have a tiny little experiment with my near-and-dear. I think your brother is coming to see you tomorrow. Oblige me by not showing him any letters from me in the sacred cause of family harmony. He is a dear lad, but he does seem totally disorganised. Year after year he goes on a holiday that brings nothing but hardship, privation, diarrhoea and a slight rash.
    Best love
    xx D

Budds Farm
17 February 1974

Charles's face is very sore and he cannot shave after his little disaster with the infrared sun-bathing lamp. Now, Louise has gone and done exactly the same thing. Have my children got a particularly low IQ?

Budds Farm
15 June 1974

I had dinner with Louise in London last week and she

was a most agreeable companion, chatting away merrily and knocking back John Haig, Moselle, smoked salmon and strawberries with impartial zest. Your poor mother worries about her incessantly, at one moment thinking she is pregnant and at another that she exists on a diet of 'pot'.

The Old Crumblings
Burghclere
[1974]

Your brother is now in Scotland working as a labourer on an oil rig. I enjoyed having him here as he is so good tempered though in some ways barely house trained. After he has had a bath – admittedly a fairly infrequent occurrence – the bathroom looks as if he had been scrubbing down a hippopotamus. However, he possesses charm and a sense of fun, and he improves his many entertaining stories by judicious exaggeration.

My father often grumbled about the scruffy and dirty appearance of the young. The Swinging Sixties had revolutionized fashion – far too casual for my father's generation. The fast route to cleanliness – power showers, automatic washing machines and tumble dryers – were still rare luxuries.

Budds Farm
6 February [mid 1970s]

Your sister is now doing shorthand at the South Berkshire

College of Education and good luck to her. Your mother thinks Louise smokes pot in her bedroom. Your brother rang me this morning: had I seen a picture of Major Surtees in a *Private Eye* article on Vassall? No, I had not. I checked up and found the individual to be Sir A. Douglas Home!

John Vassall was a spy blackmailed by the Soviets. Lupin had confused Major Surtees with the former Prime Minister, Alec Douglas Home.

Great Hangover
Much Sloshing
[Late 1970s]

I never see Louise. She has gone out of my life altogether. I really miss her very much and Budds Farm is a morgue with all you children gone. What it would be like if you were all here I hesitate to think.

Intensive Care Unit
Park Prewitt Hospital
Basingstoke
25 May 1977

Thank you for your kind and sympathetic letter. I am not unduly disturbed by what Louise has done as I am no longer surprised by the vagaries of human nature, least of all where my own blood relations are concerned. Of course I regret to some extent that Louise chose to get married, an occasion of some significance in her life, in the manner she chose. However, she has always been a determined character in a quiet way with a certain genius for attaining her objectives.

Best love

xx D

Henry had at least announced his intention of marrying my sister two years earlier. My father wrote: 'I received his statement in somewhat frigid manner, intimating total disapproval. Of course I cannot do anything to stop it.' We all rooted for them when, much later, their union was blessed in Burghclere church. My father pushed the boat out for their reception.

11b Via Dolorosa
Burghclere
9 January [mid 1970s]

Your brother is here. Someone who plays a banjo was meant to be coming down with him but happily failed to materialise.

Chez Nidnod
24 March [late 1970s]

Charlie is here. He is an expensive guest as he has an electric fire going full blast in his bedroom all day, never turns a light off and makes interminable telephone calls to far distant places. He turns on an electric fire downstairs rather than put a log on the fire. He is very good-tempered and bears up pretty well under his manifold misfortunes. There is talk of him emigrating to Zambia.

Chez Nidnod
[1974]

I hear that Charles went to the Grand National and contemplates visiting Poland. No one can say he is still at the bottom of the ladder: at the age of 30 he has still not got a foot on the ladder at all. A combination of sheer ill-fortune and egregious folly.

Lupin had a Heavy Goods Vehicle Licence and was appointed lorry driver on a relief supply mission to Poland. His passengers were the Marchioness of Salisbury and Mrs Ginny Beaumont, dedicated supporters of the revolutionary 'Solidarity' movement. In gratitude, Lupin was awarded an immense carved wooden plate – with a circular photograph of the Pope at its centre.

The Maudlings
Heathcote Amory
Berks
[Late 1970s]

Tich has been in better form and has bought a Rolls-Royce – his money is going as fast as an iced lolly on a hot Bank Holiday afternoon.

The Merry Igloo
Burghclere-on-the-Ice
[Late 1970s]

It is such a pity that so many of Charlie's friends have been to prison. It says little for their collective intelligence.

The Old Draughthouse
Much Shiverings
Berks
[Late 1970s]

Your brother has been staying here on and off, but mostly off, and we have seen very little of him. He is essentially a loner these days and I wish there was someone he was really fond of. His lorry-driving phase is over – I never expected it to last more time than it takes me to consume a hot lunch – he is going on a carpet course at the Victoria and Albert Museum! After which, he joins a rather peculiar export firm on an unspecified basis. Louise and HHH are here. They regard Budds Farm merely as a sort of hotel for their own operations. Louise is wonderful at achieving her own way.
    Love,
    xx D

Budds Farm
Friday [late 1970s]

The Carews arrived, plus dog, an hour ago and already some sort of crisis has arisen, HHH having elected to pluck two ducks he shot, on Nidnod's kitchen table.

Budds Farm
9 August [late 1970s]

I have made a resolution, which I pray I shall be able to keep,
to be much matier with HHH. Sulking simply does not help
matters. I will ask him to come on a short bicycling tour of
the Lake District.

Chez Nidnod
11 December [late 1970s]

Louise and HHH came for the weekend accompanied by
baby and dog. HHH tends to take over the house and reduce
your aged parents to the status of lodgers! He is never out of
the kitchen drumming things up for his family. Also he thinks
he has the body beautiful and at meals favours one and all
with a view of his naval which rather puts me off the cod au
gratin.

Insolvency House
Burghclere
[Late 1970s]

The tumult and the shouting, i.e. HHH, Louise, their child
and their dog have departed; likewise a platoon of Tollers and
Hanburys that came over to lunch. Your mother is peacefully
asleep on the drawing-room sofa. Like most mothers of adult
children, she tends to get on better with them when they are
not within fifty miles of her.

Budds Farm
Boxing Day 1980

I feared the worst and the worst occurred although, like the first Christmas Day of World War I, there was a brief armistice between front line troops. Louise and HHH arrived the day before Christmas Eve. That night there was a fearful and ludicrous row between your mother and HHH about how the Stilton should be cut. It was in fact HHH's Stilton, a present from myself. I tried to cool things and my reward was a Stilton whistling past my left eardrum!

The Miller's House
20 February [mid 1980s]

Twitch arrived for the night and looked reasonably healthy. He arrived in the sort of Mercedes which usually conveys six Jewish bookmakers driven by a Cypriot chauffeur in dark glasses. I think by 1987 Twitch will either be a millionaire or in Peru on the run from the police. Louise was in good form when she came down here, she and HHH are on TV next week. I don't trust TV interviewers who are out to make people like Henry look idiotic or dislikeable.

The Miller's House
17 March [mid 1980s]

There are two items that give force to the theory that this country is in a hopeless condition. (1) The popularity among the young of that repulsive thing known as 'Boy George'. (2) That ghastly TV programme, 'The Fishing Party', featuring HHH and his revolting friends – one of whom can only be described as a chateau-bottled shit – has been voted the outstanding documentary of the year! Does this mean it will be shown again? Poor Louise! I am reminded increasingly of the old colonel in the days of British rule in India who used to sing under his breath: 'There are two Bs in Jubblepaw and one of them's my son-in-law.' I can only add: 'Life is most froth and bubble, Two things stand like stone, Courage in another's trouble, Guinness in your own', etc.

xx D

Yes – the programme about four young City toffs taking a fishing holiday in Scotland and publicly airing their very bigoted right-wing views became a legend in TV documentary history. Following its first showing, it was to his credit as a hard worker that HHH did not immediately lose his job – his fellow fishermen did not all fare so well.

The Miller's House
1 April [mid 1980s]

Nidnod is trying to make a folk hero of HHH, a sort of cross between St Francis of Assisi and Joan of Arc. Louise seems in good form. Becky is a sweet little thing. I rather like her brother Benjamin who is in my opinion (admittedly valueless) a Mortimer rather than a Carew.

My mother expressed a degree of loyalty to HHH as a family member – possibly with a sneaking admiration for his boldness.

The Miller's House
Wednesday [mid 1980s]

Final notes on 'The Fishing Party'. You say that HHH has got some genuine good points. So indeed had Crippen! I am very sorry for Louise who did not put a foot wrong. I have not criticised her at all. I did some extremely stupid things in my twenties, causing pain and grief to my near-and-dears, but at least I did not perform in front of an audience of millions. You talk about 'those four boys'. In fact I think they are men of thirty. I imagine in the old days they would have been followers of Sir Oswald Mosley. It was your godfather Peter who told me he switched on to the programme and thought it was a party political broadcast for the Labour Party!
Love
xx RFM

My sister and HHH were not to divorce until the 1990s.

The Miller's House
20 February [mid-1980s]

Tea with Louise in London. Rebecca graciously accepted some sweets and then announced she was going upstairs to her room to read a book. Perhaps in certain respects she takes after me! She shows signs of being musical.

Morty's Garden of Wonderful Weeds
Spring [mid 1980s]

I hear that HHH has been offered a new job and has acquired a country estate. How nice it is to have a rich relation.

Budds Farm
19 February [late 1970s/early 1980s]

Poor Charlie goes into hospital in Hampstead next week. I am really deeply sorry for him: his life may have been one of epic futility but he does not deserve the worry and unhappiness caused by his present state of health. I think his courage and stoicism have been of a high order and compel respect. He has such excellent qualities mixed up with his capacity for folly that it is extraordinary that he has not made more of his life.

    Best love,
    xx D

My brother has since had many spells in London hospitals.

The Miller's House
15 May [early 1980s]

I hear Charlie is off to Indonesia with a Greek to buy men's underclothes.

Lupin's latest venture – manufacturing boxer shorts.

The Miller's House
12 July [1980s]

Your brother, the well-known commercial traveller (or bagman) in gents underclothes, is due for lunch but has rung up to say he is arriving in a van (where's his Mercedes?) and will be late. Hardly a surprise!

The Miller's House
Thursday, 11 August, 7 p.m. [early 1980s]

The sky is the colour of the underside of a long-dead cod and rain is pouring down. Your brother came down to lunch in good form and a quasi-suede jacket. He recently lunched with the Salisburys at Hatfield. Other guests were Enoch Powell and Mrs Hislop! He seems happy in his new flat but appears to have fallen out business-wise with Robin G-S and completely with his jolly little Greek chum. He enjoyed Spain where he stayed in a 5-Star hotel in Seville which he was surprised to find was expensive. He drove from Seville to Paris in a day, over 1,000 miles. This week he flies to Majorca. He is staying on a small boat. He is off to Thailand again in the winter.
    Love to all,
    xx D

The Miller's House
[Early 1980s]

Twitch is the only person I know who got nothing, bar one or two criminal friends, out of Eton. He would have been just as happy, or perhaps equally indifferent, at a Yateley comprehensive. He is, of course, virtually illiterate. I don't think he finds that a handicap and everyone likes him.

The Miller's House
24 February [mid 1980s]

> Charlie found snow in the Sahara. He would!
> With love from all of us to all of you,
> xx RM

The Miller's House
[Mid 1980s]

Your brother is here and seems in good form. He is putting on weight, drives a Land Rover and discusses property in terms of millions. Long may it last!

The Miller's House
[1987]

Twitch came down for lunch: he has taken to dressing like an underprivileged tramp again, on the grounds that by having only one set of clothes he saves time as he does not have to think of what he is going to wear, there being no alternative. He looks like becoming embroiled with the Hobbs family. I don't know if that is a good thing.

Lupin was to become a director of John Hobbs Antiques

Ltd. *The dramas of the notorious Hobbs family absorbed my brother for decades to come.*

The Miller's House
25 October 1987

Charlie came to lunch in a new car, a sports Audi; I hope he will drive it with suitable restraint. He talks big stuff about money and is quite the budding tycoon.

Lupin fully understood what it was to be a dearly loved son. As to what it might mean to be a deeply loving parent . . . Who was the long-suffering mother responsible for these children? 'Look what I've produced!' was one of her proud observations, often countered by 'Oh come off it, child!'
    Now you can meet this indomitable lady.

6

Nidnod

The Old Damp Ruin
Much Shivering
Berks
9 December 1980

Dearest Jane,
I hope Nidnod arrived safely. Look after her carefully and
watch her diet. Not too much liquid, please. Tomorrow is our
33rd Wedding Anniversary – a long haul with the traditional
ball and chain but not entirely without its compensations!

Best love,

xx D

Cynthia and Roger. Nidnod and Twig (my mother's name for
her husband). My mother and father. I put my mother first,
because this is her chapter.

By the time my parents met in 1947 – introduced by a
mutual friend in a London nightclub – Roger (thirty-seven)
and Cynthia (twenty-six) had already lived through the most

formative phase of their lives, the Second World War. But on that evening in peacetime London, Cupid prepared his bow.

Captivated by Cynthia's prettiness, warmth and vivacity, it took my father just six weeks to propose. Roger's charm, worldliness, wit and handsome looks put him streets ahead of any former suitors. Cynthia was entranced. They walked up the aisle of St Paul's, Knightsbridge, in December that year and following a brief honeymoon settled into their first home, 25 Launceston Place, Kensington.

After nearly twenty nearly years as an impecunious bachelor Army officer, accommodated in a multitude of 'billets', including prison camps, Roger had acquired domestic management skills. It was he who drew up lists of household essentials for their London house, from a coal scuttle to a wardrobe, and sent these inventories in loving letters to his fiancée Cynthia at her Dorset home.

Roger was an immediate hit with Cynthia's parents, her mother in particular. It was a joy for my grandmother to have a son-in-law in prospect who, in common with herself, was intelligent and cultured. Roger also gained heroic status when, by ingenious means, he removed a bat which had flown in and attached itself to my grandmother's bed. This he did by sandwiching the bat between two squash rackets before releasing it through the window. My grandparents were privileged with their own squash court.

Cynthia had to be presented to her future in-laws in London. My father would have prepared his fiancée for the glacial gaze of her future mother-in-law and the likelihood of discomforting comment. His father, mild, genial and kindly, softened this and subsequent meetings, and welcomed my mother into his family. Did sweet young Cynthia meet my paternal grandmother's criteria as a daughter-in-law? Not on your life.

Cynthia's family home was a rambling, stone farmhouse by the River Stour in Marnhull, the village where Thomas

Hardy set *Tess of the d'Urbervilles* – a romantic detail not lost on my mother. Always enchanted by fantasy and poetry, she had a flowing facility for both and throughout her life was prone to break into long recitals at unexpected moments, veering between the divine and the disastrous, applauded more often by audiences other than her family. 'A prophet is never honoured in his own country', a biblical quote she sometimes cast before us. My mother's powerful emotions found their ideal outlet in writing her own poetry; it was not a passing phase of her youth. The intensity of her poems did not find favour with my father but my mother had sufficient imagination and talent to write affecting verse that was, on occasion, delightfully coloured by her own humour. Like her mother, she was a dab hand at watercolours and pastels.

Blessed with the kind of country upbringing found in the classic children's books, Cynthia grew up on a farm, with the freedom to run wild, roaming the countryside with ponies and dogs – watched over by loving and accessible parents. It was an idyll that no later phase of her existence would ever quite match up to. Yet, as in most stories, there were shadows, and challenges to be met. Her unstable and erratic middle sister, Barbara, or Boo – 'a real character' by the time I knew her, but in Dorset days, a whole cartload of trouble – was often a draining and disturbing presence in her family.

Cynthia was the youngest, prettiest and most spirited of three daughters. A decorated officer in the Royal Scots Greys, landowner, farmer, Master of the Portman Hunt and a dedicated member of local councils and committees, Harry Denison-Pender was her loyal and doting father. He was also possessed of a famously fiery temper, and some of its sparks were inherited by my mother. Her humour, sensitivity and imagination were her bequest from her gentle but spirited mother, Doris.

As a girl, with nine indoor staff at one point, at her home,

Strangways, Cynthia was not compelled to roll up her sleeves – except to groom her pony. The war altered all that. Her wartime jobs included being a FANY (First Aid Nursing Yeomanry), working as an ambulance driver for the Red Cross and being employed as draughtswoman at an Aircraft factory – a sixteen-mile bike ride there and back every day. A young man she was in love with had been killed in the war. By 1945, she had seen and experienced much, yet retained a kind of youthful naïvety that she never quite lost. It was a part of her charm. By the time my father swept her up, she was ready to be a wife and to do all she could to make a happy life and home for him.

Newly married, in their own little house in Kensington, the continuation of rationing meant food and very many essentials were still scarce, but love, laughter and friends were in plentiful supply. In those days, there was no question of Cynthia working, other than as wife, and soon, as mother to me, born in 1949. There was a nanny and some domestic help. Labour was absurdly cheap and readily available.

One day, before I was born, my mother walked through Kensington Palace Gardens with tears pouring down her face. She had understood from my father that he might have a brain tumour and have only six months to live. Roger was suffering from a period of bad headaches – they were entirely genuine. The brain tumour, mercifully, was not. It was Cynthia's initiation into a troubled zone – Roger's lifelong concern with the symptoms of his physical health, but probably, quite often, expressions of psychological difficulties. These anxieties always received my mother's sympathy and she unfailingly took them seriously even when they aroused exasperation.

Fevered brows, aches and pains were never dismissed in our family. Bed was always encouraged as a remedy. Looking back, I cannot think of a family whose combined numbers have spent more daylight hours in bed than my own. My mother was a caring nurse and forty years on, when my father's health was truly failing, he referred to her as 'Nurse Dillwater' or 'The Minder'.

My parents hankered after the countryside. It would be much more convenient for my father's work to live outside London within easier reach of racecourses. Everyone started to flourish when Roger, Cynthia and baby Jane moved from smoggy London to Hampshire – Barclay House, Yateley.

In 1952 my mother acquired her first car, a silver Hillman Minx NJJ 166 – and also a son, the golden apple of her eye, Charles. Five years later, little sister Louise arrived on the scene. An utterly dependable and competent housewife, my mother was busy with all of us and the task of organizing our domestic staff who became like extended family members. My mother was proud of her DIY talents for fixing machines – 'It's a special knack.' She was the one to mend the hoover, not my cerebral father.

Fun-loving though she was, my mother carried the aura of one who is constantly engaged in pressing activities. With appreciative affection, it was at that stage that my father christened her 'The Buzzer'. Yet her frantic energy exhausted her. Her frequent exclamation (unacceptable today) was 'I've been working like a black all morning. I'm out on my feet!' The antidote to her nervous energy was riding in the open countryside. There was nothing to compare with the 'rapport', as my mother called it, between rider and horse – or, as she also loved to say, being '*d'accord*' with any animal. When my mother was in a position to take up hunting again, the reviving effects of riding took on a different aspect. Her adrenalin levels soared. There was palpable sigh of relief from my father when each hunting season ended, which can be felt in his letters.

Horses were at the centre of the lives of both my parents but in entirely separate spheres: my father wrote of racing and my mother rode to hounds.

The ignition key to most conversations at home was my mother. Her loquacity was considerable. She rose like a trout to the bait of the teasing of her sharp-witted husband. Her adventurous spirit was always leading her into minor scrapes. My father loved dining out on her escapades, with exaggerated invention. 'But you've got it completely wrong, Roger!' expostulated my mother, whose own anecdotal accounts might be much repeated. She too relished the fun of fabrication and should anyone question her veracity: 'What does it matter? Don't spoil a good story!'

In those halcyon days of early childhood, I remember my mother as affectionate, attractive and fun. How much I loved her company, particularly when I had her to myself.

A tomboy in sensible trousers, climbing trees and riding fearlessly, I was not. My mother found herself with a quaint little chatterbox of a child, who preferred indoors to outside, obsessed with dressing up and far too interested in what the grown-ups were doing for her own good. Enchanted by her mother's femininity, that daughter would hide in her wardrobe rustling with fur coats, evening dresses and Ascot outfits – or creep between the pink damask curtains of the forbidden territory of her dressing table to sample deliciously scented potions and creams.

Meanwhile, little brother Lupin – then known as Charlie B – manoeuvred his toy cars around the nursery floor, smiling engagingly and providing no problems for anyone. Our later and younger sister added a new pleasure as the baby of the household. I was very fond of them but as their conversational skills were not to develop for another twenty years, their company was not noticeably stimulating.

'Go and ask your mother if she's up for a lark,' my father would ask of a summer's afternoon. Picnic packed in the car, family dog Turpin's tail wagging, we would set off to Finchampstead woods. Hide-and-seek followed tea from the thermos and sausages sizzled on my mother's paraffin camping stove, which once nearly ignited a forest fire. A fire engine hoved into view and our mother was given a good dressing down. 'Perfectly ridiculous. I had things completely under control. Damn it all, I used to be a girl guide,' she exclaimed as the firemen drove away.

My mother, irretrievably known as Nidnod, gathered a few extra bonus points in the nickname stakes for certain tendencies. They need no embellishment: 'The Minister of Misinformation' and 'Mrs Malaprop', which she graciously accepted. Finally, one day when we had been guided round a historic house by a female volunteer whose cut-glass tones were a match for the Queen, my mother pressed a tip into our guide's hand, declaring in her own resonant tones: 'So lovely to have been taken round by a person of our calibre.' From that moment, my mother had yet another name – the P.O.C. or Person of Our Calibre.

The humour of our parents was poles apart. 'Having a sense of the ridiculous' was a shared standard to be met, the highest comic accolade that could be paid by either of them, but their definitions of 'ridiculous' did not always coincide. 'Do laugh!' my mother would cry, even though my father would sometimes admonish her for 'taking things so terribly seriously'. 'The world is a tragedy to those who feel, a comedy to those who think,' quoted my father. 'Your poor mother falls into the former category.' I was at times in sympathy with my mother.

'Remember I was head girl of my school, Jane. I'm not completely C3!' my mother frequently reminded me, her testing teenage daughter, in the 1960s. If a squeak of fear escaped me in the car as she overtook as oncoming traffic roared towards us, it was, 'For goodness sake, girl, I drove an ambulance in the blackout during the Blitz.' The further the war receded into the far distance, the more my mother tended to romanticize it as the most exciting period of her life. The older she became, the greater the number of boyfriends and fiancées who had apparently attended her in her youth. The past became ever more golden as the shadows deepened.

How lucky I was to have experienced the very best of my mother as a little girl. She always endeavoured to be scrupulously fair with her children and it was not until I was eleven that some small incident revealed to me that Charlie B held the master key to my mother's heart. Devastated at the time, I never held this preference against my amiable brother. He never abused his prime position then, even if he was to misuse himself in the years to come. My mother suffered much on this account, which became a regular aspect of divisions between our parents. My father was to write to me: 'Your mother loves her son not wisely but too well.' Now, the bottle was added to my mother's recreational repertoire.

Alcohol did my mother few favours. Jekyll became Hyde. Dark and dreadful evenings could be followed by days of sweetness and light, with not a troubled word recalled. Whenever my father could raise the flag for his wife and celebrate her love and goodness' he did so. Comments now published about 'Nidnod's noggin in the old martini bucket' – and this book has its share – were his way of making light of the pain of my mother's difficulties. Had my father understood how to take my mother in hand, he would have done so. He was not proactive by nature: retreat was preferable and, at times, essential.

My mother was someone who inspired affection; her own conspicuous loyalty and kindness brought her, in turn, many loyal friends. Those who worked for us tended to stay and she would remain in touch with them long after they had departed. Whenever my mother entered a contented phase and the bottles of spirits stood nearly untouched on the sideboard, her youthful zest for life, her pretty face, her warmth and generosity would smile on us all once more.

My mother outlived my father by fourteen years. She always maintained that whatever else, she was never bored by Roger. He was frequently very bored by our mother, yet he loved her deeply and depended on her completely.

My Dearest Jane . . .

Barclay House
25 January [early 1960s]

It is very quiet with you and Charles both away but your mother has not been feeling well and is not in the mood you usually describe as 'merry'. I have just signed a contract to appear on TV one evening soon. The programme lasts between 30 and 40 minutes and I am to give the commentary. I think I shall wear my Beatle wig and the sweater I knitted during the war. I am starting to grow a beard from tomorrow.

The Sunday Times
14 February [early 1960s]

I got your mother a jumbo style Valentine; it is about the same size as the 'Daily Express' and conveys some doubtless charming sentiments. Charles is still demanding a drum for Christmas and if he works on your mother hard enough, I have little doubt she will be idiotic enough to give him one. I shall insist he plays it at the bottom of the garden in the summer house.

Barclay House
17 June 1963

Next week we have a lot of parties and your poor mother is already beginning to spin like a sputnik. Have you learnt your part for the school play yet? Your mother seems rather muddled about it and I cannot quite gather whether you are in 'Macbeth', 'West Side Story' or 'Toad of Toad Hall'.

Barclay House
Sunday [mid 1960s]

Your mother is in very good form and as placid as a bowl of semolina. I think her holiday really did her good.

The Sunday Times
[1968]

I fear you had rather a disturbed period of convalescence. However we are a resilient family and no one seemed to be greatly put out for more than a few minutes by your mother stepping out of a first-floor window on to one of my better shrubs, on Saturday; then endeavouring to bring off a flying tackle on a moving car 48 hours later. Thank you for all your help on those two occasions.

Good luck in your new job and best love,

xx D

With a bandage over my nose following surgery, as my mother drove me home through Burghclere she insisted that I held a newspaper over my face so as not to attract attention.

Budds Farm
Monday [late 1960s]

I am not sure whether I shall be able to hack my way through the jungle to your residence in darkest Islington tomorrow as your mother is off to Buxted Park at dawn on Wednesday (i.e. about 11.15 a.m.) and will want to discuss arrangements to be made during her absence, that is to say whether it will be kedgeree or fish pie for supper on Friday.

Budds Farm
6 May [late 1960s]

Your mother is in bed sending out lunch and dinner invitations to persons who do not want to come here and whom we do not wish to entertain. She is off to London tomorrow; keep an eye on her. I think she has an assignation with a Newbury car-salesman, whose left shoe is always done up with parcel string so I don't suppose he'll be standing her hot lunch at the Mirabelle.

Loose Chippings
Soames Forsyte
Wilts
14 June 1970

The new family name for Nidnod is 'The Apricot' because she is always liable to end up canned. She is in fair form but can be tedious about the election. She attributes Mr Wilson's popularity solely to apathy and cynicism on my part and if the Tories are slammed on Thursday, I know who will get the blame!

Le Petit Bidet
Burghclere Les Deux Eglises
Berks
Sunday [1970]

A police car called here the other night and your poor mother managed to convince herself that the two bucolic occupants were the unexpended portion of the Kray Gang masquerading as the Basingstoke Fuzz. The subject of the call was some way short of enthralling, dealing as it did with the loss of a bicycle at Tadley's by a man from Penwood called Herbert Mortimer. By the time this trifling error in identity had been cleared up, your mother wanted to drive straight off to Reggie Maudling and lodge a complaint. However, she has simmered down since and really enjoyed herself by showing a film of allegedly wild life in Kenya – her aunt, a black cook called Tombo and three guinea fowl – to a captive audience of George, Jenny and Ian the garden boy. I'm sure you would regard this as a typical exploitation of the working class by the bourgeoisie.

Reginald Maudling was the current Home Secretary. My mother had a natural affinity with those whom she described as 'salt of the earth'. They inspired the best in her, creating bonds of mutual sympathy and affection – and amusement. That she was usually in the commanding position in these friendships and connections made them all the more rewarding.

Schloss Buddestein
Worms
[1973]

Your dear mother's greatest virtue is her loyalty. Not

infrequently she would like to bend an iron bar over my cranium and in general she finds me a very annoying and perverse old gentleman. Nevertheless, she really feels quite sad at leaving me (Query: or is it really her dog Pongo?) and going over to Jersey tomorrow for a week on the Lemprière-Robin's steamer.

My godfather Raoul Lemprière-Robin, known as 'The Buggerdier', and his wife Sheelagh were top dogs in Jersey. My mother would join them on adventurous sailing trips. Their lovely daughter Emma often stayed with my parents at Budds Farm and seemed possessed of all the virtues so absent in their own children.

[1970s]

I find a fairly large proportion of Nidnod's verbal output, which is extremely high, sheer drivel, and sometimes annoying and contentious drivel at that. Nevertheless I know I shall miss the old trout very much even though I do get a break from her views on politics, religion, Jane, Charles, Louise, Mrs Hislop, the lack of values in the modern generation and the highly undesirable qualities she finds in most of my relations.

The Crumblings
4 August 1973

It is very quiet here without Nidnod and I really miss her very much. I hope the holiday does her good.

17b Via Dolorosa
Burghclere
[August 1973]

The brief heat wave is over and the weather is dark and
clammy like a woman I used to know in Alexandria
before the war. Your mother came back on Aug 6. In the
morning there was a fearful storm and water poured into
my bedroom, the bulk of it falling on my bed. It rained
pretty well the whole day and the sky was as dark as in late
November at teatime. At 4 p.m. I set off to meet Nidnod at
the airport. I parked in a space reserved for directors of some
obscure company and proceeded to the 'reception hall'.
This was crowded with dissatisfied travellers and revolting
children. At the information desk I learnt that Nidnod's
plane was still grounded in Jersey. I thereupon bought a
copy of the *Daily Telegraph* (good on books on Thursdays)
and retired to the car for a good read. Having made myself
snug, I discovered that I had been sold yesterday's paper. I
slogged back to the bookstall where a young lady tried to
appease me with yesterday's *Daily Express*. Eventually I
bought a woman's magazine with knitting patterns rather
than have nothing to read at all. On my way back to my
car a 30-ton lorry passed me at high speed through a patch
of flood water. If I had been thrown into a pond I could
hardly have been more comprehensively soaked from my
head downwards. Luckily I only had 75 minutes to wait
in dank discomfort before Nidnod arrived, full of bounce
and ponging strongly of fish, which was not surprising as
she carried a sack containing sole, mackerel and a crab
that in size and conformation resembled a 1916 tank. We
had some mackerel for lunch the following day, Nidnod
employing an old French recipe. After a few mouthfuls,
the unexpended portions were tipped into a dustbin and

the remaining mackerel were fried in an orthodox manner with excellent result. We had the crab in the evening which was quite good and managed to survive Nidnod's special sauce!

The Old Dosshouse
[1975]

Your mother is in good form though determined to talk her full ration of complete balls; a bit more than her ration in fact. She is at present happily occupied in a row with Farmer Luckes over a hedge.

Budds Farm
[Mid 1970s]

Your dear mother has been overdoing things and is showing signs, well known to all of us, of fatigue. We had a lot of people here at the weekend and your mother treated them to interminable political monologues that made your dotty Aunt Barbara seem like Socrates by comparison.

My mother's sister Barbara (Aunt Boo) was a political activist for wide range of causes – a determined bearer of placards. My mother took a more practical public service route, becoming a local councillor, a role in which she immersed herself with customary zeal.

Sunday Times
Editor in Chief's Office
Midnight [1972]

King Chaos reigns here unopposed. If your dear mother was fighting a marginal parliamentary seat with the eyes of the world upon her, there would hardly be such an air of desperate tension and such long conferences planning the next steps in the campaign. Under the circumstances I have taken refuge in the hairy arms of demon alcohol and am heading with no little rapidity towards what the late Mr Gladstone called 'the pint of no return'. I cannot forecast how the election will go but your mother is very determined. She is rather like Lord George Bentinck who 'did nothing by halves and feared no man'. I have got to have a big elm down; the local wood-cutter sent in an estimate for the job of £125. I have told him exactly what he can do with the tree, coupled with a fervently expressed hope that he will contract Dutch elm disease himself. (I hope he is not in your mother's constituency).

   xx D

Insolvency Hall
Much Crumblings
Berks
8 May [mid 1970s]

Your mother is slightly out of hand as her party has swept the board and now controls the dream city of Basingstoke. She has just gone off to a celebration meeting.

Many Cowpats
Burghclere
[1972]

Your dear mother is taking her Council Duties very seriously
and I am the unhappy recipient of interminable monologues
on the intricacies of local government and the iniquity of all
those who do not put forward views that would have seemed
a trifle archaic at the time of the First Reform Bill. The onset
of deafness is by no means an unmitigated misfortune.

Budds Farm
12 February 1973

Your dear mother has departed for a Council Meeting carrying
enough bumf to keep her busy for a very long period indeed.
We are continually being rung up nowadays by people who
think she is the local welfare officer and that I am her unpaid
secretary. I soon dispel that particular illusion.

Gormley Manor
Much Shiverings
3 February 1974

Your mother has returned from Leicestershire and everyone
seems to be annoying her very much – family, friends,
neighbours, the NUM and the local council. I think you are
fortunate to be 346 miles away or you would be getting it hot
and strong, too!

Budds Farm
17 February 1974

Your pert sister sent me a saucy Valentine and signed it 'Mrs McQueen'. Your dear mother was convinced it had in fact come from the popular hostess of the Carnarvon Arms and I was given a fearful bollocking, with many hostile comments on my alleged drinking and amorous habits, combined with severe reminders that no member of the Denison-Pender family ever received Valentines from barmaids.

Little Crumblings
30 September 1975

Your mother is in a fearful flap over the disappearance of 2 bath towels and everyone in turn is being accused of stealing them along with a silver paper knife from her desk. She is in poor form and blames everything from World War II to the political philosophy of Barbara Castle on me. However, I mutter to myself the consoling words of the old Salvation Army hymn: 'We nightly pitch our moving camp a day's march nearer home.'
Best love,
xx D

Little Crumblings
Burghclere
[Late 1970s]

Your mother is very much engaged with horses at the moment

and this renders her a little bit touchy, particularly after 7.15 p.m. when she is liable to make Queen Boadicea look like the secretary of the Peace Pledge Union.

The Merry Igloo
Burghclere on the Ice
[Late 1970s]

Your mother has developed a disturbing belief that a sausage she cooked was stolen by a poltergeist. I have with difficulty restrained her from calling in the Revd Jardine, a Welshman with an Afro hairstyle and irregular teeth.

The Reverend was duly summoned by my mother to exorcise the said poltergeist with 'Bell, Book and Candle'. When, a few weeks later, my mother was asked how things were going poltergeist-wise, she responded, 'Oh absolutely marvellous! The vicar came round and circumcised it!'

Budds Farm
2 December [early 1970s]

Your mother came with me to Newmarket last week. In Newmarket town she put the car key in upside down, wrenched it and broke it in half! I could not get another key and as BMWs are full of safety devices, was immobilised for 2 days to my immense inconvenience.

14b Via Dolorosa
Burghclere
[1970s]

Your mother is preparing Christmas stockings, transferring things from one pile to another and making intermittent complaints that 'you're not really interested'.

Christmas could raise my mother's enthusiasm to a peak. As a grandmother, she once climbed on to a corner table in our dining room to photograph me as I presented the brandy-flamed Christmas pudding. As she raised her camera, the table buckled beneath her and a china bowl flew in the air and smashed on the ground – where my mother now lay. My husband led her gently away to her room to lie down. My father shook his head. 'Extraordinary old bird, your mother.' She bounced back an hour later, saying brightly 'Too silly!' – referring, of course, to the table.

Chez Nidnod
14 January [mid 1970s]

All quiet, for once, on the domestic front except for routine patrol activity and occasional exchanges of fire. Your mother has given up hunting for the season as her horse is lame. Quite a relief for me as in view of her antics when mounted, I always expect her to be brought home unconscious on a hurdle.

Whatever her hunting injuries, my mother was her own chauffeur – one evening arriving home bloodstained and battered after a heavy fall, she met with a very low-key response from her husband who was himself hunting at that moment – for the biscuit tin. A broken collar bone ultimately retired her from the joys of the chase.

Budds Farm
[1970s]

Your mother tried to hire a fancy dress from Nathans in London. She claims she was picked up by a commercial traveller while eating spaghetti in a café in Shaftsbury Avenue.

14a Barbara Castle Terrace
Basingstoke
[1971]

Nidnod is in good trim, fluttering about and complaining of exhaustion while making every effort to avoid repose for a single second. We had a lunch party on Sunday, a grisly situation redeemed by a first-class lunch prepared by Nidnod and a determination on my part to shove the heads of all guests into the martini bucket and keep them there until suitable signs of animation were displayed. In the evening we went to George Parkin's 80th birthday party and had a lot to drink. Your mother got in a right tangle over old Parkin's various wives and dropped one or two bricks of a somewhat weighty nature, but no one cared, least of all herself. On Tuesday a Doctor Johnson came to supper (not the crusty, right-wing lexicographer) and proved most agreeable. He is a rich bachelor who has piled up a considerable fortune by giving anaesthetics to the wealthy. I doubt if he is greatly interested in the diseases of the poor, but perhaps I am doing him a grave injustice.

Ward No. 27
Mortimer Home for the Mentally Under-privileged
Nuthampstead
Herts
[1971]

I cannot keep pace with events here. On Friday your mother
was convinced of her impending death and gave instructions
for her funeral. Later in the day she said she intended to hunt
on Saturday. Under pressure from Aunt Pam she agreed not
to hunt if the local witchdoctor, Mrs Smallbone, was against
it. Your poor mother then said she was not going to pay much
attention to what Mrs S said (a comment not far off common
sense) and that she intended to hunt. She then lectured me for
47 minutes on my own inadequacies and high moral values
implanted in those who hunt with the South Berks and Garth
foxhounds!

On Saturday your poor mother, having promised to return
early, arrived home at 6 p.m. She stopped at the Parkinsons
and the Rumbolds to recount every detail of the day's sport
and no doubt the recipients of this saga were duly gratified. At
home she announced she had been cured by Mrs Smallbone
and had no intention of going to the consultant in London.
Charles turned up with a very slight cold and was put under
a spell by Mrs S. I am apparently under the old trout quite
without my consent, for gout and various unseemly maladies.
However, your mother was in a very good temper. My
information is that the local fox-hunting mob consider she is
liable to do herself quite a serious injury one day if she insists
on jumping semi-detached bungalows on Jester.

xx D

My mother rode well and with considerable nerve. 'Full of dash
and go' herself, this was one of her highest commendations

of others. 'Gallant' and 'pluck' were favoured words in my
parents' lexicon. Of her pony, my mother's pet phrase was
'He goes like a bomb out hunting.'

Schloss Buddstein
Neubeurg
10 January [early 1970s]

I think your mother is better and in a few days time will be
chivvying the local foxes with an assiduity worthy of a nobler
cause.

The Sunday Times
16 September 1973

Your dear mother is so mild and reasonable that I am quite
worried about her. I hope she is not fading.

Budds Farm
30 September 1973

Nidnod is really looking forward to seeing you and your new
home. She is in better form than for years, quiet, reasonable
and almost relaxed. For once she is not overreacting to the
manifold disappointments, annoyances and problems of
human existence.

The Crumblings
[1974]

Yesterday, another day of extreme heat and lassitude, your dear mother gave a lunch party for 20 middle-aged trouts. Thanks to Sue, our temporary cook, it was a bountiful spread. I mixed two bedroom jugs with plonko blanco to which was added much Spanish cooking brandy and the unexpended portion of yesterday's fruit salad. The trouts lapped it up and became rather skittish in a nineteen-twentyish way. Our new 'daily', Yvonne, kept on whispering to me 'Which one of 'em do you fancy?' I replied that I was totally uninterested in anything over the age of seventeen.

Last Tuesday I attended a fearful party at Highclere Castle for local government officials and district councillors. Demon tedium was raising his hideous head almost before I was munching my first section of desiccated sausage roll. However, your mother enjoyed herself: I was merely Councillor Mortimer's husband, very much a secondary role. A man had a fit in the electrical department of the House of Tomer last week. I think seeing his bill for repairs to a kettle brought it on.

xx RM

The Old Icebox
Burghclere
[1975]

We enjoyed having your much respected husband with us and wished the visit had been even longer. He is the only person who has your extraordinary mother even remotely under control.

Scorchlawn
Burghclere
8 August 1976

Not one drop of rain has fallen here since you left. The garden
is awful and made worse by the fact that Nidnod set fire to
the orchard, destroying all the grass, two hedges and three
lilacs. Finally the Fire Brigade had to be called in. For once
we had a few pears and apples which were literally roasted
on the branch. Well there you are! Against stupidity the Gods
themselves fight in vain. Can you imagine a grown woman
lighting a bonfire under these conditions, particularly with a
nice light breeze to help it along?

*My mother had a passion for making bonfires. She would
instruct me in the art of a successful blaze – 'Remember Jane,
what you need is a hot bottom!' Once, in her late seventies,
I found her in the garden one boiling afternoon, wearing
her swimming costume and heaping debris on to a bonfire's
flames.*

Hypothermia House
[Mid 1970s]

Nidnod has been rather seedy lately. Today she said she felt
awful and was going to stay in bed. Accordingly, I unhooked
my shopping bag and went to Wash Common where I spent
£12 on ready-made or easily prepared food in order to
reduce kitchen labour. On returning home I found that the
bird had left its nest! Knowing the form I went to the nearest
public house and there was the invalid, perkily perched on
a bar stool, swigging extra strong ale and giving two local

layabouts an ear-bashing which left them with very stunned expressions.

Budds Farm
28 March [late 1970s]

Must stop now as Nidnod wants to court martial me for having muddy shoes. Easier to plead guilty and accept the punishment. She would like to restore flogging.

Budds Farm
18 January [late 1970s]

On our French holiday, I enjoyed Nidnod's picnics. At her best I think – 'A jug of wine, a loaf of bread and thou!'

Many Cowpats
Burghclere
11 January [early 1980s]

On Friday Nidnod went to the Old Berks Hunt Ball with her boyfriend Rodney Carrott. I will give you a brief description of him as he may well be your stepfather after I have been wheeled away by Camp Hobson Ltd to Swindon Crematorium (I have opted for Swindon rather than Aldershot since Swindon beat Aldershot 7–0 in the Cup). R. Carrott is in his late fifties, tall, bald as a pudding plate, and portly. He is 'in insurance' and v rich with houses in Chelsea, the Isle of Wight and Corfu.

His wife divorced him and has remarried and been divorced since. He is generous, brought down a bottle of Calvados and stood everyone drinks at the dance. He drove Nidnod in a new and enormous German car. On their return from the dance, Nidnod found she had forgotten the house keys and tried to blame me (naturally) for her misfortune. The next day they went for a ride together, their pleasure being slightly marred by R. Carrott's ancient horse dropping dead.

Best love,
xx D

The Miller's House
11 October [early 1980s]

Nidnod has gone off cubbing today. Her rapid recoveries from the sickbed make Lazarus look like a beginner when it comes to rising from the dead.

The Old Organ Grinder's Doss House
Burghclere
17 September [1980s]

Somewhat unsettled here and I don't mean only the weather. Things have been made worse by a crisis in old Doris Bean's stable. One of the two girls there was caught in a compromising posture with a young gentleman in Doris's caravan. Words ensued; the young gent departed on his motorcycle and the girl packed her bag later in the day and left too. There is now only one girl there to look after the horses and according to Nidnod the situation represents the biggest disaster since the

Titanic struck that iceberg. Nidnod is in fact threatening to cancel our holiday, and if we do go I anticipate non-stop ear-bashing on stable problems.

The Miller's House
25 December 1984

Thank you so much for the Christmas present which I shall greatly enjoy. I propose to settle down to it in front of a big fire after lunch. Nidnod is a great traditionalist; she threw her customary Christmas Eve tantrum but is in good form today despite Early Service in a small local church that could easily be used as a refrigerator. I have had some very nice presents, including the claret jug from Prince Khalid Bin Abdullah Bin Abdulrahman Al Saud. My present from Nidnod has evidently been lost in the post!

Our daily, Joy, has given me a pot of whisky-flavoured marmalade. Any hope of getting up from breakfast pissed? Best wishes for 1985.

Love to you all,
xx D

Chez Nidnod
24 March 1982

Your mother and Charles went to Joe Gibbs's wedding yesterday. Your mother bashed into a man's car in Sloane Square. He was angry and wanted to make a thing about it but Charles told him that Nidnod had just left a mental home and was liable to make a painful, even violent scene.

The man drove off in a hurry. I did not attend the wedding as those ceremonies make me feel sad; the bride, perhaps having a vision of the future, nearly fainted during the service. I joined them at an excellent reception at the Royal Hospital (fine pictures, etc.) and I was privileged to observe members of Gloucestershire's upper class in festive mood.

The wedding's glamorous couple were Joe Gibbs, son of a field marshal, and Leonie, an artist.

The Old Slagheap
Burghclere
17 December 1980

Your mother wants an electric sandwich-maker for Christmas. I hate sandwiches and I expect it will always be going wrong. My only Christmas present so far is a wallet made from the skin of some obscure animal and presented to me by Aunt Boo!

Budds Farm
19 February [early 1980s]

We are busy looking for a new house. I found a charming little Queen Anne house last week but it was turned down by Nidnod as inadequate for her ponies whose comfort and welfare rate rather closer attention than mine. Nidnod's council friend Mr W is constantly calling here for meals, drinks, etc: I don't grudge him his rations, liquid or otherwise, but he has never yet stood Nidnod even a glass of tepid

Watneys during the long intervals at council meetings. As Charlie said, he makes Scrooge look like Father Christmas.

The time had come for my parents to find a warmer, more practical home, preferably in a village. Budds Farm had always been a challenge to my father's well-being. My mother, immune to draughts, loved it and it had 'land' – at least enough to accommodate her ponies. Their next and final home in Kintbury, The Miller's House, suited my father, even if the size of his fuchsia pink fibreglass bath was better suited to a seven-year-old, while my mother luxuriated in a large avocado green bath there and found The Miller's House suburban. They were intermittently united in their pleasure of relaxed and sociable times there with friends and family.

Chaos Castle
Burghclere
[Mid 1980s]

The move is making slow headway and your mother is getting the worried look seen on the features of Emperor Napoleon when things started to get slightly out of hand in Moscow. Oddly, she has suddenly got interested in gardening and plants out lettuces and weird herbs in improbable places.

The Miller's House
1 June [late 1980s]

Nidnod has taken up horticulture and has plonked a sundial on the lawn. I have suggested a motto:

'I am a sundial and I always botch
Something that's done better by a watch.'
Nidnod is very scathing about amateurs trying to write verse. I did not tell her I cribbed those two simple lines from Hilaire Belloc!

The Miller's House
Jan 6 mid 80s

We had the Reading Crown Court Judge staying here. He completely out-talked Nidnod at dinner and repeated the performance at breakfast. I pity his juries.

The Miller's House
[Mid 1980s]

Have a good time while you're still young and the cares and worries of this rather awful world have not blunted your sense of enjoyment. Never hesitate to choose the most expensive item on the menu. Sadly, Nidnod never knew me when I was young. I was middle-aged and already getting stodgy when the organist at St Pauls, Knightsbridge, struck up 'Lead Me to the Altar, Walter.'
Best love
xx D

The Miller's House
[1990]

Your mother is in good form; I don't drive her round the twist more than once a week and if it was not for her, I would not last a fortnight.
Love to you all,
xx RFM

My father was the sole breadwinner for my mother and their three children. He was highly successful in his chosen career as a racing writer. As a major dimension of his story we join him on the racecourse, next.

7

Racing to Write

No one chronicled the events and people of the racing world
more lucidly and accurately than Roger Mortimer. He was
one of the most refreshingly candid journalists of his day
and the author of outstanding books on Turf history . . . his
technique was often a writer's equivalent to the late Max Wall
on stage: first winning the confidence of the audience, then
delivering a payoff – with a point as sharp as a stiletto.

The Times, 2 December 1991

My father's legacy has recently become the cache of his
extraordinary letters to his children, but while his comic voice
as a parent of a bygone age has readers falling off sofas with
laughter, that achievement has been posthumously awarded
to him. Roger's comic wit and acuity as a letter writer was
inevitably polished by his professional writing work. During
his lifetime, the success he enjoyed was with a specialized
readership, gaining the laurels of acclaim rather than fame.

'Stop playing marbles with father's glass eye, he needs it to
look for some work', was an old music hall song my father
was wont to sing as he climbed the stairs to his study. He
often had many concurrent writing jobs as a list in a letter to
me reveals.

'The Droolings
October 1972

My Dear Child,

Thank you for your letter which you did your best to render illegible by typing on red paper; not, I trust, a reflection of your political opinions. I look forward to seeing your house in the not far distant future but at the moment I am hard pressed. 1. Trying to complete a tome of world-shattering dreariness for Cassell & Co. 2. Bringing *The History of the Derby* up to date for Cassell & Co. 3. Launching a book that M. Joseph & Co are publishing, arranging for reviews, distribution etc. 4. Writing an article on Women's Races for the Tote Annual. 5. Writing an article on obscure Names in Famous Pedigrees for 'Stud and Stable'. 6. Advising on a racing film being made with the maximum inefficiency at Bray. 7. Hackwork for *The Sunday Times*. 8. Hackwork for the Racecourse. 9. Hackwork for Argus South African Newspapers Ltd. 10. Advising Tattersalls on how to avoid annoying their clients too much. 11. Tidying up the garden.

xx D'

Roger's output was prodigious and when pressed for time, he would pay me as a teenager – the princely sum of £1 – to dictate his copy over the telephone to the *Sunday Times*.

His innate ability to turn any incident into a good story was enhanced by working in the racing world, where unusual tales abounded. Even in his most serious work Roger was always able to tap into a seam of irreverence, expressing an unassailable pleasure in the follies, foibles and absurdities of life. This may not seem to be the key quality required of one commissioned to unfold long and definitive histories of the Turf, with titles like *The Jockey Club*, *The History of the Derby Stakes* or *The Flat*. None are suggestive of laughter.

Roger's genius lay in his ability to lighten these scholarly histories with wit and anecdotes that run like golden threads through his prose. A reader uninspired by the thought of racing histories stiff with equine biographies might discover that Roger brought the Turf alive through the human stories of the men who bred, owned, trained, rode, betted, vetted, exercised and mucked out the stables.

From its wild, uncouth beginnings in the 1600s when racing was devoid of rules or codes of conduct, the scope for deeds either daring or dastardly was boundless – compelling material for a writer who rejoiced in tales of irregular individuals and strange and scurrilous crimes.

'The Shiverings
Burghclere
[Late 1970s]

Racing has always contained some odd characters not invariably on the side of the law. One such was John Stewart who, when times were bad, used to do a bit of house-breaking in the Kensington area. One afternoon the flat-owner caught Stewart at it (there was no racing that day because of a hard frost) and Stewart lost his head and killed him. He was caught, tried and sentenced to death. To his horror he found he was going to be hanged on Derby day. He applied to the Home Secretary to have the execution put off till after the race but the stony-hearted individual declined to intervene. As the awful little procession left the condemned cell for the scaffold Stewart interrupted the parson's droning prayers to advise all present to have a really good bet on Felstead. They were his last words. Felstead won the Derby at 33/1.'

Writing in the *Raceform Handicap Book* in January 1987, this is a taste of the tone of Roger the Historian – not so different from the timbre of his letters:

> It is probably true that villainy in racing increased substantially when owners ceased to bet with each other and bookmakers came on the scene. Some of the early bookmakers would have skinned their own grandmothers had there been profit to be derived from that operation . . . Until the last quarter of the 19th century racing was crudely organised, rough and corrupt, with the number of absolutely reliable jockeys countable on the horns of a goat.

In his racing histories, my father's style was erudite and eclectic. Richard Onslow, in a 1973 review of his magnum opus, *The History of the Derby Stakes*, called him 'the most important racing historian of the present day', adding, 'the most fascinating part of this book will be the thumbnail sketches, always skilfully and often wittily written'. In the *Sunday Times* of 23 December 1973, Alan Ross described Roger's writing as having, 'The narrative incisiveness and irony of a good short story. Mr Mortimer's opening sentences are often masterpieces of compression.' To prove the point, he quoted:

> In 1824 Jem Robinson brought off a remarkable wager, having betted that in one week he would ride the winner of the Derby, the winner of the Oaks, and get married. He won the Derby on Sir John Shelley's Cedric: the Oak's on Lord Jersey's Cobweb and on the Saturday he completed the treble by leading a certain Miss Powell to the altar.

Meanwhile, Michael Thompson Noel in the *Financial Times*

on 29 November 1973 also placed my father at the top of his field, praising him for gathering in 'a sparkling catch of heroes and villains . . . [He] describes the subsequent careers of the principals – both horses and men. Some were to triumph. Some were disgraced. All are fascinating.'

To fail to share some quotes from his output as a racing writer would be a disgraceful waste of opportunity. No interest in horses or racing is needed to enjoy my father's writing, but for those who love racing, extracts may inspire a renaissance of interest in his official work.

Roger was not a country child. His family home was in London so it was probably mainly holidays with his favourite aunt, Star Mitchell, and her Irish husband Chris at Ballynure, Co. Wicklow, that offered an opportunity to ride. Point to pointing, the springtime diversion for hunting folk, became one of Roger's recreations as a young man but recollections of fox-hunting did not feature in any of his letters to me. When he did turn his pen to descriptions of the hunt, it was focused entirely upon the powerful effects it had upon my mother.

It was while at Ballynure that Roger went to his first race-meeting, at Naas, Co. Roger already had a grasp of racing events – he had been subscribing to *Sporting Life* since he was a schoolboy at Eton. 'I always read it at breakfast, thereby annoying my housemaster. I can think of six foreign countries to which I used to have the *Sporting Life* sent to relieve the awful tedium of military exile.'

Because my father later became such a fount of knowledge about racehorses, it might be assumed that was fond of every breed of horse. My mother's small, Thelwell-like ponies were in an entirely different category. He was not hostile to these lowlier equines, but neither did he display the slightest warmth towards them. His lack of interest may well be attributed to the amount of time my mother dedicated to her ponies.

Whatever his feelings, Roger would have been the first to confirm that horsemanship was not his outstanding skill. By his late thirties, riding had become an activity of the past – he had not ridden in a point to point since he was posted to Egypt and Palestine in 1937.

From his years as an impecunious Army cadet at Sandhurst, Roger became an increasingly keen follower of the Turf, more frequently as a punter on the course than as a guest at the posh end, in the members' enclosure. One of his happiest memories was at Royal Ascot in 1928, when 'my only expense was a shilling for an orange box to stand on' to get a good view.

Following the war, having spent many of his hours as a prisoner immersed in books on racing, Roger's growing expertise on the subject started to win the respect of fellow racing enthusiasts. One such admirer was Major Roger de Wesselow – a Coldstream comrade who had served in the Special Operations Executive in wartime. As good fortune had it, Major de Wesselow was in a position to offer my father his first racing post, updating records for Raceform and writing for a publication called the *Racehorse*.

So it was, on one sunny Saturday in June 1947, as a part of King George VI's Birthday Parade, that my father performed his last duty as a Coldstream Guard. It may have been the very last time that he was on horseback – he rode a chestnut gelding called Virile 'which peed during the National Anthem'.

On the following Monday morning he reported for his first day's work at the Raceform offices in Battersea. He discarded the status of Major Mortimer, the honourable soldier, to Mr Mortimer, a recorder of racing statistics. It was not a step down, but the first foot up on the ladder of a successful career that was to last for the next forty years.

My father was not driven by ambition. Back in 1947, his most pressing desire was to leave the Army. All his experiences had been within the confines and constraints of institutions – school, the Army and prison camp – and he was now in search of independence. From his earliest years he had always derived great pleasure from the power of words and the satisfaction of seeing them used well. To have been given this opportunity to apply his brain profitably in the racing world was a very promising way forward.

A long time later on 10 November 1974, in a *Sunday Times* article reviewing his racing experiences, he wrote:

> I came into racing during the post-war boom. There was plenty of money after the war but because of shortages, rationing and restrictions, not much to spend it on. If you wanted a new suit, it was not easy to get one. Today there are plenty of suits but not much money.

Racing may have been booming but my father's new profession was not an extravagantly paid one, as he commented in the late 1970s.

'The Merry Igloo
Burghclere on the Ice

The *Racehorse* used to come out three times a week and I wrote about 2/3rds of it. I always had to go to the office in London (unpaid) every Sunday, including when I had moved to the country. There was no travel allowance.'

In that same year of 1947, my father was swept off his feet by another emboldening event: becoming engaged to Cynthia. To be married to 'a writer' was an immediate cachet to my mother – she was abidingly proud of my father's intelligence and was thrilled at the idea of seeing it manifested in print. My mother always had absolute faith in my father's future success.

Roger found the racing world compelling and convivial, enjoying the thrill of the race, the spectacle of top-class horses and jockeys, and the flow of high and low life cheek-by-jowl on the racecourse. It was a vibrant, energising environment in which to work – with a constant edge of risk to it.

Race meetings bustle with movement between paddock, course, stands, tote and bookmakers – and the bar. Every one of the races, breeders, owners, trainers, jockeys and indeed the horses needed evaluation and consideration before being reported upon. A fast wit and a memorable parting shot are ideal attributes for anyone in my father's profession hurrying through the throng. Roger already enjoyed a reputation as a raconteur who sparked up social gatherings in peacetime or cheered a gloomy hut full of prisoners in wartime. Now, he could fire off his bon mots on course – and in print.

Roger's big break – not necessarily how he would have described it – occurred almost immediately when the owner and editor of the *Sunday Times*, Lord Kemsley, contacted him personally and offered him the job of racing correspondent. Roger accepted and remained in that post from 1947 for nearly thirty years.

In the 1970s, he reflected on his first employer there:

'Old Kemsley was like a more genial version of Mr Bultitude's Headmaster, while Lady Kemsley was a kindly snob with a penchant for putting her foot in it. I wonder if my career (I was getting £400 p.a. at the time) would have been different if I had not twice refused invitations to stay chez Kemsley for Ascot (Bring your wife to play canasta with Lady Kemsley). It was probably very stupid of me but ambition has never been one of my major vices.'

Roger was on his way. His writing, combining accurate information with sharp comment, anecdote and humour, soon became more widely known and enjoyed. A scrupulous researcher, he had the ability to process dense quantities of information, always remaining alert to a quirky or telling detail to enliven his material. Roger referred to himself as a writer, a racing correspondent or just a hack, not a journalist. Journalism was a profession of which he was extremely suspicious. He said that he found it awkward and invasive to ask people a lot of personal questions. His views on journalism were echoed by Balzac, whom he quoted, writing to me from 'Rabbits Larder, Burghclere':

'"Anybody who was once caught up in journalism, or is caught up in it still, is under the cruel necessity of greeting men he despises, smiling at his worst enemy, condoning actions of the most unspeakable vileness, soiling his hands to pay his aggressors out in their own coin. You grow used to seeing evil done, to letting it go; you begin by not minding, you end by doing it yourself." True, alas.'

My father succumbed with genial grace to being interviewed himself – an experience which occurred from time to time as his success increased. He once invited me, aged fourteen, to accompany him to the BBC TV studios in London, where he was appearing on a late night programme. I was whisked off by a kindly producer into a BBC lounge, where my father

eventually ran me to ground as I was holding forth, happily
draining my second large gin and lime.

I was sixteen when, in January 1966, Gus Dalrymple of
the *Sporting Life* was dispatched to interview my father for
the 'Great Racing Correspondents' series. Gus came down to
our home at Barclay House to conduct the interview:

> The place looked like one of those 'Gone with the Wind'
> houses from America's deep south. At any moment I half
> expected Uncle Remus himself to come ambling round
> the corner, bearing a tray of mint julep . . . [I was greeted
> by a] large portly man with a red and jolly face and half
> lensed spectacles perched on the middle of his nose. He
> looked like Mr Pickwick come true.

Later that month, my father observed to me:

'More about the Mortimers in "The Sporting Life" today: Mr
Dalrymple makes us out to be plutocrats living in a rambling,
Gone-with-the Wind style mansion, the walls of which are
covered with costly paintings! Can you beat it?'

Ten years later he neatly encapsulated a journalist's
interviewing strategy:

'I had to go to London yesterday to be interviewed by a
trendy young gentleman who wishes to write an article
about me. He was very agreeable but interviewers always
are; the poison only becomes apparent when the finished
article appears.'

My father's articles, hot off the press, fresh and ready for anyone to pick up and read, lay in the wooden newspaper rack in the sitting room of my parents' home.

'Oh your father – he writes so brilliantly!' his children would be told by others. We would smile shyly with pride. Our father must be brilliant, we thought, if he made his living from writing. But not one of us read a published word he wrote.

Roger thrived on the gossip of the press room as much as the exchanges he was party to in grander milieus. He particularly enjoyed his excursions to both Newmarket town and its race meetings. It is the capital of flat racing and the home of the governing body of racing, the Jockey Club.

'Asylum View
Much Twittering
Notts
10 July 10 [early 1970s]

Dearest Jane,
I have just returned from Newmarket, City of My Dreams. I left at 5.30 a.m. and arrived at 8 a.m. just in time for a plate of excellent local sausages at the Rutland Arms. I stayed at the Jockey Club Rooms; slightly Edwardian comfort – ancient valets with names like Drawbridge and Hayrick – large bedrooms with huge po cupboards – loos with mahogany wall-to-wall seats and pull-up plugs. A rather too formal garden with an unimaginative herbaceous border 200 yards long. Most of the planting must have been done by a retired drill sergeant with a passion for straight lines. Although the Jockey Club is men only, one has to change for dinner. However, when the temperature is in the top

eighties, which it was, the more daring and trendy inmates wear white coats.

Love

xx D'

Roger respected the formality which was expected in the smart social enclosures of flat racing meetings. He was of a class and generation who delighted in making the following sort of observation, in *The Times*, 26 July 1975:

> Until the last war, Ascot and Goodwood, two of the finest racecourses in this country, were each used only on four days in the entire year. At Ascot, racing was restricted to the royal meeting in June; at Goodwood to the immensely popular fixture at the end of July, an event which then marked the close of the London 'season'. For a young officer to be seen in London during the two months following Goodwood was deemed as worthy of censure as if he had been caught dining north of the Park or hunting south of the Thames.

When newly married in 1971 and living in north London, I invited my father to dinner in the late summer at our home in Highgate, which he had not yet seen. 'My Dear Child,' he said, 'a man of my sort cannot possibly be seen in north London in August.' He came, of course.

As for appearances, humans were as interesting as horses. Sartorial aspects of Ascot always got a line or two in his articles, such as in the *Sunday Times*, 16 June 1974:

> A lot of men seem perfectly happy to encase themselves in clothes that are laughably unsuitable for summer racing. Middle-aged ladies from SW3 strain their eyeballs to cracking point endeavouring to read the names on other

people's Royal Enclosure badges. There are even on view a few examples of that rapidly disappearing species, the debutante. For low comedy it is safe to rely on the usual exhibitionists in bizarre costumes indulging in their relentless pursuit of Press photographers. The racing, for those who care about it, is excellent.

By the late 1980s, Roger's view of the patrons at Royal Ascot was less than glowing:

Of course there are people who object strongly to the traditional mixture of royal pageantry and sartorial formality that form the background to Ascot. Year after year they compose letters to the sporting press about it, complaining about the clothes they feel obliged to wear and the inordinate amount of space taken up by patrons of the meeting who have come not so much to look at the horses as to gawp at the royals.

Only at Royal Ascot is a high degree of formality obligatory in certain enclosures. Most people who go to the meeting take it all in their stride but some emphatically do not. Why they continue to turn up year after year in a state of disgruntlement I cannot imagine. After all racing is not compulsory and if you don't like it and stay away, no one is going to shoot you. Some of those who grumble most about Royal Ascot are journalists. This seems a shade ungenerous as they see some of the best racing of the year free.

The Classic flat race that my father adored, and whose story he nearly made his own, was the Derby at Epsom. In the rich cast of characters in Roger's *History of the Derby Stakes* the most celebrated and infamous is Lester Piggott. My father was to make many an unprintable comment on

Lester. Nonetheless, with a record of nine Derby winners ultimately, this flawed genius of a jockey merited over thirty pages in the book.

At eighteen years old, Lester was the youngest jockey to win the Derby in the twentieth century. My father provided a telling profile:

> Lester Piggott rode his first winner at the age of thirteen. Precociously brilliant as a boy, he managed to survive more or less unscathed by a period of rather nauseating adulation by the popular Press, but sometimes his fearlessness, coupled with sheer determination to win, degenerated into recklessness and brought him into conflict with the Stewards. A few weeks after his Derby victory he was suspended for the remainder of the season because of an incident at Ascot.
>
> Piggott's brushes with authority never affected adversely his nerve or his confidence, nor did they diminish his great popularity with the racing public, who readily forgave his indiscretions, partly on account of his youth, but chiefly because his sins were the result of his burning determination to win whatever the cost.

Roger's overall view was that Piggott was a highly talented scoundrel. In 1987, the year when Lester was convicted of tax fraud, my father shared a little personal memory in a letter:

'I think it is 38 years since I went bathing with Lester P who was staying at the Royal Crescent on his own and of course at that age (19) had no car so was glad of a lift to the races. He told me some weird things about his childhood!'

For popular appeal, the greatest racing spectacle is the Grand National, which promises thrills and spills to millions, including many who rarely if ever set foot on a racecourse. Many spectators' hearts are in their mouths, especially at key moments of risk when the horses approach the course's most challenging obstacles, like Becher's Brook. Roger slipped the background history to that notorious jump into a *Sunday Times* article in the 1970s:

> For many years military men played an important part in steeplechasing. Captain Mark Becher's Army career was of a somewhat nebulous character, but he is believed to have served in the supply department at the time of Waterloo. Leading the field in the very first Grand National in 1839 when he was pitched headfirst into the Aintree brook which bears his name, he emerged to declare that he had forgotten how very nasty water tasted without brandy.

My father rarely had a bet. 'And if I did,' he said cheerfully, 'I wouldn't tell any of you. You would only ask me for more money!' If he ever sounds like a skinflint – he wasn't. He was simply prudent. In magnanimous mood after a cocktail or two, he might treat one of us to a punt and we were always receiving clutches of raffle tickets in the post. Whilst I can't recall winning so much as a chocolate biscuit by this means, I did once benefit from a paternal bet to the tune of £100 towards a holiday – a lot in the 1960s.

My father was amused by the bawdy, competitive calls of the bookies as they touted for trade from their rackety racecourse stalls. In print, Roger was forever castigating them for their greed, low cunning and absence of obligation to contribute anything back into the industry from which they made their dosh. He was a dedicated advocate of the Tote – the government-owned the Horserace Totalisator

Board, effectively a state-run bookie – and indeed acted as its publicity officer in 1959–68. Of course, Roger had plenty of gambling tales to recount, including this one in the *Sunday Times*, 18 March 1973.

I remember years ago when a young officer in the Scots Guards who owed his bookmaker something like £50, a sum he was then not in a position to pay. To resolve this little difficulty he went down to Gatwick and laid a £1,000 to £60 on a horse called The Sage who looked the complete racing certainty in a minor flat race with only three runners. The Sage was trotting up lengths ahead of his opponents and the face of the plucky punter was wreathed in self-satisfied smiles when suddenly there was a noise like a pistol shot and The Sage staggered to a halt a few yards from the winning post with a broken leg.

Soon afterwards the officer in question departed for a lengthy spell of service in darkest Africa. At least he was able to board his ship with dignity unlike another officer who, to thwart a distinctly menacing army of creditors, left for India curled up inside a big drum.

A gambling joke which always makes me laugh bounced up in a 1970s letter to me:

'The Old Draughthouse
Much Shiverings
Berks

A man took an Irish friend to see a film about racing. When the big race in the film started he said to the Irishman "I bet you a quid the jockey on the grey falls off." The Irishman took the bet and sure enough the jockey on the grey did fall off. The Irishman was paying up the quid when his friend said "I won't take your money as I've seen the film twice already." "So have I," said the Irishman, "but I didn't think he'd be such a berk as to fall off the third time."

xx D'

Betting practice changed over Roger's working life, as he recalled in the *Sunday Times* in 1974 when reforms had been instituted.

> Betting after the war, partly due the vast amount of black market money in circulation, was on a gigantic scale and on the racecourse wagers were struck that would have made most modern bookmakers, timid creatures that they are, faint clean away in horror. Without a levy or a betting tax to harass them, and being under no obligation to put any of their profits back into racing, bookmakers enjoyed a golden age.

A character called Lord Wigg was charged with the task of instigating reform of the betting industry. As Paymaster General in Harold Wilson's Labour government, he had actually spent many of his working hours in the role of Spymaster General, probing into the sexual peccadilloes of opposition politicians, and he provided key information in the Profumo Affair in 1962. He was later described, posthumously, in the *Spectator* as: 'A consummate dirty trickster who thrived on vendettas, forever straining his outsize ears for any gossip.'

He was not short of enemies, but his love of horse-racing was genuine and he achieved much for its benefit. His reputation was further sullied when he was accused of driving round Marble Arch at midnight to proposition prostitutes. The court case against him was dropped when witness evidence proved that he was merely waiting to buy the early editions of the day's newspapers.

Wigg was a consistent bête noir to my father. He was at the centre of an anecdote in a letter in the early 1970s:

'Budds Farm
8 April

I had a fairly agreeable journey to Liverpool by train despite finding myself at a table with Lord Wigg, who has persecution mania and is convinced I am plotting his downfall; and his assistant, a very creepy reformed drunk who is a macabre mixture of Uriah Jeep and Dracula. However, the situation was rendered less tense by a smart and merry old doll who turned out to be something rather high-powered from the Home Office. We had a number of very refreshing drinks together and eventually old Wigg could not keep his sulk up any longer and dipped his long red nose into a double Hennessy too. On the way home I was in a mild coma when a glorious blonde with a skirt that ended two inches below her Adam's apple kissed me on both cheeks and told me I had won a little prize in the train sweepstake. Without further ado she handed me an envelope containing £32.7.10. I promptly ordered a bottle and got to work on the blonde, but rather lost enthusiasm when I found she lived in Wembley with a bobbed-haired husband who played the guitar; surely an impermissible combination of totally undesirable factors.

Love to all,
xx D'

Aspects of Lord Wigg's character can be discerned in my

father's *Sunday Times* column in 1972, where he wrote with some irony:

> It would be nice to write that Lord Wigg's term of office as chairman of the Levy Board is drawing peacefully towards its close, but the old warrior, bellicose to the last, is not only engaged in bitter controversy with the Jockey Club, but has succeeded in making unwise statements in uniting owners, trainers, jockeys and officials in angry opposition against him.
>
> Individuals who tread the corridors of power are often surprisingly sensitive to opposition and criticism, but the extent to which Lord Wigg, normally a most likeable and entertaining character, over-reacts, is astonishing.
>
> Racing journalists who have the audacity to express views contrary to those of Lord Wigg know just what to expect by way of telephone calls, letters to themselves and letters to their employers as well.

Wigg again loomed up in my youth when he harassed my father for expressing views that did not concur with his own. My father wrote to me in the 1970s from yet another of his 'addresses'.

'c/o Clarkson's Winter Sunshine Cruises
Runcorn Wharf
Manchester Ship Canal
Lancs

Lord Wigg is very mad at present and is threatening to sue me. Foolish old gentleman; or more accurately, evil tempered old megalomaniac sod.'

I can remember Lord Wigg and Roger 'talking' on the telephone and hearing my father through his closed, study door, his voice raised in anger. To hear my father shouting was unusual – he had a very attractive voice with an even tone.

Similar blasts were sometimes issued to another racing character, a friend and sparring partner, Jean Hislop. Statuesque Jean was married to a smaller and quieter husband, John, a highly intelligent and accomplished racing writer, a former champion amateur jockey and a racehorse breeder. Jean was a very tough old bird whom my father was wont to carve up from time to time, when he felt she was pecking too fiercely. Following Ascot one year, he wrote to me:

'La Domicile Geriatrique
Burghclere
[1970s]

Mrs Hislop was slightly pissed (surprise) and accused me of sending information about her to "Private Eye". On the telephone she had terminated a long and tedious harangue by calling me a useless, stupid old man that had absolutely "had it", a sentiment with which your dear mother would doubtless agree at times.'

Although rendered shy by the reserve of John Hislop and intimidated by the formidable nature of his wife, Lupin and I, as teenagers, were amongst fortunate guests at the Hislops' Boxing Day parties. Whatever else, this couple were the most generous of hosts.

What has ensured John and Jean Hislop a gilded slot in

racing history is their joint ownership and breeding of one of the greatest racehorses of the late twentieth century, Brigadier Gerard. He won seventeen of the eighteen key races in his career. The Hislops commissioned a handsome lifesize statue in bronze of their magic horse. It stood proudly on their lawn and it was said that John Hislop made a habit of sitting on his statue's back for a minute each day.

Jean Hislop confirmed to my mother that women in racing were a tough species, and Cynthia's opinion eventually expanded to include men in racing as well. 'I go for the horses,' she would declare, 'not all those *racing* people.' A 1971 article in the *Newbury Weekly News* confirmed 'Mr Mortimer's wife hunts with the Garth and South Berks but she does not follow her husband's love of racing.' She did love racing – but on her terms.

At one point my parents were part of a syndicate, sharing ownership of a racehorse or two. Hopes had initially been high for one horse called Weaver's Loom, trained by their good friend Nick Gaslee at Lambourn. It soon became known as 'Deepest Gloom' for its signal lack of success on the course. My father would have been thrilled to know that another horse trained by Nick, Party Politics, won the Grand National in 1992.

Berkshire is a county green with racehorse gallops and gold with wealthy racehorse owners. Lambourn, a village of idyllic conditions for racehorses, boasts over fifty trainers' yards and can have as many as 2,000 horses in training at any one time. It was not far from my parents' Burghclere home. The district was well populated by racing alumni. The Hislops were just down the road at East Woodhay. Minutes away were Highclere Castle and Lord Carnarvon with his stud farm. The gentleman himself was also reputed to consider himself to be something of a stud – a trait noted in my father's letters. His son, Lord Porchester, was appointed Racing Manager to the Queen. Highclere Castle is now well known as the location for *Downton Abbey*.

Nearby Kingsclere was the training ground for a national gem of a racehorse: Mill Reef, one of the best ever Derby winners, trained by Ian Balding. Aged almost two, Ian's daughter Clare – who later would also capture the nation's heart as a television and radio presenter – was photographed sitting confidently and without support on the precious bare back of Mill Reef. Roger's piece in the *Sunday Times*, January 1973, commends this horse's sweet nature.

> When I went to Kingsclere it was Mill Reef's last night in his old home before leaving for the National Stud. When walking he was rather like some gouty old colonel but happily his temper did not offer a similar comparison.
>
> He is, in fact, a horse of angelic disposition. At his party on Sunday when several hundred local people came to say goodbye to him, he only once displayed even the faintest hint of resentment at being treated like dear old Pongo, the family dog who has never been known to growl. What other great racehorse would have stood there so patiently while small children literally crawled underneath him and every sort of friendly liberty was taken?

In the *Raceform Handicap Book* of 1989, my father wrote of a touching relationship between a horse, her stable lad – and a cat. Kincsem was a Hungarian mare, foaled in 1874, who won the Goodwood Cup. The nature of her life as a professional racehorse demanded much journeying by train and, for comforting companionship, she travelled with a cat.

Provided she was accompanied by her stable lad, Frankie, and her cat Kincsem thoroughly enjoyed her journeys. Only once was there trouble and that was at Deauville on the way home to Goodwood. Her cat was missing when she left the ship and she flatly refused to enter the train. For two hours she stood on the dockside calling for her cat. Eventually the cat heard her, and running to her, jumped on her back. Kincsem at once boarded the train and lay down.

Kincsem's stable lad, Frankie, was in charge of her well-being and it seems, she of his:

One cold night Kincsem noticed that Frankie had no rug. She somehow managed to pull her own rug off and put it on Frankie. From then on, she never wore a rug at night. If she was given one she always managed to get it off and drop it on Frankie. Frankie boasted no surname and did his military service as 'Frankie Kincsem', under which title he was buried when he died.

That is the kind of story I love from my father. Here is another from the *Sunday Times* in 1990 where he weaves together some disparate strands to great effect:

November 27 was a big day for Huntingdon. For the first time it staged a £27,590 steeplechase. On the same day its parliamentary representative, Mr John Major, was elected Prime Minister.

Mr Major is the youngest Prime Minister since the 5th Earl of Roseberry, who was in fact a Liberal. Quite apart from that, the two do not appear to have a great deal in common. Lord Roseberry owned three Derby winners. I have no reason to believe Mr Major has any particular interest in the turf. Mr Major is a cricket enthusiast and perhaps there is a tenuous link between him and Lord Roseberry in that the 6th Earl captained Surrey and awarded the great Sir Jack Hobbs his county cap.

Mr Major apparently aims to establish a classless society and his admirers regard it as a point in his favour that he never went to a public school. Lord Roseberry was very happy at Eton, where he had a brilliant career, and as he lay dying at The Durdans, his house at Epsom, he had the Eton Boating Song played on a gramophone.

The non-conformist wing of the Liberal party was anything but keen on Lord Roseberry's racing activities. He himself said that they did not seem to mind all that much when his horses lost; it was only when they won that a real fuss was kicked up.

Mr Major's admirers will doubtless be pleased to learn that racing is becoming more and more classless. One has only to glance down a Royal Ascot racecard of 25 years ago and one of today to see that the aristocracy has largely opted out. Gone are the colours of Lord Roseberry, Lord Astor and the Duke of Norfolk, etc., etc., while those of Lord Derby are seen all too seldom . . .

I have always thought Huntingdon rather a dull town, perhaps rather like Bedford which was described by a US airman during World War II as resembling a cemetery with traffic lights.

The last time I attended Huntingdon races I ran a novice chaser there which I backed at 4-1. Approaching the final fence with John Francome in the saddle, with several lengths clear, he over-jumped, crumpled on landing and that was that.

The end of a perfect day came when we got lost going home. My wife was driving and I thought something was wrong when we passed Oliver Cromwell's statue for the third time.

I have said that I rarely saw my father close to a horse. His own trusty steed was his typewriter. A few yards from my room at home, the hottest news in racing – as well as much of its history – would be compiled and dispatched to the nation from his study. Yet racing was an esoteric and rather intimidating world to me, full of people speaking an unintelligible language. However, I was aware of the huge pride at home when my father's first major book was published in 1958: *The History of the Jockey Club*, which I have since read. It teems with as many compelling characters as a Charles Dickens novel.

It would be untrue to say I never went racing – very occasionally I had the fun of accompanying my father. The great perk was to have my father's company to myself for the car journey back and forth, where my constant longing to be grown-up was gratified by the nature of the conversations I was able to enjoy with him.

For excitement, there was the occasional privilege of standing beside my father in the BBC broadcasting box. I regarded this as a huge honour, which could only have been improved upon had I been handed the microphone and invited on air to make a comment. Strangely enough, I wasn't. For several years Roger was employed by BBC radio to provide commentaries on the line-up of runners prior to a race, and for the post mortem following the event. He worked alongside Raymond Glendenning initially and then the BBC's first full-time racing commentator, Peter Bromley. These were the few occasions I was permitted to spend in my father's company on the racecourse. It was his workplace so I would be left to my own devices – from the age of around eleven – but with a member's enclosure badge pinned firmly to my lapel.

It wasn't all fun and games. One boiling summer's day, my father took me, aged thirteen, wearing my best frock and clutching my autograph book, to the 'Celebrities' meeting at Sandown. 'Enjoy yourself and meet me back at the car at 5 o'clock, my dear child,' said my father as he melted away into the crowd. The day was long, hot and, far worse, devoid of a sighting of a single star. I was hoping at least to see Adam Faith who was reputed to be a keen racegoer. Back at the red hot car at the appointed hour, thirsty and cross, another age passed before my father appeared. When he finally trundled cheerfully into view, he said: 'Sorry I'm late, dear, but I got delayed by Elizabeth Taylor in the bar.' It was one of our more silent journeys home.

If I have ever made a contribution to the joys of racing, it was in Northumberland. My parents came to stay and I escorted them to a icy, wind-blown winter meeting at the little country course at Hexham, way beyond Roger's normal territory. We spent a lot of time imbibing whisky macs in the bar, roaring with laughter at a joke, the meaning of which I never quite discovered, but the hilarity was contagious. In a later article on the aesthetic aspect of racecourses, Roger concluded: 'Goodwood and Hexham are the two most beautiful courses in the country.'

In 1972 my father won the Lord Derby Racing Writer Award. In the awards programme, Brough Scott wrote an perceptive profile of my father, concluding : 'Roger Mortimer is modest about everything he has done, with one vital exception. When his elder daughter was at school, he used to write to her so often and so amusingly that she used to hand the letters around. Did he take pride in this? "Yes I think I write a very good letter."'

My Dearest Jane . . .

The Maudlings
Heathcote Amory
Berks
[Late 1960s]

Four perspiring days at Ascot which I think your dear mother enjoyed, including dinner with the Majendies one evening; Paul with his socialist bird Miss Mallalieu who is trying to educate him. I fell for Miss Mallalieu whose socialist principles did not prevent her from having a merry drink with me in the Royal Enclosure the following day.

From Yateley days, my first real friend in the shape of a boy was Paul Majendie, then at Oxford and later a successful journalist. In 1991, my father wrote again, in an article, of Miss Mallalieu:

> Of those individuals recently elevated to the House of Lords, the one in my view worth keeping an eye on is the charming and attractive Ann Mallalieu QC. Unlike many left-wingers, she is a keen fox-hunter. She contributes lively articles to the *Field* and is a dedicated follower of the Turf. Ann Mallalieu might one day make a very useful member of the Jockey Club.

Budds Farm
[1970s]

Great lunch with the swells before the Irish Derby – lobster,

Newly commissioned Coldstream Guard's officer Roger, 1930.

Roger as a POW in autumn 1940 – the first
of five he would spend in prison.

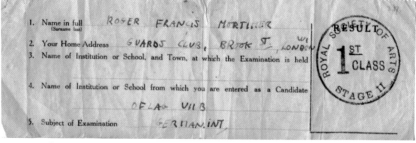

1. Name in full (Surname last)	ROGER FRANCIS MORTIMER
2. Your Home Address	GUARDS CLUB, BROOK ST, LONDON W1
3. Name of Institution or School, and Town, at which the Examination is held	
4. Name of Institution or School from which you are entered as a Candidate	OFLAG VIIB
5. Subject of Examination	GERMAN INT

ROYAL SOCIETY OF ARTS
RESULT
1ST CLASS
STAGE II

Roger's first class exam pass in German, in prison.

Army Form B.2606.
(REVISED)
MILITARY
IDENTITY CARD No.   A   421246

Surname MORTIMER
Christian Names (and rank or designation at time of issue) ROGER FRANCIS MAJOR
Sex MALE
Personal No. 44922
Height 6'1"
Colour of Eyes Blue
Colour of Hair Fair
Other Distinguishing Marks (if any) –
Date of Birth 22.11.1909.
Signature of Issuing Officer John Richardson Mole Major.
Date 10.8.46.

Signature of Bearer
RF Mortimer

Roger's military ID card, 1946.

Roger and Cynthia's wedding day in 1947.

What have I got here? My mother and me at my christening, 1949.

My father and me
in Dorset, 1951.

Me at Barclay House, 1952.

Grandpa Denison-Pender, my father and me at Barclay House, 1953.

Duffle coats for me and Lupin in the snow, late 1950s.

Grandpa Denison-Pender with me, Lupin and Lumpy, 1960.

My father and me on the beach, 1960s.

My teenage self in the garden at Barclay House, 1964.

Lupin shows some bottle – with me in 1968.

Pongo, and Moppet on the sofa, 1960s.

Happy family outing, 1950s.

My mother Cynthia, pretty in yellow, 1950s.

What a radiant lady – Nidnod in the 1960s.

Nidnod and Turpin, 1960s.

Aunt Pam (Ham) and Uncle Ken (Honkel) in Oslo, late 1960s.

Grandpa Roger with little
Piers at Budds Farm, 1975.

Brothers Piers and Nick, 1977.

A bit bigger than me! Piers and Granny Nidnod's pony, 1975.

Grandpa Roger and baby Nick, 1977.

Solicitous Grandpa with Nick, his arm in plaster, and Piers in one piece at The Miller's House, 1983.

My father and me celebrating Christmas in Northumberland, 1988.

The happiest
holiday in
Provence –
my parents,
1987.

My parents on the beach, 1960s.

Roger in classic pose – reading the paper – beside Lake Como, 1960s.

Roger penning a piece in a racecourse Press Room, 1969.

May 6

Dearest Jane,

I have just sent a small present to P.F.
Torday which I hope will be useful.While engaged in purchase
of the same,I discovered that The Pent House at Camp Hopsons
is where the trendy Newbury set goes for elevenses each
morning.It is sunny and nearly warm today.Oh for some
rain.The garden is a mere dust bowl.Even the weeds are
giving up the struggle for existence.Cousin Tom's horse

Jupiter Pluvius won the Chester Vase and is now fancied for
the Derby.I have come to the conclusion that words I
particularly dislike include bland,mellow,chuckle,
Democratic,dainty,meaningful,purposeful,sporting,wee,
crisp and gown.

Are you sure you know the meaning of(can even pronounce)
words such as recondite,esoteric,superrogation,archetype,
pragmatic,empiric,ochlocracy,viable,carminative,oblate,
nympholepsy,fardel,drupe?

lck 70s

Monda

Dearest Jane,

I have received your letter which you did not honour with the dignity of a 1st class
stamp.However better late than never(often untrue)and I read it with pleasure.
Not much news from here.We went out to dinner on Saturday and I
met a tall lady from Venezuela and a bald man from the Foreign Office
who fancied his chances.On Sunday we lunched with Mrs Cameron;also present
a South African lady(white) and a very agreeable man who had played Rugby for Ireland.
I drank too much port and eventually demon doss enfolded me in his hairy arms.I gave
your mother lunch at Kingsclere today:the Crown has been tarted up and the soup there is
excellent.Tonight we dine with the Badgetts and a tiresome fat woman will be there who has
a vituperative tongue and once informed that Mr P.had murdered his third wife.I have
been busy in the garden,having concocted a top dressing which the weeds will probably
like if nothing else.The new ironmongers in Kingsclere

                            Budds Farm.

Good Friday.

   Dearest Jane,

          I suppose you are now a fully paid-up member of that weird mothers'
world that revolves around nappies,wind and five o'clock feeds.And the best of British
Luck to you.I have had many questions about you in the Carnarvon Arms and a stout lady
wanted to know if P F.Torday had been "induced".Not knowing what she meant,I said
"possibly"and left it at that .Your dear mother is still in a very exalte mood
and is under the happy but doubtless mistaken impression that the child's existence is
due solely to her.Louise is in rasping form and swigged down a double whisky before
lunch without turning a hair.I think she would make a very good female golfer.Your
extraordinary brother has gone to Ireland to fish.I must say he never commits himself
to the obvious with regard to his own way of life.It is pouring with rain and we have
all been crouching round the fire with the alternative of Show-Jumping or Elvis
Presely on TV.Talk about a choice between the dagger and the bowl of poison.I have
been re-reading Madame Bovary which is quite one of my favourite books.I had a very
good dinner with the Bomers when your mother was away.Sarah complained of the
difficulty of buying a magazine with handsome male nudes in so I got her the gala
spring number of "Health and Efficiency"which ought to keep her quiet for a bit ;
although in fact the gents pictured playing ping pong or sawing up trees were not,in my
view,much improvement on Farmer Luckes or Mr Randall.Aunt Joan is coming down to
Burghclere by coach with fellow members of the Marylebone Pottery and Ceramics Club.
God knows what they hope to find here.One of my older friends,Dorothy Kemp,died last
week aged 95.Her late husband played cricket for Oxford against Cambridge in 1878.
I have been mildly amused by the Marcia Williams affair--just a paupers Watergate,
really.I always adore the hypocrisy of the Left and their shrill squeals of indignation
when they are caught out making a bit of money on the side.The first whine is always
about newspaper persecution;and is at least partially justified.I dont seem to remember
much complaint from the lefties,though,when the Tories were getting far worse hell over
the Vassall,Profumo and Lambton cases.I'm rather sorry for poor old H.Wilson.He's been

duck, strawberries, hock and a lively conversation with a tough, entertaining old bag whom Belper used to consort with in the 1920s. She has wisely abandoned sex for gardening. Lunch today with a charming old queen who has a marvellous garden; dinner with a lively widower whose one eye gleams with lecherous anticipation when he sees your dear mother – so good for both of them. Amusing lunch with millionaire Jock Whitney. He opened as follows: 'I have just had a heart attack and am on a very strict diet. However if you will twist my arm a little, I will probably give in and we will consume a number of very large dry martinis.'

Love

xx D

Hypothermia House
Burghclere
[1970s]

Yesterday I took the coach to London and went to the Hyde Park Hotel for the Horserace Totalisator Board's Annual Lunch. Many self-important individuals, including MPs and union bosses. I had the ill fortune to sit next to an arrogant, pompous old bore Sir Gladwyn J. He took a quick look at me, decided I had nothing to offer (true, possibly) and turned his back for the entire meal. On my other side was a racing character I don't much like. The Chairman, Woodrow Wyatt, was once a leftish Labour MP but is now a jolly 'Establishment' man. His speech was not unamusing.

Budds Farm
6 May [late 1960s]

Charles came both days to Ascot and rather enjoyed himself. He has a pleasant life here; he rises at 9.45 a.m., plays
the gramophone and smokes till lunch; smokes and plays the
gramophone till tea; watches the cornier programmes on TV
till the labours of the day overwhelm him at 9.30 and then
retires to rest.

Budds Farm
10 February 1968

My Sports Editor on the 'Sunday Times' is leaving. I shall
be lucky if I ever get anyone so indolent and disinterested
again. In twenty years not one word of praise or blame. Only
the wage packet on the dot each month. What more can you
want?

La Maison des Deux Gagas
Grand Senilite
France
[1973]

My relations with the Sunday Times continue to deteriorate.
The Sports Editor, John L., who believes what he reads in the
New Statesman, proof of his puerile intellect, told me he was
not in the least interested in racing. I replied that it was rather
akin to the literary editor saying that all biographies bored
him. I also pointed out in plain terms that the top brass at

Thomson House is distinguished chiefly for bad manners and incompetence. There the matter rests at present.

My colleague Tom D. of 'The People' (do you remember him telling crime stories to you and Charles during a rough crossing to Le Havre?) committed suicide the other day, the pain from his spinal cancer having worn him down. Because he accelerated the inevitable end, his employers are endeavouring to reduce the amount payable to his widow. I would gladly strike for a case like this; I fear though that journalists are only stirred by threats to their personal affluence. Quelle cochonnerie!

I am battling with two books at present, one for Cassell, one for M. Joseph. I keep on getting them muddled up but no one seems to care. I hope the Cassell book will appear in October; in my opinion it is a rare bargain at £8. Whether anyone else will think so is by no means certain.

On Sunday I lunch with Jim Joel at Childwickbury. He is a bachelor, nearly eighty, worth at least £40m. The son of a desperado who made a fortune by questionable means in South Africa, he is the mildest, kindest and most generous of men.

In World War I, Jim Joel was a dashing Hussar. Shortly before the great battle of Arras he was short of a charger and his father sent him out a horse that had been placed in the Middle Park. Despite lack of military training, the horse survived the battle, was taken back to England and won a couple of small handicaps there.

I have been invited to see his horses but I expect we shall look at his pictures and china. He is my favourite millionaire and in a diffident way tells hilarious stories of his youth.

Best love,

xx D

Budds Farm
23 July 1973

I lunched with Jim Joel yesterday in full Edwardian splendour. Four of us to lunch and a butler and 2 footmen in attendance. Israeli melon; lobster mousse with lobster claws and a rich sauce; choice of chicken pie or lamb; gooseberry fool; peaches, cherries and raspberries.

Schloss Buddestein
Worms
1973

The Sports Editor, John L. has made overtures to me re writing a leading article for the 'Sunday Times' on the malaise of this country at the present time. My recent expostulations seem to have made an impression. However, I have declined. Ancient cobblers should stick to their last (whatever a last is).

Budds Farm
31 October 1969

I may have had a bit of good fortune as some optimist wants to produce an American edition of one of my books so with luck I may be able to buy myself a couple of new shirts and a packet of Wills Whiffs. I look forward to seeing you soon and hope you will entertain me by hamming the part of the up-and-coming female tycoon.
    Love
    xx D

Budds Farm
Thursday [1970]

Nidnod and I went to Oxford to see William Douglas
Home's new play 'The Jockey Club Stakes'. Of course it is
not noticeably avant-garde – rather derrière-garde in fact –
but it is not unamusing and the audience received it well. It
opens in London on Wednesday. I can't go to the first night
as I shall be at Newmarket but I can get a couple of stalls
any time I like. Do you want to come? You are welcome
to but I think it would hardly be your cup of Horlicks as
it is all 'establishment' jokes about the Jockey Club and
Eton. William D. H. is very kindly giving me a percentage of
the profits for my help so I hope to God it runs. It will get
ghastly notices from the trendy critics who prefer themes on
lesbianism and incest in draughty cellars but I can only pray
that it gets by as 'The Secretary Bird' did. I have just received
rather a fat cheque from my publishers plus the news that my
last book is being reprinted so I enclose a v. small sum for you
to have a drink or buy some new smalls.
    Love
    xx D

The Turf Club
January 1969

Typical business lunch. Two men from Cassell's, one from the
Jockey Club, my agreeable literary agent + myself. Endless
drinks, too much to eat, and total avoidance of topic for
which we had met. Result: two wasted hours in uncouth W1
district and nothing accomplished. I concluded by saying that
at the current rate of progress we might meet in the geriatric

ward of an 'Eventide Home' at Woking. This was reckoned poor taste!

Chez Nidnod
14 Rue Prinker
12 September 1973

This afternoon I have to go and see a bearded man at Cassell's. He likes me as much as the head of El Fatah likes Moshe Dayan; his sentiments are reciprocated in full.

Maison du Vieux Crapaud
Burghclere
1 January [early 1970s]

Yesterday I went racing at Windsor but found I had arrived a day too soon! Surely a portent of impending gagadom; or perhaps déjà arrive. I went to a pub and ordered an expensive ham sandwich which to my disgust was smeared with margarine of a revolting nature. When I timidly expostulated, the genial host threatened to send for the chucker-out. Later I saw an elderly man trip and fall when trying to catch the Slough bus. I recognised him as an individual called Gunner Bennett (real name Joseph Stavinski), a heavyweight boxer who came and taught boxing at Windsor Barracks in 1936. I called out to him and he was pleased to be recognised and to have a drink and a chat. He looked, unlike so many old boxers, happy, healthy and prosperous. My next step was to visit the rather posh Windsor and Eton Art Gallery. Having £250 to invest as the result of some work done, I thought

I would buy a small picture. I had a long look round and narrowed the choice down to three of the type I used to buy from Harry Sutch for £50–£150. Their respective prices were £5,400, £4,700, £3,700. Thanks awfully! With a light laugh which might have been interpreted as a distinct sneer, I pissed off into the January gloom.

Love to all,

xx D

The Crumblings
Cowpat Lane
31 January [early 1970s]

I had to sign three copies of my book at Newbury on Saturday and was instructed to write a very embarrassing little message in all three, rather suggesting I loved the owners of the book, who in fact were all men I had never set eyes on before. It's awful the things I have to do for money; I wish I drew the line somewhere.

Budds Farm
14 October [mid 1970s]

I have just had an article published dealing with the law of libel (Chapman v Jockey Club) and only hope that I got some of the facts right. Libel is not a subject on which I claim to be well informed. I am a bit nervous myself as recently owing to a misprint in my copy a certain individual was described not as a well-known breeder, but as a well known bleeder.

Budds Farm
March 1974

We had an enjoyable stay at Tetbury with the Popes for Cheltenham. The browsing and sluicing is of the highest order. It is a man's world there. After dinner the ladies are herded into the drawing-room and the men sit round the fire in the hall, swilling port. The sexes only meet again to bid each other goodnight.

The Popes – military John (a terrific tease) and charming Liz – were a most handsome and hospitable couple. They were superb riders and true friends of my parents.

The Old Tudor Doss House
Burghclere
[1970s]

The Sunday Times have given me a 33 per cent pay rise. I wish they had thought of it earlier. A book I was editing for George Allen and Unwin has been cancelled due to the enormous cost of coloured photographs. However, I have got some assignments from magazines I had never previously heard of.

La Domicile Geriatrique
Burghclere
Sunday [June 1980s]

And the rain comes pitter patter, pitter patter down, beating flat the few flowers in the alleged herbaceous border and soaking my Japanese-made-special-offer shirt from J. Levine of Atlee Crescent, Chingford. I went to Ascot all four days; in these hard times the dresses would not have been too smart for a rural dean's garden-party in the remoter part of Lincolnshire. I lunched twice at Ascot with Mr K. Abdullah (oil tycoon) who has a private lunch room at Ascot and is rather apt to dish out Arab appetisers that look like dog turds. Mr Abdullah comes with a friend who owns half Bombay and always has such a terrible hangover that his lunch consists of mineral water and a digestive biscuit. I don't suppose either gentleman is all that interested in women; unlike the African Chieftain who visited Queen Victoria and informed her he had thirty-one wives. The Queen graciously asked how he occupied their time and received the answer, 'I fok them.'

Peter Willett's younger son, Stephen, was a chef in the Grundy Stand and I saw him in a tall chef's hat (or more accurately a chef's tall hat) and sporting a heavy dragoon's moustache.

I use the Abergavennys' private stand at Ascot, much frequented by elderly members of the racing 'establishment'. Cheeky juniors refer to it as the Intensive Care Unit! We have been asked to the Queen Mother's 80th Birthday party and of course your mother wants to go.

Love to you all,
RFM

Chez Nidnod
27 September [early 1980s]

I am getting rather chummy with a certain Mr Khaled Abdullah, a dusky sportsman who has a few dozen oil wells at the bottom of his garden in Saudi Arabia. He gave me lunch the other day and he has asked me to write a speech for him. Can I ask him in return to settle my central heating bill for 1980/81? Also present at the lunch were an armed 'minder' and a plump Mr Hazar who is richer than Mr Abdulla and behind a mask of buffoonery never misses a trick. He prefers racing in France as it is 'More elegant'!

The Bog Garden
Burghclere
[Early 1980s]

Very odd people go to Ascot these days and I would not be surprised to meet Crippen and Myra Hindley in the Royal Enclosure.

Dr Crippen – my father's favourite murderer – surfaces a few times in his letters.

The Grumblings
Burghclere
[1970s]

There is a pompous man called Boucher who, though very rich, always sells his best mares. He was rather annoyed at the Newmarket Sales when someone said to him: 'Lucky Mrs Boucher has not got four legs or she'd be in the sale ring, too.'

Q. If a jockey wears a jock strap, what does a jockette wear?

A. A fan belt

Budds Farm
23 April [1980s]

My horse was beaten by 6 inches at Wincanton on Monday, a difference of £500. I shall now have to delay buying a new hat.

The Shiverings
Burghclere
[Late 1970s]

I am glad to see my latest effusion is included in Truslove and Hanson's Christmas catalogue of the best books recently published. I only hope some sucker will be enticed into buying one. Oddly enough the book got a long and flattering review in the 'Irish Press' which I think is the organ of the Sinn Fein party.

Love to you all,

xx D

Budds Farm
[1970s]

'Oh give me a man to whom nought comes amiss, one horse or another, that country or this.'

That was of course written about hunting but it is the general attitude towards women adopted by a fair number of males of my acquaintance. I think the author was Adam Lindsay Gordon who was always sloshed and broke, was exiled to Australia and committed suicide there. He remains

Australia's national poet. I wrote about him years ago for some magazine.

c/o Marquis de Sade
Chateau de Belvoir
14 b Kitchener Road
Holloway N14
[1970s]

I received a very disobliging letter today from a Sunday Times reader. It began: 'I suppose you think you're being funny.' There were other accusations besides, not all of which were totally justified. We are a very odd race. No Englishman will admit he is deficient in humour or ability to appreciate it; yet how many nasty arguments, even rows, begin 'I suppose you think you're funny' or 'Are you trying to be funny by any chance?'

Budds Farm
November 1974

I finish work with the Sunday Times tomorrow. A very agreeable young gent came and took at least 177 photographs of me, all in the rain and with me wearing a cap two sizes too small. Your mother was very busy trying to fit all the animals in. The photographer stayed till 2 p.m. talking to your mother but as I left at 12.45 that did not greatly worry me.

The Merry Igloo
Burghclere on the Ice
[Mid 1970s]

When I joined the Sunday Times the circulation was about 400,000; it was quite pleasant to work for if you did not mind exiguous pay; fuddy-duddy, paternal, and a cosy family atmosphere. Lots of staff parties at which the sports writers all got pissed and the literary and artistic contributors started feeling each other.

Under Thompson, the Sunday Times staff parties were really awful being chiefly a shameless display of arse-licking by keen 'executives'. I once had dinner with Rees-Mogg and found very little in common with him. Harold Evans (The Dame) is a gritty little fellow from Middlesbrough with a class chip on both shoulders. Sir Dennis Hamilton was the classic example (still is, no doubt) of a smiling shit. If he squeezed your arm and said how much he enjoyed and admired your work, you knew your job was in serious jeopardy. I think he hailed from Newcastle and was pushed ahead in the Army by Field Marshal Montgomery in the war.

I preferred the old Kemsley staff – Ernest Newman (Wagner's illegitimate son); James Agate, who had been to a male brothel with Proust: H. V. Hodson, the Editor, who looked like a diplomat in a pre-war play by Somerset Maugham; and a weird old crow called Valentine Heywood, an expert on titles and decorations. There was also an amusing cricket writer, Robertson-Glasgow, who suffered from periodic depression and eventually cut his throat after breakfast one day with the bread knife.

Most of the people Evans introduced to the paper were Australian Trotskyites (like the 'Insight' team) or abrasive little fellows from northern newspapers. Also a conceited little shit called Michael Parkinson.

I have been working for 'The Racehorse' since June 1947. I was made editor at one stage but only lasted 3 weeks, my ignorance and ineptitude being impossible to conceal.

Best love,

RM

Harold Evans and Michael Parkinson – two media icons in the ascendant to whom my father would give no quarter.

Budds Farm

21 November [early 1970s]

I have just had a letter of farewell from the Editor of the Sunday Times. It is typical of him and his dreary publication that it was addressed to the house we left some years ago, Barclay House, Yateley.

Budds Farm

26 January 1974

I am going to do a short stint with the Sunday Times; quite like old times again. The do-ray-me will come in useful, my capital having depreciated by £90,000 in ten months. (Gentlemen, charge your glasses. I give you the toast – 'Wedgwood Benn'.)

Anthony Wedgwood Benn, legendary far left Labour minister (1974–9) and one of my father's pet bêtes noires.

Via Dolorosa
Burghclere
[1975]

What with Arabs, Trade Unions and Mr Wedgwood Benn, life
is particularly disenchanting at present. I have been working
12 hours a day completing a book of monumental boredom
and feel mentally exhausted. The job is now finished and it
only remains to correct 1,297 pages of proofs. Today I have
just done a rush job – an article on stallions of obscure origins
that have proved successful in the Antipodes. Not the summit
of hilarity for writer or reader.

Schloss Schweinkopf
Grosspumpernickel
Neuburg
[1970s]

A magazine I have never heard of has hired me to write 2 five
thousand word articles on English racing from 1900 to 1925.
I knocked them off in a couple of days and now feel rather
anxious about getting paid. The editor's signature seemed to
indicate that his name was Soupfeather which sounds a trifle
improbable but of course you never know.

Budds Farm
11 June [1970s]

There was a fight in the press room on Derby Day between N.
Dempster of the Daily Mail and a fat man from the Express's

William Hickey column. Dempster dragged Fatty round the press room by his neck and Fatty pulled the 'Mail' telephone out by the roots. It was a lively scene much enjoyed by one and all. Dempster won on points.

Insolvency House
Burghclere
[Late 1970s]

Louise is reading more than she did. I have lent her 'Madame Bovary' which I hope she will enjoy. Did you know I had a mare called Madame Bovary, 33 years ago, in partnership with John Hislop? She won a race and bred a large number of winners. When she ran at Windsor, I did not own a car and just took a cab off the Kensington rank and told him to drive me to the racecourse. It only cost about £3. (Up until the war we used to get 4 postal deliveries a day in London, the last one at about 9 p.m.)

Budds Farm
[1970s]

Your mother enjoyed Ascot, even the ordeal of having lunch next to a plump Liberal peer who is an ex-parson. I got lumbered with a tall, gloomy Swede who owns a salt mine. A man in the Royal Enclosure sported an umbrella advertising French letters and was asked to leave.

14b Via Dolorosa
Burghclere
Sunday [late 1970s]

We stayed with the Popes for Cheltenham. Lady de Mauley was at the races and while the Gold Cup was being run she talked vivaciously about clothes and the price of temporary cooks. I have discovered that Lady de M is known locally as 'The Duchess'. Mrs Pope was highly complimentary about you and your husband. Frankly this is beginning to annoy me and I hope to unearth someone who took a very strong dislike to you both, particularly to Paul whose popularity is getting on my nerves.

P.S. I enclose £5 as I hear you had a bet on my horse. I would have advised you not to risk a penny on him as the ground was awful and his little feet went into the mud like tent pegs. Also his usual jockey was away, injured. Don't pay any attention to what your mother says about racing.

Love to you all,
xx D

Budds Farm
[Late 1970s, on pig paper]

I have more or less finished a book (to be published by Guinness Superlatives Ltd) to celebrate the 200th Derby next year. I look like having three books on the market soon, all of almost unsupportable tedium. I am thinking of writing a novel about military life in the 1930s. There will be a very odious character called Major Hurstbourne-Tarrant with a wife called Muriel who seduces the innocent young narrator in the Railway Hotel at Fleet after the final night of the Aldershot Tattoo.

The Old Crumblings
31 January 1970s

Today a publisher, whose name eludes me, invited me to compile a history of racing throughout the world since AD 1200. I estimated it would take me till 1993 to complete the book and that the rate of pay worked out at £26 per annum. Under the circumstances, I felt obliged to decline. I must now write my speech for this ghastly dinner at Stratford-upon-Avon tomorrow. At least 250 people present and I am terrified as I speak about as well as your mother's dog Pongo plays the French Horn. Thinks: is it better to get up sober and stammering or totally sloshed and rashly over-confident?

Little Grumblings
Roper Caldbeck
3 July 1970

Mrs Hislop's horse Brigadier Gerard has won two nice races and is now worth at least £25,000! We went to a 'small' lunch party with the More O'Ferralls at Kildangan Castle; your dear mother was tucking into really admirable groceries between Clive Graham (racing journalist 'The Scout' on the Daily Express) who had not shaved, and the US Ambassador, who had. Very potent Calvados cocktails beforehand. I sat next to a tough old blonde who had been on the shadier side of show business and a lady belonging to the Guinness family. One old gent present had flown to Ireland next to Miss Bernadette Devlin and fell for her in a big way; I doubt if he will get to first base, though.
    Love
    xx D

The More O'Ferralls had established a fine racing stud at Kildangan, while Bernadette Devlin was an Irish Republican activist and youngest woman MP (Independent, 1969–74) ever elected .

La Maison du Hangover Horrifique
Burghclere
[1970s]

Come to Burghclere if you wish to be where the action is! On Wed we had a dinner party before the Fancy Dress Ball – guests dressed to represent a racehorse's name. Present were Mrs Mortimer (Petite Etoile), Major Mortimer (Red Rufus), Mrs Surtees (Spanish Steps), Major Surtees (The Benign Bishop), Mr Greenward (I'm a Driver), Mrs Greenwood (Raise a Native) and Mr Cottrill (Blue Cashmere).

  Best love from your affectionate father,
  xx RM

During his forty-five years as a racing writer my father witnessed many changes in the sport. His own epitaph was 'The dogs bark and the caravan moves on, but never let it be forgotten that racing is meant to be fun.'

  From the racecourse to home: my parents lived in a total of four different houses during their long marriage. It's time to go home with them now – before setting forth on a Mortimer holiday or two.

8

Happy Home and Hairy Holidays

Chez Nidnod
Burghclere
[1970s]

Dearest Jane,
I am writing this with the window wide open; autumn
sunshine is pouring into the house and smoke from bread that
got jammed in the toaster is pouring out.

xx D

My father was a true home-lover – home was also his principle
office though not a quiet one. He enjoyed the surrounding
presence of his wife and family in the house, finding them
available when he took a break. The general hubbub they
created did not dim his concentration – a quality he had long
ago cultivated in environments loud with people, on a busy
racecourse for one, prison camp for another. It is only now

that I wonder if he might sometimes have hankered after the retreat of another workplace.

His hours of leisure were largely spent at home. Barclay House was the one he loved the best. It was there that he enjoyed his happiest phase as a husband and father of a young family. His health was OK and his career was in the ascendant. Life was full of promise. There were many good friends and neighbours, and we felt part of the Hampshire village of Yateley. We lived there for sixteen years. It was only pressure from a big property developer that induced my parents to sell up – very profitably – and move to Berkshire and Budds Farm, a house my father never liked. My mother loved it. Their final home was the Miller's House in Kintbury. My father liked it – my mother did not.

My father's physical antidote to the sedentary nature of writing was gardening. His first garden had been created from scratch, with pride and hours of his own hard labour. Barclay House backed on to a large garden. Paths threaded their way around its colourful features: a herbaceous border, beds of shrubs, roses and bright annual plants. A late summer border blazed with his favourite dahlias, fronting a long greenhouse, whose warm, damp interior glowed with sweet tomatoes. Apple trees flanked the wide path through the expansive kitchen garden and beneath them spires of lupins followed generous clumps of springtime polyanthus and primroses. I was not infrequently ticked off for picking them. We had a 'garden room' in the house where my mother arranged flowers, legitimately.

There were two large lawns to mow. Fierce games of croquet were played on the bottom lawn, led by my father, with Pimms and lemonade to follow. On the top lawn, the ancient mulberry tree growing at its centre provided the focal point around which our family life revolved. Trikes and bikes were ridden around it; lunch and tea parties for dolls, dogs, cats and people were relished on rugs on the grass beneath it. My little sister in her large antique black pram slept in its shade, my mother basked on her sun lounger, my father snoozed on his deckchair, book open in his hands. Prickly relations were humoured with sherry beneath the mulberry's leafy canopy, which was sometimes hung with its dark, nefarious fruit, waiting to be converted into jellies and ice cream by my mother. On a June evening during Ascot week my parents sometimes held a cocktail party; the mulberry tree stood proud above a white-clothed table, jugs of Pimms and big bowls of strawberries and cream. A small waitress, I wove in and out between the adults in their delicious haze of cocktails, Chanel No. 5, cigarettes and chatter.

Of all the gardeners who assisted Roger in our three different homes, there was not a single one who measured up to his unexacting standards. Their most productive role was to provide material for amusement. His favourite was, as in a children's story, the dependably cheerful, apple-cheeked, twinkle-eyed Mr Randall, 'Old Randy' at Budds Farm, for whom weeds grew ever more vigorously when he had sprayed them.

When I was unwell in bed, as a little girl, my father once decided to cheer me by bringing a terracotta clay flowerpot up to my bedroom in which sat, not unduly bewildered, a large toad. Two other little creatures my father brought to my bedside sprang straight from his imagination – Porky the Pig and Bruno the Bear – in stories which were neither repeated nor committed to paper. Porky was good-natured, greedy and always 'Up for a lark' – and always getting into scrapes. Bruno was the straight man whose job as a sensible, self-righteous bear was to point out the error of Porky's ways. If my father preferred scallywag Porky, it was Bruno's hat which he wore when addressing real-life money matters. My brother and I received this cheery little edict, delivered by hand, one April evening in the mid 1960s:

'This morning at 8.10 a.m. the central heating was switched on and there was electric heating in the kitchen, which was empty. There were electric fires switched on in three bedrooms although it was a mild April morning.

The electricity bill is very large indeed and is sometimes over £30 a quarter. In these times of high costs and high taxation I am compelled to ask for a little restraint. From now on the central heating will be switched on by your mother or by me. Until the winter comes round again, electric fires in your room and in Charles's are totally unnecessary and I forbid them.

The telephone is being used with an abandon that might lead one to believe that all calls are free. They may be so to you but not to me. All those local calls add up to a very big total and I want them cut down. If you have long-distance calls please find out the cost and notify me. If you have had any such calls in the past three weeks, please let me know.

Please be careful about leaving lights on when leaving a room. Over the months the amount of money wasted in this respect is considerable.

The time is fast approaching when you will be living away from home. It is no bad thing, therefore, to practise a little economy. Please remember that basic income tax is 8/6d in the £ and for some of my work I only receive 2/6d in the £ owing to supertax.

Yours ever,
RM'

'He who pays the piper calls the tune,' quoted my father regularly. A decent-sized home in the country, private education for his children, social entertaining and holidays abroad may sound reasonably posh but did not signify loads of dosh – or what my father called 'treacle'. Bills hung in a heavy chain around his neck.

217

However, my father enjoyed little shopping expeditions for treats, sweets and ice creams and eclectic household items, which gave him great pleasure – not least for the shopkeepers he encountered, like 'the bearded lady' in the village shop at Finchampstead. Sometimes, after a trip to London, when he was feeling flush, he might come home bearing a smart new holiday outfit for my mother, in bright colours – shocking pink, turquoise or orange. He showed commendable patience in occasionally taking me, an indecisive and uncertain shopper, to buy a new outfit. In common with most men from a military or services background, Roger was always keen to keep moving and get on. It was exactly the same when we later went round gardens together – no loitering or lingering to bask in the scent of a perfect rose.

Lists of my father's household chores – 'fatigues' – would crop up in his letters.

'Barclay House
9 October [mid 1960s]

I must now do the boiler, get the drink up from the cellar for a dinner party, select the glasses, chop up some kindling wood, lay the fire, fill the log basket, fill the coal bucket, fill the cigarette box, clean my evening shoes and scrape tomato soup stains off my dinner jacket, pick some flowers, chuck out the old ones and telephone fifteen boring people. A man's work in the home is never done.'

At the end of the day my father sank into his expansive armchair to read a book – newspapers would have been devoured at breakfast time. Beside him like a monument was his large Bakelite 'wireless', tuned to classical music on the 3rd Programme in the evenings. Later in the 1950s, a television was purchased – viewing strictly rationed. My father would turn on *Tonight* with Cliff Michelmore, whilst I sat impatiently, praying that I would be allowed to stay up and watch a proper programme like *Emergency Ward 10*. I can remember being astonished that my father, with his low boredom threshold, was prepared to gaze at that craggy-faced individual, Malcolm Muggeridge, and listen to his seemingly interminable pontifications.

Comedy programmes – well, of course my father adored them, either on TV or the wireless: *Round the Horn, Hancock's Half Hour*, Jimmy Edwards, Harold Lloyd, *Dad's Army, Till Death Us Do Part* to name just a few of them. Maybe they put him in the mood to later ascend the stairs to his study and write his children another letter.

My Dearest Jane . . .

Budds Farm
8 April [late 1970s, on pig paper]

Charles is spring-cleaning the kitchen with praiseworthy zest and has unearthed many curious and sometimes not wholly desirable links with the past. When I went to fill the log basket this morning, a rat of remarkable size was perched on a pile of wood and making himself very much at home.

The Sunday Times
23 October 1972

I trust the Yorkshire air is suiting you and that you are not lonely away from the Smoke. Your mother tells me you are making your house very nice. I think she visualises you as a future President of the WI and Paul as joint-master of the Bramham Moor.

A little cottage near Harrogate was our first home in the north. My father always expressed interest in my home life but, in terms of letters, I only fed him a trickle of responses. It was quite a challenge to respond rewardingly to such a polished letter writer – and laziness played its part.

Loose Chippings,
Soames Forsyte
Wilts
14 June 1970

We have had a four-week heat wave here and the garden now looks like the remoter part of the Sahara; I have twice seen a mirage on the croquet lawn. Your poor mother has joined an allegedly smart 'Country Club' at Silchester. I was taken to bathe there on Thursday and while doing the breaststroke rather gracefully side by side with a Junoesque Swedish au pair girl, one of your mother's fellow members went through my small kit and removed every penny from my trousers.

I was taken round Mrs S's garden last Wednesday. It is enormous – 19 acres – and full of rare shrubs. She is mildly eccentric and goes in for astrology, faith-healing and water divining. Her husband walks two paces in rear and keeps his mouth shut. I once saw him handling his garden fork in a manner suggesting that it would give him greater satisfaction to plunge it into the torso of his ever-loving wife than into the richly manured soil where he was standing. The house is lush but vulgar, with a touch of the Regent Palace Hotel and one of the more expensive cinemas in Birmingham.

Love,

xx D

The Old Troutery
30 January [early 1970s]

I hope you enjoyed your visit to the Lake District and have undergone cultural experiences of value. I always associate the Lake District with Gaffer Wordsworth and torrential rain. Needless to say, I have never been there. What indeed do I know of England bar Aldershot and London, W1 and SW1? The answer comes in unquavering tones: SFA. Do you ever read a rather inferior periodical called 'The Spectator'? It recently contained a longish letter by Diana Gunn defending pornography. Somehow I cannot envisage that ethereal creature really enjoying a cinema bleu but I think the point she makes is that she does not wish other people's little pleasures to be curtailed. I dare say she is right. I doubt if pornography does much harm and is usually hilarious rather than erotic.

Your dear mother has grown some lovely hyacinths and is justly very proud of them. I believe Hyacinth is quite a common name among the male Prussian aristocracy. There was a very odious officer in the SS (a body most Prussians of the old school avoided like the plague) called Graf Hyacinth von Strachwitz. I know a rather pompous old boy who carefully conceals the fact that he was christened Narcissus. It has been very chilly down here and my consumption of whisky macs has bordered on the impermissible. All the trendy racing set are off to the Seychelles. As for myself, I hope to have luncheon one Monday at quite a good hotel in Bournemouth. When I went there just before the last war, there was an old man of immense pomposity staying there called Colonel Cornwallis-West. He had been very good-looking in his youth with a penchant for elderly ladies. When 24 he married Winston Churchill's old mother who was in her late forties. She was a bit young for him so he took on a swarthy old actress called Mrs Patrick Campbell. On account of these exploits he was known as 'The Old Wives' Tale'.

Best love,

xx D

Hyper-sensitive and of swan-like beauty, Diana Gunn and her husband Peter were both writers.

Budds Farm
[1973]

I hope you have been able to buy your house in Hexham and that you are furnishing it in lavish and luxurious style so that you can entertain for the local Hunt Balls and Conservative Rallies. Here, my dahlias are very good; the rest of the garden is curling up at the edges like a British Railways sandwich.

La Morgue
Burghclere
[1974]

I am very, very bored today. It is too wet to take the dogs out, let alone garden, and I am up to date for once with all my work. I wish I had a very large supply of extremely potent drugs: all I possess is one aspro tablet somewhat soggy from a long sojourn in a damp sponge bag. I may be driven to going out and having a drink with Mrs Hislop.

The Olde Igloo
Burghclere
17 January [1970s]

Thank you for sending my glove. It was careless of me to leave it behind and has resulted in slight frostbite in the exposed hand. We have been more or less under siege here but conditions were only really unpleasant for three days when we hardly had the heating on at all and there was no hot water. My car was stuck in the garage for over a week, the post van could not get down the lane, and of course there was no hope of a tanker being able to fill up the oil container. However, we had no lack of logs, alcohol or sustaining groceries. Many other people had a far worse time. Mr P has not been able to get rid of his alcoholic mother-in-law and I doubt if he ever will. She does not do many miles to a bottle of John Haig. Nidnod rather enjoys a crisis and is quite happy unblocking sinks etc. provided I remember to applaud.

Love to you all,
RM

Detention Centre 392
Burghclere
1 February [1970s]

It is raining hard here and doubtless we shall have floods here soon. The de Mauleys are punting over for lunch. Thank God January is over. It has been a hideous month for most people. Owing to the gravediggers' strike, local corpses are being placed in the deep freeze of Jackson's Stores. Your mother has a new boyfriend, a retired naval officer in spectacles who lives at Wash Common. He is of a serious nature and was obviously put out when I said there were more dotty admirals than dotty generals, there being a great many bonkerinos in both categories. Not much local excitement except the case of indecent exposure near the old bandstand in the Victoria Park. Lucky to have much to show in this weather! As John Pope used to say, it's a case of more wrinkles than inches!

A good friend of my mother, Lady de Mauley had a certain glamour – and grandeur. In their earlier phase as committed pony-club mothers, their mutual competitiveness added an edge to their friendship.

Very Near the Overflowing Drain
Burghclere
11 May [1980s]

How is your garden progressing? I think you have, fortunately, quite a flair for cultivation, and as a certain lady observed to that restless fellow Napoleon, 'Vous ne savez pas quelle bonheur on peut trouver dans trois arpents de terre.' (You do not know what happiness can be found in three acres of earth.) Your mother has decided to try her hand in the garden and has pinched a favourite corner of mine for her own efforts. She has quite a good eye for the garden, much better than I have, but she is very impulsive and allergic to advice. We have hired a Mr Fisher to come in and do housework once a week. He is a saucy old toad described by his wife as 'a marvel with a Hoover'.

xx D

Your Garden This Summer by Enoch Dungfork (alias RM)
Radishes are no trouble but encourage wind.
Beetroots are not much trouble bar for thinning out. Who wants to eat beetroot, though?
Peas get eaten by birds and it is cheaper to buy them.
Marrows are easy to grow on rich dung. They look smashing at the Harvest Festival but are somewhat dreary to eat.

The Bog Garden
Burghclere
[1981]

I am conscious of not having written to you for rather a long time but I don't in fact write much during the summer. I'm too busy and hardly have time to sit and think. 'Rest! Rest!' said Florence Nightingale. 'You have all eternity to rest in.' In addition I am compelled to face what Churchill called 'the surly advance of decrepitude'. Doctors say gardening is bad for the elderly who use, and strain, muscles never otherwise employed. By dint of much labour I got the garden in quite good order for Ascot week.

    Best love,
    xx D

Home Sweet Home
Sunday [1980s]

The garden is very horrible, all straggly and windswept. I sometimes think I prefer concrete. I *loathe* Sundays. I think this is a hangover from the miseries of Sunday at Eton.

Le Grand Hotel de Bon Confort et de Repos (I don't think)
14 January 1973

Our new 'daily', Lorraine, is an agreeable woman but does not realise the perils inherent in trying to engage me in conversation when I am reading 'The Times' newspaper at breakfast.

The Bracket
Much Slumbering
Beds
[Mid 1970s]

The husband of our daily Lorraine says he wishes to God he was a bachelor! I think he's got something there.

Many Cowpats
Burghclere
[1972]

There is nothing to report in the garden bar the presence of a large and extremely likeable toad who looks like Reggie Maudling without his spectacles.

Budds Farm
29 April 1973

The garden is tidy but brown and dry; there is a big friendly toad in the lupins called Nigel. He looks pensive and ill-pleased with the world for which I can hardly blame him.

The Grumblings
[1973]

Mr Randall has just trapped a very tiresome female mole called Ulrica who was ravishing the lawn.

The Miller's House
[Early 1980s]

Old Randy is here today: judging from what he achieves, I imagine he plants weeds rather than hoes them.

Chez Nidnod
The New Caravan Park
Burghclere
[1970s]

There have been some trendy parties in Burghclere lately with much stripping of improbable individuals – our doctor being one of them. Nidnod is worried that we are excluded from these bucolic saturnalia.

The Old Damp Ruin
Much Shivering
Berks
9 December 1980

My social life is on the upsurge: I have been asked to a bridge competition to partner a lady of 87. Yesterday I had the urge to cook and made a chocolate cake. Much to my surprise it has turned out a stunner and I am asking some charming ladies in for elevenses.

I am shopping in Whitchurch this morning. I am very popular there. (Query: Why? Answer: I am younger and jollier than most of the inhabitants.) Last week I went into the general stores and sang:

'How much are the crumpets in your window,
The ones with the holes going through?'

That went down very well.

Little Shiverings
Burghclere
[1980s]

I have bought a new motor, a very cheap Citroën made of cardboard and tin. It has a dashboard like a Lancaster bomber, not one of the knobs being remotely applicable to everyday motoring. Your mother has bought a fridge: I have stumped up for a new carpet for the downstairs loo, the present carpet looking too much like a map of the Solomon Islands.

[Late 1970s, postcard]

I hope you're all having a good time at the seaside. Yesterday I got sloshed at lunch at the Walwyns and spent a lot of money at the Lurcher Show. Colonel Mad came to lunch here on Friday. He is an alcoholic diabetic. The cat made a huge mess in the bath this morning. I sent a cheque to Louise and her dog Chappie ate it. Nidnod on very good form.

xx D

Colonel Mad was Private Eye's *name for Jeffrey Bernard. In his 'Low Life' column in the* Spectator *he once applauded* Roger's History of the Derby Stakes *as the best racing book ever written. My father asserted that it was only the booze that impeded Jeffrey Bernard from being a top racing writer. When Jeffrey temporarily decamped from Soho to Berkshire, without a car, he wrote himself a letter every day thereby ensuring a postal delivery to his cottage – and a lift in the post van to the local pub, ready for opening time.*

Chez Nidnod
25 September [1970s, on pink pig paper]

Thank God I have only 748 pages of this porcine writing paper left. I'm not sure Lloyds Bank really like it. A hideous start to the morning: I woke up, switched on the wireless and the Croydon Salvation Army Band was playing 'Jesus wants me for a Sunbeam'. I then tottered to the bathroom and had to evict from the bath a platoon of exceptionally large and healthy spiders whose attitude was distinctly hostile. However, morale was restored by drinking champagne in the sun with the Bomers. I went blackberrying yesterday and was accompanied throughout by an amiable bullock. We are now on good terms and he answers to the name of Nigel.

Chez Gaga
Burghclere
[1974]

I called on the vicar last week and found him nude except

229

for an exceedingly scant pair of Eton blue swimming trunks, and a beret. I unloaded a great deal of jumble on him for the church fete.

Chez Nidnod
Sunday [late 1970s]

I hear you have been seen at the local hunt ball. I always thought you might end up by becoming a typical member of the Northumbrian sporting community and I shall not be surprised to hear of you taking riding lessons before long. I never really liked hunt balls all that much; hideous memories of wheeling enormous women round the Corn Exchange floor to the strains of the 'Blue Danube'; slightly intoxicated young men making what they believed to be hunting noises and going down on the floor to worry the hearthrug. Since my photo appeared in the local paper, I am almost a celebrity and am treated with rather less disdain than usual in Jacksons Stores and the local public house.

Best love and my respects to your ever loving husband,
RM

Budds Farm
Spring 1974

Your dear mother took me to a party given in a draughty village hall by the Kingsclere and Whitchurch RDC. Sweet sherry in minute glasses, pickled onions, presentations and speeches. I was cornered by a voluble Welsh parson who was a great hand-kisser; he might have kissed mine but for a largish biro stain.

Castle Chaos
Burghclere
22 October [late 1970s]

The dahlias have been wonderful. I really grow them to annoy garden snobs who affect to despise all colour in the garden bar white and grey, and who mutter 'Surrey stockbroker' when they see a herbaceous border.

La Maison des Deux Gagas
Grand Senilite
France
[1973]

My herbaceous border, which was looking proud and handsome, has been battered to the ground by a storm of the sort that upset Ovid so much as left Rome for exile: 'Me Miserum; quanti montes volvuntur aquarum' etc. (Ah me! What mountain waves around me flow.)

Home Sweet Home
Thursday [late 1970s]

The usual restful morning here. The cat wakes me up at 6 a.m. and I let her out. Preparation of the cat's breakfast is delayed by inability to find the tin-opener. My dog then demands to be let out and disappears into the shrubbery, leaving me shivering at the front door in my Marks and Spencer pyjamas. I decide to have a hot bath but find the water tepid. Shaving is frustrated by the battery in my razor being on the brink of extinction. I try and cut my toenails but develop acute cramp in one leg. I then do the boiler and find the fuel has not been delivered as promised and in fact has run out. I fill the log basket, clean the grate and lay the fire. I eventually settle to a peaceful breakfast, the table nicely laid, sausages, toast, marmalade and coffee and 'The Times'. Peace, perfect peace at breakfast can only be achieved with loved ones far away. I am just perusing the obituary column when Charles arrives from London. At any rate he does not try to be jolly at breakfast for which I am truly grateful.

c/o Bishop of York
Ebor Castle
York
[1970s]

I hope you will be here next weekend for the local fete. There is a folk-song competition for local teams and I look to you to assist the Harts Lane team. Our song is 'Farmer's Itch' and starts off:

> 'As I were going down Cowpat Lane
> With a crappity pudding for parson,
> I was suddenly seized with a hideous pain
> And terribly sick the green grass on'

This is an old Basingstoke traditional song and it is inaccurate to ascribe it to the late Reverend Enoch Durge, Vicar of St Vitus's Much Polking.

Budds Farm
Whit Monday 1975

Mr Randall is the most industrious man I know; also easily the worst gardener. His seeds never come up and if they do something fatal happens to them soon afterwards. Even spinach and beans experience a terminal sickness under his care. He really ought to be a GP. Given a free hand, he would soon put the brakes on the population explosion.

Slight and dapper, Mr Randall had a comely and voluptuous wife reminiscent of Ma in H. E. Bates's The Darling Buds of May *– with a similarly large and merry family. There was a warm understanding between the Randalls and my parents.*

Chez Nidnod
Burghclere
Monday [early 1970s]

A very grey day. To use a vulgar Canadian expression, it is raining 'like a cow pissing on a flat stone'. In many ways England is a good country to live in but it is a disadvantage that there are only about twelve really fine days every year. The lack of sunshine accounts for the well-known English melancholia, accidie, liverishness and almost total lack of joie de vivre. No wonder the English invented gumboots and mackintoshes; and probably galoshes, too. English cooking, toad-in-the-hole, for example, and roly-poly pudding, is a reflection of the English climate. It is typical that cricket – allegedly our national game – cannot be played when it is raining. I have known several former captains of the England XI, and all have been alcoholics due to sitting around in dank pavilions all day waiting for the rain to stop and with nothing to do except play poker and drink. The house is being painted by Mr Thorn and his assistant, the latter being an unemployed actor with earrings. I think he might get a job in the chorus of The Pirates of Penzance.

Best love to you all from all of us,

xx D

The Old Drippings
Burghclere
February [1970s]

A thaw is now in progress: this is to be welcomed even if it does mean I am required to wear a mackintosh in the upstairs lavatory. Mr Thorne, alleged to be a plumber, says we need new water tanks and that the water here is undrinkable, particularly when bats and mice drop into the tanks and are drowned. Personally, I rather like the fruity taste of our water and the light-brown colouring. I believe in the old saying 'What doesn't sicken will fatten.'

17b Via Dolorosa
Burghclere
6 February [late 1970s]

I have come to the conclusion that I don't like Budds Farm much, if at all. There is an unfriendly atmosphere and I have always felt slightly ill and vaguely unhappy here. I now have a growing desire to transfer into one of those large country houses where elderly persons have their own room and a couple of sticks of their own furniture, and eat plain and simple communal meals with a book propped up against the teapot or HP sauce bottle. Doubtless the other inmates would be as boring, querulous and unsociable as oneself. Those institutions are really a queuing-up point for the ferry which old Charon (I trust a member of the Transport and General Workers Union) punts at intervals over that murky stream called the Styx. However, at present my dog Cringer keeps me here. At least Mr Randall is happy. Last night he went to Shepherd's Bush (Remember the headline 'Police comb Shepherd's Bush for missing girl'?) and saw a BBC programme featuring a woman with out-of-door teeth named Rantzen. I think it was what journalists call a 'chat show'.

Morty's Garden of Wonderful Weeds
Spring [early 1980s]

My Good Child,

What are you up to now? I hear rumours of you writing books on gardening (the blind leading the blind), on cooking, even on children. Why not combine cooking and children and go flat out for the cannibal market? The next thing I suppose will be to learn of you playing water-polo for Morpeth Mermaids.

I was offered the Sunday Times gardening column in 1953 but refused on the grounds of absolute ignorance. I have been doing a frantic morning's gardening; my plants look unhealthy and I feel ditto.

Love,
xx D

When that book – An Idiot's Introduction to Gardening – *came out, my father wrote to me with succinct approval: 'Easy reading means hard writing.'*

235

Budds Farm
18 April [early 1980s]

Your mother and I continue to look at unsuitable houses and today we visit an Italian-style bungalow with enchanting views of the industrial quarter of Andover, the Florence of Hampshire.

'Eventide' Home for Distressed or Mentally Afflicted Members of the Middle Classes
Burghclere
[Early 1980s]

Our search for a new house continues. I have seen four which suited me but your mother imposes the veto with the regularity of the Russians at UN, and with the same air of dogged finality.

Budds Farm
7 June [early 1980s]

Our search for a house continues. To my surprise Nidnod took a fancy to a former pub called 'Trip the Daisy' 6 miles from Swindon, hardly the City of my Dreams. It is a charming house but no garage and no possible access to the property for a car. The garden is far too big, including a rock garden which always reminds me of Sunningdale. Personally I would prefer a really modern house on the grounds that a house is something to live in, not look at.

The Miller's House
[Early 1980s]

Your mother has decided she likes the Miller's House after all; good news. It is now forgotten that I discovered it and that her initial reaction was to say that she wouldn't be seen dead in it! We have hung some pictures: it is not worth disagreeing with your mother. Emily the hen is settling down well and will soon join the ranks of those animals whose comfort takes precedence over mine. To celebrate the sale of Budds Farm, I have ordered a new pair of trousers from J. Byrne, Bespoke Tailors, overlooking the Newbury cemetery.

We have a walled garden here or a bit of one. I doubt if it would have reminded Alf Tennyson of:

> 'Many a sheeny summer morn
> Adown the Tigris I was born
> By Bagdat's shrines of fretted gold
> High-walled gardens green and old.'

I am now off for some jolly shopping in Marlborough – a coal scuttle, loo paper, alka-selzer, the 'Spectator', bread, Worcester sauce, picture nails.

The Richard Crossman Ward for Decayed Gentlefolk
Park Prewitt Hospital
Basingstoke
[1970s]

I bought a pair of scissors in Boots the other day and they broke in half five minutes later. When I went back to complain, the pert young lady assistant asked if she could see my toenails as they must be extraordinarily tough! I said she could see my toenails if I could see a bit of her. 'What sauce!' she said, bridling roguishly and we were really getting on quite well when a gimlet-eyed supervisor came along and we both slunk away very shiftily. I must be off, so in the words of the old Golders Green folk song it is 'Hey ho and away we go with pretty Herbert Samuel' (Trad.).

The Old Lazar House
Kintbury
Berkshire
Wednesday [February 1980s]

I am browned off with this winter. Cold weather is tolerable when you are active but it's a proper bugger when your activities are confined to filling log baskets and coal scuttles, producing kindling wood and cleaning grates. Luckily I learned a lot about domestic fire-lighting at Eton. In my day boys had their first experience of frostbite at school; no wonder many of them grew up with purple noses of what one of my masters called 'an incarnadined proboscis'. My father had gruesome stories of having to break the ice on his wash basin at Marlborough. In those days there were no urinals and each boy had a po under his bed.

Love to all,
xx D

The Miller's House
1 April [1980s]

What a ghastly Easter. Freezing cold and nothing to do except drink and stoke the fire. I was reduced to drinking Grand Marnier at 11 a.m. Luckily our guests were easy and gave no trouble. I refuse to garden when the temperature remains below 48 degrees. Even so I must go and plant out some special-offer pansies which look about as miserable as I feel.

The Miller's House
April 1988

I have been planting chrysanthemums called 'Sunburst' which are very expensive and decidedly ugly, rather like a certain type of woman.

The Miller's House
Sunday [1980s]

My typewriter has just packed up. Il ne manquait que ca! I can't remember if I owe you a letter. I now combine physical decline with mental instability: no wonder poor Nidnod is browned off with my growing inability to cope with life. I don't much care for it myself. 'My husband loves gardening,' I sometimes hear Nidnod say to some old buddy. This morning I have been hoeing the gravel, a fatigue I regard with strictly limited affection. Old Randy is away for a fortnight and the weeds seem to know it and sprout ferociously.

Best love to one and all, your decrepit parent,
xx RM

The following is an extract from my father's single and unappreciated contribution to Kintbury Parish magazine: 'Gardening for the Elderly'.

Sometimes I have heard dedicated foxhunters, after a couple of dry martinis, express the hope that they will eventually meet their end in the hunting-field. So far, I have only met one gardener desirous of expiring quietly in the herbaceous border and she, sadly, was run over by a No. 14 bus in Knightsbridge while endeavouring to reach Harrods during sales week.

The Miller's House
Spring [Mid 1980s]

Last week I bought 4 pictures in Kingsclere and a wicker garden chair in Great Bedwyn. In Little Bedwyn I discovered a most attractive pub, more like a French café, which dishes out excellent prawns and suchlike goodies. Come and have a tuck in with me there.

    xx D

My father took a fortnight's paid holiday with his family every year and looked forward to it. My parents were united in their enthusiasm for holidays. We all loved the seaside, at home and abroad. Lupin did not enjoy the sun, latterly preferring to remain in his hotel room reading Sherlock Holmes. As the years rolled by, my mother's inclination was for action, my father's for repose.

> Martha swallowed a jellyfish and Jane she got the cramp.
> Mother in law began to jaw because the sea was damp
> Neighbour Jud got stuck in the mud and a crab got hold of me
> And away sailed the bathing machine a-sailing out to sea.

This was an old music hall song chanted by my father on every seaside holiday. For him, Edwardian holidays by the sea had been a reality. It was on our seaside holidays in 1950/60s France, that my parents' happiness together seemed to blossom, or at least to green their boughs. 'The French know how to live!' my mother declared as she navigated from the Michelin map for my father steering the family car (Wilf Wolsey, Reg Rover or Victor Vauxhall) coastwards through the lush, pastoral landscapes of Normandy and Brittany.

Beguiled by the romance of the simple life, my parents murmured daydreams of retirement – a little blue-shuttered cottage beside an apple tree, cats and dogs basking in the sun, hens pecking among the beans and dahlias, a plump pig grunting from its pen. They were enchanted by rustic sightings of ancient Messieurs and Mesdames in faded checks, denims and clogs, cajoling a cow down a lane. Then the sudden appearance of a 'pert Mademoiselle', buxom on a bicycle, would turn my father's head in a more youthful direction. The absence of grand aspirations in my parents' fantasies was endearing. They dreamed not of chateaux or villas but of cosy cottages.

'The roses round the door make me love mother more,' quipped my father as we passed another rose-clad farmhouse. At the sight of a churchyard crammed with gravestones, he would invite us to join him in this recital:

> There's a ten foot wall round the cemetery
> Which is foolish without a doubt
> The people outside don't want to get in,
> The people inside can't get out.

Cafés and bars along the route served drinks all day long. This suited my parents well. Within an hour of arriving in

France, aged nine, I was introduced to a delicious aperitif, a tiny tumbler of Cinzano, an experience simultaneously sharpened by the sting of a French wasp on my leg.

My father's essential accessory on every holiday was a miniature leather suitcase, in which he kept travel documents and money. My heart always warmed to the sight of his substantial form, purposefully striding into airports and hotels, carrying this doll-sized case. A particular sweetness settled over my father on those sunny seaside holidays in France, away from work and grey and brown-gravy England, the plop of bills on the doormat at home.

The 'Book Box' was another holiday treat. My father would make a judicious selection of books for each of us, packed into a box which was to remain unopened until we had crossed the Channel, which on some occasions was not by ferry to Le Havre or Cherbourg, but flying from what was basically a field near Folkestone in a 'Silver City' plane which carried cars as well as passengers.

These were not the holidays described in my father's letters. We were with him! It was as my parents got older, and their children less compliant or absent, that he shared his holiday experiences, good and bad, in his letters.

When combing my father's letters for holiday stories, the unexpected revelation was how frequent were my mother's absences from home on her own excursions. There was some magnetic force in my mother which attracted potential drama on any expedition. A magnet inherited and magnified by Lupin.

There was a glint in my mother's eye as she prepared for her trip to the equestrian events at the 1956 Stockholm Olympics, an invitation she had accepted from a Swedish millionaire of my parents' acquaintance. He had taken a big shine to my mother. My father allowed her to go on condition she was accompanied by her aunt as chaperone.

The remaining evidence of the trip is my mother's flickering cine film of the distant Olympic flame and horses jumping in conditions of what appears to be pitch darkness.

Staying in Cyprus with my Aunt Pam and Uncle Ken, Brigadier Darling, in command of a British anti-terrorist campaign there in the late 1950s, my mother was not averse to the idea of being close to the front line, but her sister and brother-in-law kept her under control. 'Your mother!' my uncle would roar. Military protection could not prevent her from contracting sand-fly fever from the beach where she regularly snorkelled, delaying her return home for several weeks.

In Oslo, in the 1960s, my mother again stayed with my aunt and uncle, who was now NATO commander of Northern Europe. Their official residence was Oslo's former Bunny Club with a mural of palm trees and flamingos adorning the drawing-room walls. Sometimes well-inebriated groups of party lovers rang the doorbell late at night, ignorant of the new, dignified occupants of the 'club'. They were not the only nocturnal disturbance. Bursting into my uncle and aunt's bedroom one night, my mother entreated them to rise at once. There was an emergency – outside in the city, riots were taking place and the sky was lit with explosives, which could only signify that, as in other European capitals at the time, student revolution was at hand. It was a firework display, the opening event to a Norwegian national festival.

At another festival, on a family holiday in Sardinia, my mother rang the hotel to say that she and my ten-year-old sister had missed the bus back following their excursion to a carnival in the middle of the island, two hours' drive from our hotel. They were stranded overnight, all lire spent, in an area notorious for ruthless bandits. They were rescued by a friendly local family and supplied with food and a bed to share for the night, arriving back safely by lunchtime the following day. My mother's fury with my father for making no apparent attempt to rescue them cast a pall over the remainder of the holiday. For his part, my father had been fully confident that his wife's penchant for misadventure was invariably balanced by her resourcefulness in overcoming ensuing difficulties.

My mother emerged from such incidents intact. Fate dealt her a much unkinder hand when she was knocked unconscious, badly bruised, and robbed in the bedroom of one of Kenya's poshest watering holes – the Muthaiga Club Hotel – in 1970. Her usual fearlessness was set back for a time. The long-term effect of this horrible experience was to raise her mildly racist tendencies to full heat.

Occasionally the long-suffering General Sir Kenneth and Lady Pamela Darling, nicknamed Honkel and Ham, accompanied all of us on holiday. Having no children of their own, the teasing and banter of these family occasions gave them light relief from the unstinting deference they were accorded in military life. 'What's going on here!' my uncle would roar as he entered a room, rather hoping for something inappropriate, and in this he was usually rewarded. My bossy aunt could unbend into fits of giggles, no more so than when, after a long lunch of sangria and paella in Menorca, the whole family danced in a crooked row along the waterfront singing 'Mad dogs and Englishmen go out in the midday sun'.

One day in Menorca we set off for some secluded little cove to swim, but my father had forgotten his bathing kit. He decided to trip lightly into the balmy waters in his birthday suit. He was some way out to sea when a large coach arrived above the beach and from it, clucking like hens, emerged a stream of Spanish nuns, evidently also on a little seaside outing. Gleefully, we combed the beach for camouflage for my father. A collapsed cardboard box was scraped off the sand and born aloft to him in the sea; he slipped it over his head, emerging triumphantly with his elegant fig leaf in place.

Holidays can be both challenging and consolidating to friendships. Raoul and Sheelagh Lemprière-Robin were two great friends with whom my parents happily holidayed, given that their destinations were not always rewarding and could be rife with testing incidents and discomforts, plus at least one spat between my mother and Mrs Lemprière Robin, a lady of equally definite opinions.

In the mid 1980s my parents invited me to join them for a week in Provence. I was appointed map reader – but sacked after one hour in France, when my mother was compelled to reverse back up a motorway slip road. Our hotel restaurant was an early specialist in *'cuisine minceur'*, not quite my father's choice of robust fare. 'What *are* these fucking sheep's balls?' he exclaimed as a minute meatball he had failed to spear on his fork shot off the plate. But like the French holidays of my childhood, it turned out to be one of the happiest of times. 'It is surprising what fun you can be,' said my mother to me kindly. Such was my sadness at saying goodbye at the end of our holiday, I found myself in tears in the taxi as it sped from the airport.

By the time my father entered his seventies, his evident appreciation of my mother's companionship and capabilities seem to echo the happiness of their earlier days. They were often accompanied by their little dogs who sometimes proved less troublesome than their children. Increasingly, his letters were to be coloured by memories of the holidays of his youth. In addition, he was intrigued by the holidays that others chose to take.

My Dearest Jane . . .

Loose Chippings
Soames Forsyte
Wilts
14 June 1970

How are you getting on with all those hirsute, noisy, argumentative Greeks? Have you made nice friends yet with any shipping magnates that would be suitable for the position of my son-in-law? Don't lie about in the sun too much as it is bad for the skin and you will come back looking as if you were off to a fancy dress party as a prune.

My 'sabbatical' summer in Greece, mostly on the isle of Samos, renting a house at £4 per month!

Little Crumblings
Roper Caldbeck
Bucks
3 July 1970

I sent a long letter to you at Poste Restante, Vathy and another was addressed by your ever-loving mother. She has been confusing everyone by saying that you are at a well-known Greek hotel called Poste Restaurante! Can you beat it?

Budds Farm
[Early 1970s]

Is it true you are off to Paris? When I was just 18 I lived in France for 6 months. I was a nice, shy lad learning French before embarking on the Spartan rigours of Sandhurst. I had an aged tutor whom I mobbed up: with luck he used to lose his temper and throw me out and I spent long and happy days in Fontainebleau or at Barbizon. In those days Frenchmen had beards, bowler hats (straw hats in summer), button boots and short tailcoats. Usually pince-nez. The franc was very shaky and the exchange was about 380F to the £. My ever-loving parents kept me brutally short of treacle but occasionally I saved up £3 and went off to Paris for 36 hours where I had the time of my life and broadened my outlook. I went to France a dear little innocent boy (more or less) and was luckily seduced by the postman's wife who was also usherette at the local cinema. I suppose she would be about 92 if still alive. Still, one had to make a start somewhere. I lived at Fontainebleau and spring in the forest there was something I still remember with pleasure. Did it never rain in those days? O mihi praeteritos referat si Jupiter annos! (If only Jupiter would restore those bygone years to me. Virgil, *Aeneid*.)

I must remember to send old Mabel a birthday card. I think she is 87. I have seldom had happier times than when Mabel and I and my sister went to stay in rooms at Brighton (9 Holland Road) during World War I. No wonder I still retain affectionate memories of the West Pier and Maynard's sweet shop. I remember as if yesterday all the slot machines on the West Pier, my favourite being the execution of the Irish Traitor Sir Roger Casement. I also remember with pleasure the busty lady who gave swimming and diving displays from the pier. Brighton then was full of wounded soldiers and I amassed a marvellous collection from the cigarette cards they gave me. If only I had kept them I would be sitting on a goldmine. I once saw an elderly lady fishing on the pier. A gust of wind removed her hat and her wig inside it. There were happy days sitting in a deck chair on the pier reading the adventures of Tiger Tim in 'The Rainbow' and consuming a 2p bag of raspberry drops and listening to the band of the 60th Rifles playing excerpts from Chu Chin Chow. The food was very nasty at the height of the U-boat campaign: no potatoes (only swedes), cocoa, margarine for butter, and a repellent sticky liquid in lieu of sugar. Enough of this senile and unprofitable drooling.

    xx D

Mabel was the first woman Roger loved – his nanny.

The Miller's House
[Mid 1980s]

I'm glad you had an enjoyable holiday. Le tourisme in France is more agreeable than it was when few plugs pulled and nervous old ladies always cleaned their dentures in mineral water.

Budds Farm
Thursday [mid 1970s]

Last week I paid my first visit to Brighton since I went with you and saw all those appalling commercial travellers. This time the place was inundated with Trade Union representatives who of course, being members of the new aristocracy, had all the best rooms in the hotels and the best tables in the posh restaurants. At the Old Ship your mother and I shared a bed the width of a stretcher, on the 5th floor. My head was balanced on the bedside table, your mother's feet were on the floor. Demon Doss was conspicuous by his absence. However, we had an agreeable morning on the pier, your mother reading the 'Daily Express', whilst I purchased postcards of an indelicate nature. We then had two quiet and pleasant days with the Grissells. On the way home we lunched at a flash public house which sold contraceptives.

xx D

Brighton was an easily accessible and nostalgic playground for my father. Outrageously saucy seaside postcards were always sent, signed by 'The Archbishop of Canterbury' and 'Dame Harold Evans'. His POW friend, Michael Grissell and his wife Rosemary lived at Brightling Park in Sussex, which today combines a family farm and racing stables. Their elder son Gardie was to ride in the Roger Mortimer Memorial race at Sandown in March 1993 – which he won.

Budds Farm
[Mid 1970s]

We are just off to Wales, land of male voice choirs, perpetual rain and appalling food. I hope we shall not be kidnapped by Welsh Language Mobile Guerrillas.

Moles Paradise
Burghclere
16 September [1970s]

Your mother showed immense pluck in plunging into the frigid waters of the Atlantic. She also showed perspicacity in choosing the most expensive items on the hotel menu. However, she looked after me and the dogs devotedly and

I grudged her nothing. As usual, she was at her best when laying out a picnic. The beaches were marvellous, the bathers rather less so. If I could have 5p for every pendulous stomach, distorted breast, hernia or varicose vein that I saw, I would be under no compulsion to do another stroke of work. My experience of Welsh shopkeepers is that they are more avaricious, ill-mannered and disobliging than their counterparts in Newbury which is saying a good deal. For my real view of the Welsh, read Dr Fagan's little oration on sports day in 'Decline and Fall'. On the whole, though, I prefer them to the Scots: they are less self-satisfied and their congenital slyness is rather amusing.

xx D

Budds Farm
17 September [mid 1970s]

The Surtees had an agreeable 14 days in Salzburg, where it rained continuously, and Vienna. They wanted to go to the 'Magic Flute' in Vienna but no seats were available under £60! I'd have told the opera authorities just what to do with their flute, magic or otherwise.

Eventide Home for Distressed Members of the Middle Class
25 July 1979

I hope you enjoy the opera. I'm not desperately keen on it but I enjoyed 'Aida' in Cairo as the leading tenor was slosherino, caught his robe on a big nail and was left singing away in rather murky combinations with a trap door at the back. I made my appearance as a Roman Centurion in the Aldershot Tattoo of 1931 with the massed bands blasting out the Grand March from 'Aida'. I got stung by a wasp one night but that's show business.

Budds Farm
August 1979 [on pink pig paper]

I'm glad you enjoyed your culture trip to Glyndebourne. I do rather hate 'La Bohème'. I was taught at Eton for a short time by John Christie, the founder of Glyndebourne. He frequently appeared for Early School (7.30 a.m.) in evening clothes, which of course commanded our respect.

Hypothermia House
[Mid 1970s]

I'm so glad you enjoyed your holiday in Devonshire. It is a delightful county but I could never work there as I find it impossible to keep awake. I do not believe for one moment that Drake was playing bowls when informed of the approach of the Armada: it is much more likely that he was having a couple of hours zizz on his hammock. In 1931 I was at Okehampton on a machine-gun course; it was hardly a well-chosen locality for that purpose as the ranges were always shrouded in mist so we used to go fishing instead. One day I was shown round Dartmoor Prison, a dreadful place, damp, chilly and depressing in the extreme. I was told that the food was all boiled, the objective being to impart just sufficient nourishment but render the meals as boring and unappetising as possible. I was shown a gang of blackmailers who were serving sentences of life or twenty years. They were the backbone of the prison chess team! Soon after my visit, there was a mutiny at Dartmoor and the convicts gained temporary control. The Governor had a vat of hot porridge poured over his head and was lucky to escape with his life.

Love to all,

xx RFM

Chez Nidnod
Burghclere
[Late 1970s]

I expect P and N enjoyed the seaside. Piers, I suppose, is just reaching the age when a bucket and spade holiday represents the summit of human happiness. In human existence is there anything to equal the pride and joy obtained through promotion from a wooden spade to an iron one? At that age one isn't finicky about the weather. I enjoyed Aldeburgh in 1919 despite the jolly east winds from the Baltic. A boy called Paul Lindo instructed me (not altogether accurately) on the facts of life, in a bathing machine.

Budds Farm
31 May 1977

Pam and Ken are off to the South of France. I would like to see the General on one of those nudist beaches. Will he permit your aunt to be topless?

General Sir Kenneth and Lady Pamela Darling – my uncle and aunt.

The Old Damp Ruin
Burghclere-under-Water
3 January 1980

Your mother wants a joint holiday with the Darlings next summer. NOT my scene, not nowadays anyway. I need a younger lady and a less energetic man.

The Miller's House
Kintbury
12 July [mid 1980s]

I hope you had an enjoyable holiday in Italy. I rather prefer the Italians to the French but that does not signify a great deal. Like most Englishmen, I love France but detest the French almost as much as they detest us. The Italians are okay as long as they stick to Art and Agriculture. It is when they strike military attitudes that they tend to become absurd. The best thing about the French is the French language which is excellent for clarity of expression.

Maison des Gagas
Kintbury
[Mid 1980s]

I am delighted to hear you may come on holiday with your aged parents. I appoint you ADC, Baggage Mistress, Resident Clown, Nidnod's Keeper, Reserve Chauffeuse and my partner at the Hotel The Dansants. Time of departure: May 12 approx: length of stay, 8 days approx: destination, v. expensive hotel in Beaulieu, France. Finance: I will be responsible for your travel costs, room and food. I may even stand you a drink or two.

*A near perfect holiday with my aged parents in Provence.
At home or abroad, my mother's vocabulary was spiced
with French expressions: 'We are absolutely d'accord!';
'très sympathique'; 'au fond'; and so wistfully, 'A partir c'est
toujours à mourir un peu.'*

The Miller's House
[Mid 1980s]

I'm quite glad you weren't with us on our holiday in
Portugal as it was fairly bloody. The villa was modern, v.
comfortable and well-furnished, sited on top of a hill with
a wonderful view. A charming garden, an excellent pool
and a female cook nearly up to NAFFI standard. But the
two and a half mile track leading to the villa was hideously
rough, full of pot holes, chasms and boulders. Every drive
down it was an ordeal and the car stopped ominously once
on the way to the airport. It rained every day bar one. The
local towns were as dusty and squalid as the less fashionable
parts of Slough. The Tavernas dish up filthy food grudgingly.
The recommended fish restaurant was closed. Many fat
Englishmen clad in very short shorts – revolting. Nidnod
got flu, a temperature and was dosed by a Frog doctor.
The Lemprière-Robins got bad colds and I weighed in with
diarrhoea. A steep cobbled hill fucked up my knees. We had
no papers, TV, radio and passed the time with bad bridge.
On Thursday we left at 7 a.m. and at the airport, where it
was raining hard, we found a 6-hour delay due to shortage
of crew. When at last we boarded the aircraft it did not
take off for 75 minutes. At ghastly Gatwick the L-Rs found
they had missed all Jersey connections. I got separated from
Nidnod and the situation was tense till I suddenly saw her

with, thank God, our taxi-driver, who had waited 11 hours for us. We got home, knackered, at 10 p.m.

xx D

See you soon. Roof is leaking!

The Olde Igloo
Burghclere
17 January 1980s

Nidnod asks me 'Why can't we go to Australia, everyone else does?' That's quite an easy one to answer. I'm studying a brochure for a train trip in the utmost luxury (and at enormous cost) from Victoria Station to Venice. As Nidnod gets bored (naturally) staring at me every evening across the sitting room, would not demon tedium raise its hideous head if compelled to gaze at me for two days in a Pullman car? The Cottrills are in Barbados, the Lemprière-Robins are off to Ceylon, the Darlings to South Africa. Mrs Roper Caldbeck is off to Portugal, Major Surtees to Cologne and the Draffens to Bournemouth. No one I know can afford to go ski-ing any more. Brig Lemprière-Robin is put out because his daughter's young man wears three earrings.

Bankruptcy Row
20 May 1981

Just back from France; weather marvellous, groceries variable. Your mother shook me by ordering a lobster dish at a small seaside restaurant that cost me £26! Nice work, Nidnod!

The Miller's House
[Late 1980s]

I hope I enjoy our Danube trip. At all events I don't reckon
to be seasick. Whenever I see the ocean I think of poor old
Ovid leaving Rome, 'Me Miserum, quanti montes volvuntur
aquarum.'
Best love,
xx D

*Ovid's 'Ah me! What mountain waves around me flow' was
one of my father's favourite quotes.*

*My parents' many friends bob up like corks throughout
my father's letters, and brief biographical detail is usually
attached to one or other of their appearances. Social life and,
more essentially, friendship, are the focus next.*

9

Round the Table with Friends

Friends are for life and life is for friends.

Anon

A treasured letter can sometimes vanish inexplicably into the ether. One such was when my father wrote to me in sympathy following the premature death of a good friend. Etched in my memory from that letter is the line : 'Of all the words in the English language, "friend" must be the nicest.'

As the letter writer he was, my father maintained and retained many friendships throughout his long life. He never, to the best of my knowledge, fell out significantly, if at all, with a single man or woman whom he embraced with that status – friend.

Desmond Parkinson and John Surtees, stemming from their years together as POWs, were two of Roger's closest friends. Once married to their respective wives, friendship sprang up between my mother and Mesdames Surtees and Parkinson. That there was the odd exception is unsurprising given that there were to be three Mrs Surtees and four Mrs Parkinsons.

Women were very susceptible to Desmond, whose effortless sex appeal was enhanced by an enigmatic reserve which was also highly desirable in his professional life – he worked in the Secret Service. Eminently approachable, easily blending into an apparently ordinary commuter's existence and a home-lover who mowed his lawn at weekends in Silchester, there was little in Desmond's peaceable demeanour to indicate that his domestic life was one punctuated by regular turmoil. My mother was devoted to him.

A bon viveur and an eminent connoisseur of wine, which was his trade, John Surtees had the most delicious smile and whilst conservative in habit and outlook, exuded an aura of mild mischief. He too was very attractive to women. The friendships with the Surtees and the Parkinsons were facilitated by being relatively near neighbours, within dining distance of my parents.

Loyalty to friends rated very high with my father. Since he relished gossip – grist to the mill to any writer – discretion overall was possibly not his strongest virtue. The great circus of characters my father encountered on his social and racing rounds made unwitting contributions to his locker of anecdotes. Many lapped up my father's wit, delighting in it, unless they found themselves speared on the sharp nib of his pen. Even then.

Friendship is one thing – marriage quite another. For Roger, John and Desmond, marriage did not prove to be easy. The deep mutual understanding and tolerance established in their shared prison-camp existence made these old friends entirely relaxed in each others' company. As husbands, my mother largely held prison responsible for their emotional flaws.

The company of women delighted Roger, who warmed to a pretty face in which kindness, humour and intelligence might be discerned, so long as when her lovely mouth opened it did not spout forth any fanatical or insistently earnest views. As for sex, his letters are stuffed with references to it, most usually in tales of the comedic or tragic peccadilloes of his fellow man or woman, including occasionally his own. The tone and language of their telling is in the voice of one for whom sexual passion seems some way down the list of human compulsions. Affectionate rather than passionate, his view of male/female relations found their best expression in the cartoonists he loved: James Thurber, Osbert Lancaster and Andy Capp.

Providing you were not a doctor of a different skin tone, a trade union activist, a left-wing female feminist student, a lecturer at a provincial university, a 'commerssial' traveller, as he used to say, or a long-haired, unwashed friend of his children, my father was amenable to most forms of social connection. He was always on the lookout for good conversation.

From his letters, often soaked in cocktails and popping with wine corks, it would be easy to form the view that my father and mother were both rampant alcoholics. For my father, a stack of work was never more than a glass away. I often saw him merry, maybe mightily so, but never drunk. My mother's smile was brightest over a cup of tea to which she hadn't added a slug of gin or brandy. When she was on form, her own spirits were quite vibrant enough without alcohol to convert them into a hotter pickle.

Both as host and guest, my father was what he occasionally called 'Little Mr Popular' – a raconteur who charmed and mildly shocked others around the dining table. He often wished people would go home almost as soon as they had arrived and he never outstayed his welcome elsewhere. He did not evaluate a successful social occasion by the hours given up to it – the last thing he wanted was a lunch that lasted until 6 p.m. or a dinner till 1 a.m. Had he been such a guest, the chances of him having the time to digest and relate his adventures in his letters would have been much less likely.

My Dearest Jane . . .

The Sunday Times
[Mid 1960s]

The Maxwells have moved, a loss I can stand with a fortitude bordering on indifference.

La Maison des Deux Gagas
Grand Senilite
France
1973

If you were empowered to ask 12 characters from history to dinner, whom would you ask and why? I fancy the following:
  1 Shakespeare 2 Queen Elizabeth I 3 Marquis de Sade 4 Moses 5 Jack the Ripper 6 Oscar Wilde 7 Gertrude Laurence 8 Cleopatra 9 Fred Archer 10 Jane Austen 11 Marquis de Gallifet 12 M. R. James
    xx RFM

Barclay House
14 March [mid 1960s]

I have a trying week in front of me with two very tiresome dinner parties in London. I have got to the age when I have no desire to entertain other people or be entertained by them. I would far sooner read a book or just think.

Chateau Marcuse
Cohn-Bendit
Deauville
France
[Late 1960s]

We had six people to a dinner party last week. Not a success as Mrs Hislop, who declined champagne and demanded neat gin, was in one of her less attractive moods. She arrived late and announced to one and all that she was 'pissed'. During the cod au gratin she gave a blow by blow (or ball by ball) account of how she shared a bath at Goodwood with Lord Belper, a story totally lacking both in general interest and aesthetic content. Mrs Cameron stayed the night this week and treated me to a monologue on pre-marital sex in Scandinavia, during which time I sank into a very deep coma indeed while at the same time maintaining – I hope – an expression of lively interest and concern.

Lord Belper was a racing man and roguish old friend whom my father claimed had never got over the divorce of his parents. Lupin's riposte was that there were many more individuals who never got over knowing Lord Belper.

SS Bernadette Devlin (and God help all who sail in her) somewhere off Clacton
[Early 1970s]

On Friday I went off to lecture the Garth and South Berks Hunt Supporters Club in a white building, once the Women's Staff College, at Frimley. Your mother emphasised it was a very smart and formal affair. She came decked out like the Deb of the Year's mother at Queen Charlotte's Ball and I was in evening clothes with only faint traces of Heinz tomato soup on the flies. Unfortunately your dear mother had, for a change, got hold of the wrong end of the stick and everyone else was clad as for hunter trials at Tweseldown on an inclement winter afternoon. I felt like the manager of a provincial cinema who feels obliged to stand in the foyer wearing a dinner jacket before the 1.45 p.m. performance. However, it all went off alright and I had a very good supper, sitting next to an elderly lady who would have made an admirable commanding officer of the 11th Hussars.

I am off to dine with Schweppes tomorrow. I have had a card asking if I prefer oysters or caviar.

Best love,
xx D

Budds Farm
6 May [late 1960s]

Mr P now seems to be bedding down with Mrs Scott, ex-wife of the individual who pissed off with the second Mrs P. Mr Parkinson has many virtues but is a very poor picker.

Maison du Vieux Crapaud
Burghclere
1 January [early 1970s]

Had dinner with the Parkinsons; Desmond's daughter Anna Louise, now at Clare College Cambridge, is a sweet and intelligent girl who does not thrust her obviously 'advanced' views down the narrow gullets of elderly bourgeois guests.

Anna Louise, daughter from Mr P's first marriage, became a BBC journalist and a writer. Anna sent her mother a copy of my earlier book, The Coldstreamer and the Canary, *describing the POW experiences shared by both of our fathers. Her mother, now in her eighties, was moved by the emotional wartime revelations of her first husband as a very young man. During their marriage, like many others of that period, Desmond had maintained his stiff upper lip.*

The Crumblings
Cowpat Lane
31 January [early 1970s]

Mrs Hislop gave me a most indecent Christmas card made worse by a highly suggestive message inside. Your mother later retrieved it from my wastepaper basket but luckily she did not know who it was from or there would have been a minor explosion. It was not a traditional happy family Christmas chez Hislop. On Christmas Eve, their younger son invited his mother to fuck off (twice), declined to apologise, and shortly afterwards was given £25, shoved into a Newbury Kwiktryp Taxi and requested not to darken the portals of the parental home again. Not quite the sort of scene conjured up by the Revd Harold Anymore-Empties in his annual Yuletide Sermon.

Love,
xx D

Budds Farm
9 March [1970s]

Mr and Mrs Hislop came over before lunch on Sunday; Mrs H is a real old tippler and knocks back glasses of virtually neat gin with the carefree nonchalance of a healthy baby lapping up Ovaltine.

Gormley Manor
Much Shiverings
3 February [early 1970s]

I had lunch with J. Surtees at some smartish midday club and drank a great deal of port, felt dangerously skittish for about 35 minutes afterwards and extremely unwell for 24 hours after that. We lunched with the Maxwells at Sandown. Peter Willett sat next to a rather hairy black beetle who revealed himself as William Hickey of the Daily Express.

Peter Willett, a family friend in Yateley, was also a distinguished racing writer. He and my father shared many car journeys to race meetings and, more significantly, worked in tandem on a number of books. Having not seen him for over forty years, I tracked Peter down and went to see him. When parents are gone, all too often so are their friends, particularly when you live a great distance away. It was a joyful and unexpected bonus to rediscover Peter, aged ninety-two, still driving and fully on the ball.

Loose Chippings
Soames Forsyte
Wilts
14 June [late 1960s]

I got very sloshed at Martin Gilliat's annual fiesta, so much so that I accepted an invitation from my old friend Helen Adeane to go to the Garter Service at Windsor Castle tomorrow. Not my tasse de consommé at all and the fact that I let myself in for it is further proof, if such was needed, of the evils of drink. Dinner at the Turf Club (£24.18s.7p) with the Surtees and the Burnaby-Atkins. Your poor mother got a bit edgy and I thought she was going to crown me with a bowl of imported French strawberries. Yesterday I had to ring up Mr Jock Whitney, one of the richest men in America but quite 'civilised' (to use a favourite adjective of your mother's!). I rang up at 11.30 a.m. and the call was answered by a valet who, to my delight, used the royal 'we'. 'We had a very late night, Sir, I regret to say, and we are not awake yet. I think it is advisable that we should sleep on.' I am lunching with Mr W next week.

Martin Gilliat was the Queen Mother's Private Secretary with a reputation as a munificent host. Helen Adeane was wife of the Queen's current Private Secretary, and the aunt of Carolyn Lloyd, aka HT, my oldest friend, who regaled me with stories of Lady Adeane's filthy sense of humour and passion for practical jokes. To complete the trio of courtiers in attendance, Freddie Burnaby-Atkins was another entirely delightful POW friend of my father and, at that point, Princess Margaret's Private Secretary.

14b Via Dolorosa
Burghclere
[Early 1970s]

Went out to dinner and we sat down at 10 p.m. by which time
we were all sozzled. Two elderly guests were quite delightful.
Less delightful were a common (horrible word but it fits) little
publisher of rubbishy books and a wife who took a great
dislike to me from the word go and did not attempt to conceal
it; and a one-eyed tycoon with a wife who writes knitting
articles for women's' magazines and smokes pot and indulges
in LSD to show how she is in sympathy with 'the young'.

Schloss Schweinkopf
Grosspumpernickel
Neuberg
[Early 1970s]

Many Thistlethwaytes are due to lunch here on Sunday; they
always cheer me up and to some extent restore my faith in
human nature. Did you see that poor Anthea Dingwall had
died? I shall always remember her biting my ear when I was
ordering rice crispies and two bars of sunlight soap in Tices'
Grocers. Bye-gone, happier days!
    xx D

*In those Yateley days, I used to pop through a hole in the
hedge to play with my next-door neighbour, Anthea Dingwall.
She was the youngest of a big family, whose company I
enjoyed because they were all older and, to my mind, more
fascinating than my own family, and far more overtly and
constantly affectionate to each other. My father, who liked*

them well, nonetheless mocked at their endless embraces, an unlikely version of which he received in Tices' Grocers from poor Anthea. Her fine military father, Johnny, was gigantically tall, well over six feet.

Budds Farm
31 October 1972

I went to a wedding on Saturday; with natural reluctance and only because the bride's old Mum, Ag Clanwilliam, is an old girlfriend of mine and I have never met a member of her sex with a sharper or more rollicking sense of the ludicrous. I had some fun with her ever-loving husband, Gilly, too, when we were both young, enjoyed the good things of life and were only mildly handicapped by the fact that we never had any money at all. It was typical of Gilly that when he did not have enough treacle to buy a pair of spats for a canary, he bought the biggest Bentley that ever had been made and which, when driven from Camberley to the Bag of Nails nightclub, required the petrol tank to be refilled at Staines. I suppose the sort of night life available at the Bag of Nails and the Old Forty Three simply does not exist nowadays. I sometimes wonder what happened to the girls at those establishments; some married into the peerage and others, more wisely, into the beerage.
   Best love,
   xx D

Gilly Clanwilliam was an Army officer contemporary of my father to whom my father was devoted, along with his wife, Ag. They had six daughters. I wish I had known them.

Clarkson's Winter Sunshine Cruises
Runcorn Wharf
Manchester Ship Canal
[1970s]

Last night I went to the Lords Taverners Dinner at the
Café Royal which was followed by a boxing tournament
afterwards. The dinner was really bad; I sat next to a rather
haggard person called Boulting who is in the film trade.
He seemed very agreeable. The dinner with Schweppes was
excellent but otherwise of quite relentless tedium. We seem to
be going out to dinner almost every night and my one evening
shirt is showing disconcerting symptoms of battle fatigue.

*The twin Boulting brothers, John and Roy, were both
successful film directors and producers.*

The Sunday Times
16 September 1973

A woman came to dinner who is the pillar of the local
Conservative party and looked like a cockatoo with a slight
smell under her nose.

Budds Farm
23 September 1973

I called on Major Surtees in London and got quietly sloshed
on port in the middle of the afternoon. How agreeable it is
to have a few old friends one can talk to with uninhibited

frankness. We know each other far too well to try any bullshit or the commoner forms of self glorification.

Hypothermia House
Burghclere
October [late 1970s]

On Sunday we went out to dinner with Penrhyn Pockney and his wife.

We arrived punctually at 7.45 as requested but dinner was not dished out till 9.15 by which time I had consumed a great many of Mr PP's excellent cocktails. I have no recollection of the food I ate or whether I participated, tastefully or otherwise, in the conversation. I do remember kissing a blonde lady and claiming her (untruthfully) as a relative. I did not get the impression that my hostess was all that sorry to see us go. The following day was a buffet lunch given by Mr Parkinson to celebrate his 60th birthday. We were invited for 12.30 but owing to a sharp tiff in the cook-house between Mrs P and her mother, the latter of whom exists on a purely liquid diet, the groceries did not appear till 2.30; by which time one and all were up to their tonsils in gin. Among the guests was a sinister man from MI5 and a rich brewer with a very thin wife; also a small general accompanied by a wife whose consumption of drink was hardly assisted by the occasion which in fact I enjoyed very much.

Penryhn Pockney (his real name) is married to Jane (des Voeux), sister of Elizabeth Aird and Susan Caldecott, my mother's cousins and also local friends.

Budds Farm
[1970s]

It is 4 p.m. and Nidnod is wrapped in deep slumber on her
bracket. She fancies a spell of Egyptian PT after lunch and
today she has a good excuse as last night she was prinking
about on the dance floor till 2.30 a.m. We left here at noon
and I had engaged a very nice room at the Jockey Club at
Newmarket where we had a good rest and some zizz. We
were due to dine with Henry and Julie Cecil at 8.30 p.m.
and were just leaving when Nidnod noticed a message on the
bedside table stating that dinner had been postponed till 9.30
p.m! Luckily some of the picnic had not been consumed as
we were getting peckish. The button came off my shirt collar
but by some miracle I had brought a spare evening shirt with
me. We duly arrived at the Cecils, neither of whom had ever
spoken to me or Nidnod before. Both said they were too tired
to go to the dance! There were about 11 people to dinner
including old Bunty Scrope's wife (née Sykes). There was also
a rich widow whose mother was descended from Pushkin.
Henry Cecil has immense charm and is a brilliant trainer; his
ever-loving wife has great charm. Plenty to drink. We went
on to Cousin Tom's dance; a superb affair held in Tattersalls
Sales ground. The weather was perfect; two days previously
there had been the worst thunder storm at Newmarket
this century. The decor was fabulous and the flowers most
beautifully arranged. You could sit outside the whole evening
if you wanted. I am told Charles Blackwell was v. sloshed but
never saw him. Your mother bore her years very gallantly
and was pleased with her hairpiece until Twitch turned up
and with exquisite tact, told her it looked as if a rat had died
on her head. Anyway, Nidnod tucked into the win or lose
with a will and she really did enjoy herself, cutting pre-war
capers with Lord Desmond Chichester and Arthur Budgett.

There must have been several hundred people there, a lot of whom I actually knew. We left at 2.30. We came home this morning; Nidnod had a nasty hangover and in the car was reduced to drinking pineapple juice out of a tin can. Suddenly autumnal here. Out to a big lunch party tomorrow; Nidnod is basking in social sunshine.

Best love,

xx D

Tom Blackwell was my father's first cousin – more of him later – and Charles was his son. My mother was not at ease with the Blackwells but gratifyingly my parents were able to enjoy Tom's exceptional party together. Henry Cecil, one of the greatest racing trainers, died of cancer in June 2013 and was honoured by a minute's silence at the opening of Royal Ascot a week later.

Budds Farm
20 February 1973

Mrs Cameron has been here for six hours and has not yet drawn breath or spoken a word of sense so I am going to wash my hair.

My father was not always in tune with the Scandinavian views of Agnete Cameron, fine, forthright, Danish godmother to Lupin.

Budds Farm
[1970s, on pig paper]

The Surtees had a supper party for 30 in their barn. The

browsing and sluicing were beyond reproach and I enjoyed myself with a platoon of recently unmarried women. A very agreeable young gentleman who is just going to Eton said he supposed I had been in World War I which makes me about 84. I often feel it but it is disenchanting to realise I look it as well. On Friday I went to a huge party given by Ian Cameron who is High Sheriff. All the Berkshire Mayors were there: unlike the Metropolitan Police, they could hardly be described as a fine body of men. A band composed of members of local schools played Cole Porter and Noël Coward and played very well too. A trombonist of about fifteen rather took my fancy and I was later able to offer her a sausage on a stick and a stuffed tomato but there was not much time for enlightening conversation.

Ian Cameron was the stockbroker father of David Cameron, Prime Minister.

Moles Paradise
Burghclere
16 September [1970s]

I went out to dinner last night and sat next to a tedious Australian lady who nudged, pinched and pummelled me all through the meal. There was also an Australian doctor present who reminded me of another Australian doctor of whom one of his patients observed to me: 'I reckon the doc's got fuck-all grip on medicine.' An old friend of mine who is 79 is getting married in Newbury next week. His previous wife went clean off her onion. The last time I saw her she clasped Cynthia to her ample bosom and started singing fortissimo 'Oh you beautiful doll, you great big beautiful doll'!

The Sunday Times
23 October 1972

We went to a Sunday Times Beano on Sunday. It was hot and boring and I knew few people there. However, your mother established meaningful relationships with a left-wing writer on football and a cartoonist called Scarfe whose pictures are usually quite incomprehensible to me. However, he was one of the few present, male or female, who had bothered to shave. In fact he looked like a promising merchant banker.

Chez Nidnod
[Mid 1970s]

Old Lord Carnarvon came to dinner and was reasonably affable and totally untruthful. He tells me he has been asked to lecture to the boys at Eton. On what? One might well ask. He has frequently told me how pretty he was as a boy and how he was constantly having to repel the advances of other boys. Obviously the first part of his statement is untrue; as for the second, I can't see him repelling any advance had he been fortunate enough, a fairly improbable supposition, to have one made to him. Yesterday evening we had drinks with ex-Chief Constable of Berkshire, who treated his guests as if they had been brought there 'to help the police with their enquiries'. Also present, a very big horsey lady and a very small shiny Colonel who rescues stray dogs. Also a man from the Daily Telegraph who looked rather like a black slug in a string vest but it was quite a jolly old party.

Lord Carnarvon had been keen to acquaint me better with one of his grandsons (not encouraged by me) and his generous, strategic gesture of hosting a nineteenth-birthday dinner for me at Highclere Castle was somewhat overwhelming.

Budds Farm
[1980s]

The lunch party (Parkinsons, Elmes, Hislops) went off very well on the whole; the browsing and sluicing left nothing to be desired. Jean Hislop had two whacks of everything and approved of the claret. Attired in a tweed plus four suit, she was on her very best behaviour and most agreeable company.

I may change my name by deed poll to Kissinger-Mortimer as I now have a full-time job trying to reconcile Major and Mrs Surtees. Luckily I am partially deaf as both sides believe in very lengthy explanations in which all facts unhelpful to their own case are rigorously omitted. Of course it is rather flattering to be asked for one's advice which is invariably given regardless of the fact that it is ignored, even resented, if not in accordance with the listener's cast-iron prejudices.

Guy and Brita Elmes were long-standing friends and good news.

Budds Farm
[Late 1970s, on pig paper]

There is a local row on here as someone managed to insert an advertisement in the Newbury News: 'Strong experienced man required to trim large bush. Apply Mrs Jean Hislop, East Woodhay House.' Umbrage has been taken. I know the perpetrator. Poor old Jean, she does go out of her way to make enemies. After all, one makes quite enough of them in the normal course of events without deliberately trying to augment the number.

HM Office for the Deciphering of Ancient Documents
19 Sludge Street
November 1975

Last night we dined with the Budgetts: excellent lamb and plenty of uninhibited conversation covering such topics as Harold Wilson's sexual habits, the nudes at Newbury Art School and the problems inherent in trying to organise laundry arrangements for stable lads.

Arthur Budgett was a top racing trainer with the distinction of two Derby winners to his credit.

Little Crumblings
Burghclere
30 September [1970s]

I attended a party given by Mrs Brunskill (formerly Mrs Parkinson No. 1) in Wapping. Her flat is part of an unattractive building but it is very pleasant inside with a big balcony overlooking the river. The guests varied from 8 to 80 and in costume from bourgeois formality to the filthy jeans and sagging braces favoured by a farouche individual of indeterminate sex. The food was good and plentiful but the drink tasted as if it had been drummed up earlier that day at Staines Gasworks. There was a band that played intermittently in a distant room and happily they could seldom be heard. I wore check trousers and shirt and a blue linen jacket coupled with an expression of extreme affability which enabled me to

form a rather beautiful friendship with a lady dressed up to
represent Little Lord Fauntleroy.

Le Petit Nid des Deux Alcoholiques
Burghclere
[1970s]

The Parkinsons are coming to lunch with Francis Reed,
who always looks as if he is due to play left back for Naples
Tramways, and Lady Gault. To loosen them up, they are
getting a good, rich, Bloody Mary, the usual mixture being
gingered up with orange and lemon juice, celery salt and
tomato ketchup. We went to Nika the Squeaker's birthday
party in darkest Fulham. We picked up your brother, who said
he had been invited. I thought it odd he was in day clothes
and not a dinner jacket: on arrival I discovered that he was
not actually a guest but hired to wait and wash up!

*Francis Reed was one of Roger's good POW friend. Nika
Rumbold, mother of Nick, Charlie and Cassandra Hurt, was
a brave, bright and sparky friend of longstanding.*

The Old Dosshouse
Burghclere
[1980s]

I had dinner with Major Surtees at his flat in Parsons Green.
He asked tenderly after you. Conversation centred largely
on incidents in our past which at the time seemed either
hilariously funny or remarkably enjoyable. Whether anyone

else would have employed similar adjectives is improbable. Terms such as 'sordid' and 'irresponsible' would more likely have been used. Once one is married one is forever driving down a road with a clearly defined 30 mph limit, a limit all too rarely exceeded and then the pleasure is diminished through the unfortunate possession of a middle-class, Protestant conscience.

Best love,

xx D

Chez Nidnod
14 Rue de Vache-Crappe
Burghclere
[1980s, on pig paper]

For once we are having some dry, warm weather and aged locals are wearing pith helmets and wonder how long it will be before the monsoon starts. Your mother dragged me off to the Newbury Agricultural Show and my submissiveness was duly rewarded by a glass of warm Cyprus sherry with the President. I purchased a hamburger sandwich; it was like consuming a tepid slug. On Saturday the Cottrills had a joint birthday party at the Swan, a trendy Lambourn pub kept by an enigmatic ex-journalist from the Daily Express called 'Jamey'. He greeted me as if I was his dearest friend which in fact I wasn't. The dinner featuring smoked salmon and roast grouse was excellent and a good time was had by all those present. Your mother went to two weddings last week. She has a macabre taste for those bizarre and rather barbaric ceremonies. Is there anything more tedious and embarrassing than the typical wedding reception speech? Some old family friend, demi-sloshed, bangs on interminably and manages to combine utter banality with saloon-bar vulgarity.

Humphrey Cottrill was a high profile man of the Turf, ultimately racing manager to Prince Khalid Abdullah. He and his wife Lola were racing friends held in warm regard.

Home, Sweet Home
[Mid 1970s]

We went out to dinner last night with the Roper-Caldbecks. Amongst those present were a lady like a bull-mastiff; a jolly old General whose speech was filtered through a walrus moustache; and the General's lady, a formidable dame with a glass eye of piercing blue. The browsing and sluicing were excellent.
 Best love,
 xx D

Slightly formal, Harry and Dorothy Roper-Caldbeck were a kind, hospitable local couple with Portuguese connections.

Hypothermia House
[Mid 1970s]

An old friend of mine proposes to remarry his first wife. To marry her once was a grave mistake; to do it a second time verges on insanity. However, he may be saved by the fact that she is at present mixed up with an alcoholic Swede.

The Merry Igloo
Burghclere on the Ice
[1979]

We have been invited to the opera to see 'Die Fledermaus' on Jan 1st, a celebration for J. Surtees's 60th birthday. When I first met him he was a youth of 20 with a lot of fair hair and a hole in his leg inflicted by the Germans at Calais. I myself was suffering from burns and malnutrition and the only shoes I possessed were cardboard clogs with wooden soles. Luckily bourgeois education in this country prepares one to endure physical discomforts.

Chez Nidnod
4 January [1980]

We went to John Surtees's 60th birthday on Monday. We saw the 'Fledermaus'. At the interval, Nidnod thought it was all over, wrapped herself up and made for the exit! I enjoyed it except for an additional act by an elderly Swedish soprano who looked like a centurion tank on the way to the scrap yard and sang very flat. Afterwards there was supper for 12 at John's elder daughter Anna's house in Fulham; highly organised and very good. Many old friends. I drove your mother home and we reached our own shack at 2.30 a.m., unusually late for me.

Kind regards to you all,
Love,
xx D

Budds Farm
7 June [early 1980s]

Poor Mr Parkinson is lumbered with 2 mothers-in-law billeted on him. No. 1 is quite nice but totally gaga and has just been sacked from a Home at Goring for being 'a disturbing influence'. No. 2 is penniless, a fearful bore, an alcoholic and incontinent.

Little Shiverings
Burghclere
[1980s]

About a fortnight ago I rang up John Surtees and was told by his wife he had not come home. Jokingly I said, 'Has he done a bunk at last?' Unfortunately he had, the first I knew of it. I'm sorry that mutual antipathy has destroyed Maison Surtees.

Desmond Parkinson has got rid of his mother-in-law at last.

The Old Lazar House
Kintbury
[Late 1980s]

The ex-Mrs Surtees and her very agreeable new husband called in here the other day. They seemed happy.

Both my parents loved warm and attractive Anne, ex-Mrs Surtees, now Mrs Higgins.

The Olde Leakyng Cabin
Burghclere
December 1980

I went to a bridge party on Thursday where my partner was a local lady of 87 who appeared to know no one below the ranks of Earl and Countess. She asked if I knew a certain peer and I replied that I knew him quite well but had never yet had the good fortune to catch him properly sober. This upset the old girl who was about to tell me how terribly decent he was whereas in fact he is a bombastic shit.

The Miller's House
12 July [mid 1980s]

Last Sunday I attended a drink and light refreshment party in aid of SSAFA and was, despite my stick, the sprightliest man there. Our host, a genial sailor, had no idea who I was and addressed me as 'Colonel Miller'.

The Miller's House
[Mid 1980s]

Your godfather Peter Black writes to me most weeks; life in Jersey verges on the grim but at least he is not short of treacle. I was stung by a hostile bee while staking a plant (helenium) called Moerheim Beauty (I think). Mr Randall is just off on a coach tour of the Adriatic. I have heard nothing of the Darlings lately: I write to my sister-in-law Pam once a week, my sister Joan once a week, P. Black once a week,

Raoul Lemprière-Robin once a fortnight, Freddie Burnaby-Atkins once a fortnight. I was quite proud of my output until a kind friend suggested I was a ghastly bore, sending dreary communications and expecting the unfortunate recipient to reply.

Godfather Peter Black invited me to stay, age thirteen. I was dazzled to be met at off the train at Chester by his super-glamorous wife, Monica, her mane of auburn hair up in a chignon, sporting a mink coat and shod in crocodile stilettos. Back at their house, I tucked into a dinner of lobster Neuberg, fillet steak, then chocolate mousse, washed down with vintage wines. Queasily, I made my way up to my luxurious bedroom, knowing I had arrived in paradise.

The Miller's House
22 August [1980s, in red ink]

I have just received my annual summons to the Blue Seal dinner at the Savoy. When I was elected in 1946 the Blue Seal had so much treacle put away that the dinner and all drinks were free. Nowadays you hand over £40 to an official known as The Chaffwax as you enter the premises. Therefore I don't go. Apart from which most of my contemporaries are dead, undergoing major surgery or are residents of private asylums on the outskirts of Worthing. The Senior Member is Lord Amherst who was elected in 1919. He was a chum of Noël Coward's and on the fringe of the stage. The next senior is John Codrington, the well-known landscape gardener. I think he is ninety.

The Blue Seal was an ancient military dining club.

Chez Nidnod
Kintbury
3 September [mid 1980s]

Last Sunday was a very hot day (87 degrees F) and I went to a barbeque lunch where with singular folly I elected to ward off heat stroke and dehydration with copious drafts of gin and vin rose. I felt so ill the next day I placed myself in intensive care, i.e. I lay on my bed reading crematorium catalogues and imbibing iced soup brought to me none too willingly by Nidnod. The following day my condition was declared to be 'stable'.

Chaos Castle
Burghclere
[Early 1980s]

Yesterday we had a superlative lunch with old Harry Middleton. His marriage was of brief duration but he had a teenage daughter there yesterday, blonde and very saucy in a pink bikini. All the guests, except your middle-class parents, were upper class. I sat next to lovely Rachel Willoughby de Broke with whom I fell in love in the Newbury Corn Exchange in 1929. I was running well out of my class as she was taken up by Prince Ali Khan and the King of Belgium. Also at lunch was a somewhat royal individual who runs the polo at Windsor. I enjoyed it all very much and after a good deal of gin let my tongue wag somewhat indiscreetly. Drink unfortunately always tempts me to be clownish!

A popular friend and racehorse owner, Harry Middleton, had been assistant head of BBC Outside Broadcasting, including racing coverage. In the bikini, his daughter Laura later married Peter de Wesselow, grandson of Roger de Wesselow, who gave my father his first job in racing in 1947.

The Miller's House
17 March [mid 1980s]

I've just had an Easter card from the Very Revd Basil Madjoucoff; if only all my friends were as faithful. I first met him in the table tennis saloon at the YMCA, Jerusalem, in 1937. This YMCA, built with American money, is a huge phallus-shape building containing every luxury. Basil is an Armenian and those of his fellow countrymen who had not been sliced up by the Turks were pretty hot at ping-pong and Russian billiards.

If anyone is interested in the extraordinary story of the Very Revd Basil Madjoucoff, ask Lupin!

The Miller's House
December [mid 1980s]

A huge parcel from America today containing a Holy Calendar and pictures of sacred birds from the Very Revd Basil Madjoucoff. It is 50 years since I beat Basil in the final of the table tennis championship at the YMCA in Jerusalem.

The Miller's House
[Mid 1980s]

Fairly warm and occasionally sunny: we have a lunch party today and I have put chairs out in the garden although au fond I know it is not warm enough. The trouble is that I want our guests to see the garden which frankly does credit to Nidnod, now 'une horticulturaliste enragee', and myself. No weeds and some lovely roses and clematis. Children and dogs spell death to conversation; Thank God no children around today and I have incarcerated the dogs. Among the guests is David McCall, the same age as myself and living precariously after a hideous operation. He was my greatest friend at Eton and oddly enough I cannot remember ever discussing sex with him, a subject that comprised about 65 per cent of adolescent conversation. I think we stuck to racing. He had no money at all and his education was paid for by an uncle. His father went off to Dublin one day for a haircut and lunch at the Kildare Street Club and was never seen or heard of again! David began work as an insurance clerk at £110 a year and I gave him his first business, i.e. insuring my mackintosh for £3. Happily he soon went into racing as a bloodstock agent and is now a millionaire. Also coming are the Van Straubenzees (I fancy Mrs Van S.) and the Gaselees (ditto Mrs G.). I have mixed a drink called a Dr Bodkin Adams, named after the Eastbourne GP who is believed to have done in 400 of his wealthier geriatric patients. He was acquitted of murder because of the inadequacy of the prosecution led by an Eton contemporary of mine who was cordially disliked by one and all. For lunch we are having haddock mousse, boeuf à la something or other, meringues followed by Blue Vinney cheese, washed down with plonk rouge supplied by a friend of Charles, and some port churned out by a descendant of Dr Warre, the famous Headmaster of Eton. I have had a haircut and am wearing a white jersey (so far only one jam stain) and some poncy white shoes bought at a disposal sale in Marlborough. Talking of stains (quite an amusing topic) there used to be a fat punter at Ascot who always let it be known when things were going well as the soup stains on his waistcoat were real turtle.

    xx D

As the new owners of my parents' former home, Budds Farm, the Van Straubenzees played a small but significant role in our family history.

The Miller's House
April 1988

We went out to dinner last night. As we approached the house of our hosts, I said to Nidnod, 'If Lady C. is here, I intend to drive straight home.' Alas, another lamentable case of lack of moral courage and she ruined my evening. She likes me slightly less than a cat likes a bull terrier and always infers I am suffering from a terminal disease – possibly wishful thinking on her part. I unfortunately forgot to put my teeth in and Nidnod was furious. She is getting her own back with frozen bully-beef for lunch and those biscuits like bus tyres they issue to arctic expeditions. Do you remember the one good restaurant in Newbury, La Riviera? It has been sold to new owners and is now called 'The Last Viceroy'. I am trying it out with Freddie Burnaby-Atkins on the rather flimsy grounds that he was in fact ADC to the last Viceroy.

    Best love,
    RM xx

'The Browsing and Sluicing were excellent', wrote my father on nearly as many occasions as he claimed to have been poisoned by meals of a 'repellent' nature. Neither a gourmet nor a gourmand, Roger appreciated good food and he largely depended on my mother to produce it. When left to his own devices, he was a cook of some originality.

'Gormley Manor
Much Shiverings
[Early 1970s]

I drummed up many nourishing delicacies during your mother's absence including a giant pie composed of salmon fishcakes, fish fingers, onions, haricot beans, Muscadet and potatoes. I had three helpings and fell into a restful coma afterwards.'

In their earliest years of marriage, my mother, a novice in the kitchen, did her best despite the limited ingredients available due to food rationing. Their happy ménage was nearly brought to a premature halt when she served a bowl of steaming boiled pig trotters – unadorned – at a dinner party. A homemade pâté in Yateley a few years later reduced the dinner guests to silence, until my father broke the ice – 'I wondered what had happened to that dead rat in the cellar, dear.'

In much later life, my mother could take an hour to fry an egg, rendering it into an unrecognizable specimen on my father's plate. In order to be well prepared on other occasions, dishes were cooked so many days in advance of consumption that interesting bacterial variants might be on the menu.

Between these two polar points in my mother's cooking

career, she produced quantities of absolutely delicious and imaginative dishes to which I owe my own pleasure in cooking. She relished the adventure of new recipes, taking herself off on day courses at the Cordon Bleu school at Winkfield. She was a fine sauce maker!

Cooks were hired from time to time, with varying degrees of success. Our daily food in the late 1950s was transformed by our tiny Italian cook, Fernanda. Enticing aromas of herbs and garlic wafted from the kitchen; sheets of homemade pasta hung over the back of a kitchen chair, awaiting Fernanda's sharp knife to cut them into strips of tagliatelle or squares of ravioli.

The microwave was invented for my mother. She adored electronic gadgets – an earlier favourite was the electric carving knife which made Sunday lunches sound more like a chainsaw massacre. Once the microwave arrived, the suggestion of preparing even the simplest dish was greeted with 'But I'll do it in the microwave!' My mother was inspired to write an ode to her microwave which she stuck on the kitchen wall. When a microwave engineer was called out one day, he read it and, hugely impressed, took a copy back to his company who promptly rang my mother to offer her a job as a microwave salesman. She settled for £20 of free microwave equipment.

By the 1980s, going out to a local restaurant or pub became a popular pastime for my parents. Only a few hostelries escaped my father's crusty critiques on paper but luckily for them, not in the press.

Gathering round the table to eat together as a family provided happy memories – but was not infrequently the stage set for domestic fall outs. My father became practised in quietly leaving the room, but not before he had uttered the last word. Sometimes it was a simple one: '*Pax*' – Peace.

My Dearest Jane . . .

Barclay House
19 October [early 1960s]

Your mother leaves for Germany on Tuesday and I am left to hold the fort, so to speak. However, I always manage to look after myself pretty well and make myself reasonably comfortable.

Barclay House
25 October [early 1960s]

It is somewhat lonely here with only the inscrutable Moppet the cat for company. I am doing some nice steady work in the cook-house and last night drummed up salmon fishcakes and scrambled eggs, followed by bananas, vanilla ice and cream, the meal being swilled down with a bottle of Chianti. Tonight I am doing a little casserole of chicken cooked in Burgundy, preceded by a rich broth into which I have thrown everything from the unexpended portion of a pork chop down to the remains of a tin of Kitekat. 'What doesn't sicken will fatten,' as the old saying goes! Everyone is kind to married men living on their own and I have a stack of invitations as thick as the telephone directory; I may even accept one or two.
    Love,
    xx D

Budds Farm
6 May [late 1960s]

I made a new cocktail last night, orange juice, grenadine, vermouth, brandy and a splash of crème de menthe. It is guaranteed to make a week-old corpse spring lightly from its coffin and enter for a six-day bicycle race.

Budds Farm
[1970s]

Charlie and I had the Bomers to dinner last night. The menu, daintily executed by me, was as follows. 1 Salmon Chowder (i.e. tinned salmon from Jackson's Stores jinked up with eggs, red pepper, oatmeal and the unexpended portion of a bottle of Hungarian Riesling (9/- a bottle – don't miss this astonishing bargain). 2 A rich pie of minced beef, minced pork and haricot beans generously sprayed with a rich kidney and Chianti sauce. 3 Raspberries, strawberries and bananas, well iced, and floating merrily in a sea of brandy and orange Curacao. To prepare for this repast we had all shoved our heads into a trough containing a very powerful cocktail.

The Bomers, Colin and Sarah, much loved next-door neighbours at Budds Farm, were serious foodies who saved shillings in a jam jar in their kitchen for the purchasing of a pot of caviar. My mother loved Sarah for her sweet and sympathetic nature, as did my father, with the added bonus that he could enjoy literary discussions with her.

Budds Farm
23 June [late 1960s]

On return for a pleasing family lunch, I found your brother
had stormed out after a row with Nidnod; he did not appear
till teatime. Your sister had had a row with Nidnod, too,
and declined to have lunch as well. I wanted lunch badly but
found it quite uneatable, so a good time was had by all, I
don't think!

The Sunday Times
Tuesday [late 1960s]

On Sunday evening we had supper at the Carnarvon Arms. I
was slightly alarmed when a squat, hairy man accompanied
by a long bespectacled woman arrived with an electric organ
and set it up, but in fact he played very agreeably – mostly old
tunes for moth-eaten listeners and I had a little difficulty in
preventing your mother joining a man with Guinness on his
moustache who was singing – if that is the right word – the
choruses.

Schloss Blubberstein
Montag [early 1970s]

It continues sehr nasty weather down here, immer Regen
and Sclamm! Der Herr Oberst Thistlethwayte and his family
came to lunch yesterday and a reasonably good time was had
by one and all. Louise cooked the mitagessen and dished up
a huge capon with mushrooms, carrots and peas that was
really quite excellent. Vortrefflich!

Noel and Ann Thistlethwayte and their children were good family friends.

Schloss Schweinkopf
Grosspumpernickel
Neuberg
[Early 1970s]

Your sister chain smokes Marlboro cigarettes and declines to take exercise. I took her to supper at the Marquis of Granby, near Brightwalton. The browsing and sluicing there are more than adequate and I had some delicious onion soup. Louise had enough pâté maison to load a barge, followed by a cheese soufflé that would have satisfied a platoon.

Budds Farm
[1970s]

Last Sunday we went to lunch with old Mrs D. (85) who has twice received extreme unction but has made astonishing rallies just as the District Nurse was placing pennies on her eyeballs. Her wit and precision of speech remain undiminished; she is merely a trifle more sceptical. Unfortunately luncheon, not prepared by her, was of a singularly repellent character. We started off with a gigantic raw beetroot each, covered with what looked and tasted like Erasmic, a shaving soap.

Budds Farm
12 October [mid 1970s]

In a public house last week I was induced to consume a highly coloured circular object designated 'a Scotch Egg'. I am not a fan of the Scots but do they in fact merit this particular insult? Mine contained four inches of garden string and the beak of a fully grown hen. Is this usual or was I just unlucky?

Budds Farm
20 February [1970s]

Your brother gave a dinner party for 12, the food prepared by himself. Trust him to be eccentric, the repast started with fried cheese on toast.

Budds Farm
12 May [early 1970s]

I had a good dinner at White's on Monday: to wit, a couple of perfect martinis first; poached salmon from the River Dee with cucumber and a rich cream sauce; Welsh lamb with new potatoes and young beans; fresh strawberries with kirsch and cream; and, I forgot, a lovely clear gravy soup first with not a single winking eye of grease on the surface. All this washed down with an excellent hock, a faultless claret; followed by port (I think Taylors 1924) and brandy.

Chez Nidnod
Burghclere
[1972]

Thank you so much for the nice birthday gift which was much appreciated. Just the thing for my jaded palate. I am getting quite like my great-great aunt who when she was 91 used to souse her chocolate éclairs with Worcester sauce to get a kick out of them.

Le Petit Nid des Deux Alcoholiques
[1970s]

Your mother is cooking as if her life depended on it and weird smells and greasy black smoke are escaping through the kitchen window. She could always get a job in a crematorium.

Budds Farm
[Mid 1970s]

I went to Cousin Tom's Derby night dinner at White's. 17 guests including the ineffable Lord Goodman. Vintage Bollinger before a dinner of cold soup, salmon soufflé, cold duck in aspic and stuffed with foie gras, new potatoes and asparagus, bombe surprise with fresh raspberries. Drink included Chablis, a delicious 1961 Claret, Port, Brandy.

Lord Goodman, a leading lawyer, held many prestigious positions in politics and the arts.

'Eventide' Home for Distressed or Mentally Afflicted
Members of the Middle Classes
Burghclere
[Late 1970s]

After Charlie Rome's funeral, four of us caught the inter-city
at Darlington at 5.33 p.m. and looked forward to a leisurely
dinner and some British Railways claret to cheer us up. We
advanced on the dining car at 7 p.m. and found it empty bar
a few members of the staff reading newspapers and playing
cards. 'No dinners after 6.15,' we were told. (Passengers had
not been warned of that decree.) 'Is there a second sitting?'
we asked. 'The staff does not like second sittings,' we were
informed. We then went to a sordid installation termed a
'buffet-bar' where I ordered four whiskies and soda and four
sandwiches. A surly individual replied that there might be a
little whisky but there was no soda, no sandwiches, nothing
at all to eat, and that in any case he was closing down as
he wanted to do some paperwork (what?). I have written
to complain but I don't suppose I shall even get an apology.
However, Mr Surtees took me to his flat in Chelsea and
regaled me with lentil soup, cheese and Burgundy.

xx D

*Aged 20, Charlie Rome was captured in the same year as
my father, 1940. Forbidden to attempt to escape because of
his conspicuous height, he taught fellow POWs, including
Roger, to knit. To celebrate his twenty-first birthday in
prison, he was given an extra potato. I witnessed the happy
reunion of these two at a dinner party in their old age,
communing like a wise pair of bespectacled owls in their
velvet dinner jackets.*

The Olde Leakyng Cabin
Burghclere
December 1980

My luck is in: I hear I have drawn a small carton of petit beurre biscuits at the Jacksons Store raffle. On Christmas Day we go to the Darlings for lunch. Let us hope she can be induced to light a fire in the drawing room. The more I think of it, the more I wish I was having Christmas at a kosher hotel in Eastbourne. I have had Christmas at some weird places including Bethlehem, Trieste, Alexandria, Spangenberg and Cadogan Gardens.
    Love,
    xx D

Now a hotel, Roger's family home was in Cadogan Gardens, SW3.

Budds Farm
[Early 1980s]

The Hounds of spring may be on Winter's Traces, but life here can hardly be termed satisfactory. The temporary cook arrived on Monday. She is a divorcee of about 35 and by no means bad looking. She has hunted, yachted, ridden in point to points, piloted a glider and cooked for a leading Newmarket stable. She talks incessantly. Unfortunately she cannot cook. Last night the Bomers came to dinner. Disaster! We started with stuffed tomatoes (unspeakable) and then boiled pheasant which might have been boiled crow. Sarah Bomer was sweet as usual. Nidnod was in a fearful mood. Unfortunately Nidnod has invited guests all this week, thinking (quite reasonably) that this expensive cook could provide some edible nosh. I have been ordered to read less and laugh less!

Best love,

D

Budds Farm

28 March [late 1970s]

I went to a dinner (men only) at Nicky Beaumont's at Ascot House. Very comfortable, nice furniture and altogether agreeable. Excellent 6-course dinner of which I recollect asparagus, lobster, English lamb, mushrooms on toast. Sluicing on the same high level. Guests mostly old characters connected with racing.

Nicky Beaumont was Director of Ascot racecourse. With his wife Ginny, he returned to his home county of Northumberland when he retired. Full of character and always up for a laugh, the pair of them were full of good cheer and kindness.

The Miller's House

27 February [mid 1980s]

Lunched yesterday with Gilly and Ag Clanwilliam and had a marvellous treacle pudding which I greatly relished.

The Miller's House
12 July [mid 1980s]

Nidnod made me give her dinner at 'The Blue Boar' the other night; the food made a transit camp at Catterick seem like the Connaught.

The Miller's House
27 April [mid 1980s]

The hired cook is a success; v. good food but wasted on me as I prefer kedgeree, fishcakes and kippers.

The Old Lazar House
Burghclere
27 August [early 1980s]

Your mother enjoyed her holiday in the Channel Islands. She came back with two jumbo crabs which we had for lunch today. She did them very well (a cayenne pepper sauce) but my stomach was in a state of mutiny some hours later. A slight fracas occurred when two geese entered the kitchen and made some huge messes. The conservatory has been invaded by an army of dung beetles. A vigorous counter attack with an ancient spray killed them off and I now have the task of removing about 7,000 corpses.

Chez Nidnod
15 August 1981

V. hot here and everyone agreeably limp and lethargic. Nidnod thinks she is in Malay and gives us paw-paws for breakfast, a fruit previously encountered by me only when reading pre-1914 stories by Somerset Maugham.

[1988, postcard]

Filthy smoked salmon at the 5 Bells. Might have been the Aga Khan's galoshes.

The Old Organ Grinder's Doss House
17 September [early 1980s]

Yesterday I took Nidnod to Marlborough, bought her a book and gave her tea at the Pretty Polly Tea Rooms which provide the largest and richest teas, and the most expensive, in the south of England: also a bewildering variety of ices. I would like to take the boys there. Very good strawberry jam and cream.

The Miller's House
[Mid 1980s]

We had lunch in the Three Swans at Hungerford where we had whitebait cooked as badly as only an English pub could cook it. I then asked for some cheese. I might as well have asked for a fried chimpanzee. 'Ploughman's lunch', possibly a 'cheese sandwich', but they had never heard of anyone ordering 'cheese'. I must go down to my evening repast – vegetable soup and a slice of toast. I shall soon be caught pinching Otto's dinner.

Eventide Home for Distressed Members of the Middle Classes
25 July [1980s]

As for your vegetarian cooking, I am convinced it would be a howling success with feminist readers of the Guardian; most men like something with more blood in it (disgusting brutes)! It is extremely kind of you to ask a tedious relic of the past such as myself to stay. There are certain obstacles to be overcome but I hope to be able to accept your generous invitation (no courgette and peaspod puddings, if you don't mind).

Your affectionate father,

xx

Grandparents, aunts, uncles and cousins were a different kettle of fish – it's time to swim alongside them.

10

Blood is Thicker than Water

Blood may be thicker than water but it is also a great deal
nastier.

E. C. Somerville and Martin Ross,
Some Experiences of an Irish R.M. (1899)

As he arrived in the world, my father encountered his first
relation. His mother. It was not an encouraging start.

His mother's appreciation of her son was marginal and her
criticisms generous. Her known pleasures lay in expanding
her hat collection, pampering her poodles and sharpening her
tongue. Some balance was achieved by the kindly nature of
his gentler father. Little Roger did not give his parents much
trouble. He got on well enough with his elder sister, Joan, my
grandmother's favourite.

That my grandmother had grown up in a family of
thirteen children had done little to mellow her outlook. She
was not unintelligent but she may have been blighted by some
inner and untold unhappiness, poor lady. Her father, Thomas
Blackwell, was well liked and a highly respected business
tycoon. Latterly known as the 'Jam King' he was the Blackwell
of 'Crosse & Blackwell', purveyors of fine jams, pickles and
conserves since the early 1800s. His second wife, my father's

grandmother, was reputed to have been in love with a poor curate when her parents pressed her into marrying another suitor, the older and more prosperous Thomas Blackwell.

Various Blackwells surfaced intermittently in our family life. My father's first cousin Tom, a true friend and ally to Roger, was generous and a shrewd financial adviser. They both worked in the racing world – Tom, a member of the Jockey Club, owned a stud near Newmarket. Although he had two children, Charles and Caroline, from his marriage to the glamorous Bunny, before she took off for pastures new, Tom was very definitely a man's man and one of the old school. There are more question marks over his jovial bachelor brother, John, assistant head at my brother's prep school, a great golfer and well loaded. My father enjoyed them both. My mother enjoyed neither of them. Tom and John's mother, Aunt Shirley, all kindness and fluff, bobs up like a cork in my father's letters along with Aunt Margery Blackwell, a sedate spinster who lived in Gerrards Cross. A former beauty with a lovely voice, she had cancelled each of her three weddings at the last minute in terror of the impending honeymoon. My grandfather was usually delegated to inform the unfortunate husbands to be.

Aunt Joan grew up as a brisk Blackwell in manner and habit, occasionally glowing with a jolly show of interest in her nieces and nephew. One Boxing Day, teenage Lupin and I found ourselves sitting in the drawing room alone with Aunt Joan. Thoughts on our social life suddenly struck her and turning to my brother she asked brightly, 'Any balls, Charles?' The phrase entered family history. Aunt Joan had been released from the obligations of her mother's drawing room by the Second World War, flourishing as a WRN and later as swimming teacher at the Francis Holland School. She was a competent and keen photographer. Her friends were called 'chums' and had names like Bunty and Pixie. She married the charming, urbane Reggie Cockburn, barrister. She was his second wife in what was well known as a marriage of companionship rather than consummation. It was not until after her death that I learned that she had several step-daughters – and received the impression that it was nearly news to them as well. She had an unerring ability to promote the excellence of almost every child she knew to my parents, apart from their own. Nonetheless, she was kind enough to me.

If passion and warmth did not beat powerfully in the Blackwell breast, my father's Aunt Star Blackwell was a compensation. Abandoning her first marriage to elope with an attractive Irishman, Chris Mitchell, to live in a beautiful Georgian house in Co. Wicklow, Ireland, she was beloved by both my parents. Aunt Star had a huge sense of fun. I leave her profile to my father later in this chapter.

Neni (Enid) and Pips (Phyllis) were my mother's aunts. Aunt Pips was something of a surrogate grandmother in the absence of her sister Doris, my granny, whom I lovingly remember from all the occasions I stayed with her. She died when I was only three.

Aunt Pips had style and verve. Slender with perfect posture and well dressed, she was a talented horsewoman who hunted side-saddle. A black-and-white cine film of Aunt Pips tells the story – in her formal riding habit, smiling behind the black net veil attached to her top hat, merrily puffing a cigarette through the net. She loved the young but tragically had lost her only son to appendicitis aged twelve, followed later by the death of her beloved husband, Norman Loder – a great friend of the poet Siegfried Sassoon, whose signature appears on every other page of their visitors' book. Aunt Pips's second husband, Lindsay Shedden, was a cool dude – tall and slim. I remember him in his eighties, stylish in jeans and a large sombrero in their garden at Rose Cottage, Somerby, in Leicestershire. Uncle Lindsay was married four times – one of his wives was the Duchess of Rutland.

Never judgemental, Aunt Pips was popular with all of us. Her sister, Aunt Neni had been very pretty and so was her little house and garden at Manton in Rutland. There was nothing to suggest that her life had been dominated by tragedy. Her wild and handsome only child, Michael, like a brother to his first cousin, my mother, had been killed by an accident on a motorbike, aged eighteen. Her husband, Uncle Ted Kemble, a former county Chief Constable, later committed suicide.

Relating to relations was often tricky – not necessarily eased by the absence of children on all sides of the family. We had only one first cousin, a good egg called Alex Fellowes, who became a headmaster and happily married father of four. Alex was the only son of my mother's middle sister: the notorious Barbara, Aunt Boo, famed for her political protests and variety of lovers. My mother did not appreciate Aunt Boo's shenanigans but, when he grew up, Lupin did. He carried out small services on a large scale for this aunt, responding to persistent telephone appeals round the clock. He enjoyed Aunt Boo! The contrasting sensibleness of her elder sister Pamela could be depended upon. Pam and her soldier husband Ken were a great team, if a strict one, as aunt and uncle, aka Ham and Honkel. This did not in any way restrain my father from poking fun at their foibles, not least my aunt's deplorable dress sense and her stringent application of domestic economies. He was not to know how generous she and my uncle would later be to my brother and sister and myself. Ham's one indulgence was the Du Maurier cigarettes which she smoked in quantity. Both polo players in their youth and dedicated riders to hounds into their old age, Ham and Honkel had a great passion for horses. I can remember trembling as their two enormous grey beasts – appropriately named Slam and Jeep – thundered around us in a field. Their chosen dog was always a whippet. My uncle rose through the Army to the ultimate rank of General Sir Kenneth Darling, straight as they come.

At the head of the family was our widowed maternal grandfather, seemingly the incarnation of Father Christmas all the year round, forever distributing gifts. Grandpa, Harry Denison-Pender, was the grandson of a charismatic and remarkable man, Sir John Pender, responsible for the laying of the first transatlantic telegraph cable across the Atlantic, investing his own money in the undertaking. By his death in 1896 he had founded thirty-two telegraph companies which amalgamated into Cable and Wireless.

Grandpa lived in a comfortable Victorian mansion at Hook in Hampshire, attended by a cook and uniformed parlour maid, and our Christmas Days were spent, magnificently and memorably, with him. Crippled with arthritis, his daily pastime was to study racing form and place quantities of small bets on meetings around the country. His hospitality, enjoyment of children and pleasure in practical jokes were the traits he had in common with my father.

The roll call of relations continued with other players who every now and again took centre stage.

My Dearest Jane . . .

Budds Farm
[1970s]

I cannot recollect a single really enjoyable expedition with my mother as she was always finding fault with my manners and appearance, possibly with good reason. When she came into the nursery, fortunately not often, I felt like an awkward recruit at the commanding officer's inspection of barrack rooms.

The Sunday Times
4 March [mid 1960s]

I had a letter from my mother yesterday complaining of her life and hard times on £4,000 a year tax free, more than I have for all of us. I refrain from further comment.

Gar, my grandmother, once gave me a £5 cheque when I first lived in London and paid her a visit. I wrote to thank her and abjectly apologise for having promptly lost it. She replied: 'No more cheques for you. That will teach you not to be so stupid.' Grandpop had died when I was 8 years old. He used to perform magic tricks with half crown coins and bring us sweeties in the form of Melbury's Newberry Fruits.

The Miller's House
[Late 1980s]

The school holidays seem to start earlier and earlier. My summer holidays never began till after Goodwood, the first week in August. My ever-loving family were very quickly bored with me and I can hardly blame them. My mother strongly disapproved of a boy my age reading books. I should have been practising my service at lawn tennis or caddying for my father on the golf course.

Budds Farm
[Mid 1970s]

The stockbroking firm of 'Roger Mortimer & Co' has

been 'taken over' and the name vanishes. Would you like a painting of the Mortimer founder? It would do for a little used lavatory or to cover a soup stain on the wall. I enclose a photograph of my parents' wedding in 1906. The best man, John Grisewood, was my godfather, who swindled my father out of a large sum of money then retired to the United States to enjoy it. Father looks browned off already – I don't blame him.

Budds Farm
Cowpat Lane
[1972]

The Midland Bank, trustees for my parents' estate, forwarded to me a rather pert letter they had recently received from an individual called Sir Tresham Lever now posing as a lowland laird and living in the house once occupied by the Scott side of my father's family. Lever has recently acquired two fairly indifferent paintings of Sir Walter Scott's parents that used to be in my father's house and which I flogged to the St James's Club after my father's death. In a rather lordly way Lever asks, 'Who is this man Mortimer and how did it come about that he possessed such pictures?' Rather saucily, he described the Scott family as 'having gone to seed': his criterion for seediness being lack of money and any form of ostentation. I have sent a note to Lever, adding that his first wife (originally a Miss 'Poodle' Parker, if you please) was a friend of my father and my mother and came often to our house.

An ancestral connection on the Mortimer side with a cousin of Sir Walter Scott endowed us with some historical treasures. Notably, a fine portrait of Sir Walter Scott after the original by Henry Raeburn, and enough crested blue and white Spode china to equip a banqueting hall; my parents' dogs ate off the plates. My mother was a more enthusiastic reader of Sir Walter's novels and poetry than his distant relative, my father.

Cage 3
Sybil Thorndike Geriatric Ward
Basingstoke Infirmary
Tuesday [early 1970s]

Do you think your Aunt Barbara is now madly in love with Harold Wilson and Ian Mikardo because of their opposition to the Common Market? Mikardo is a man of truly hideous aspect. 'Be careful of that fellow Mikardo,' Winston Churchill once said. 'He's not nearly as nice as he looks.'

Aunt Boo was such a dedicated anti-Common Market campaigner that she brought a fistful of leaflets to distribute round the guests at my 1971 wedding reception, along with a little toy elephant mascot and her current partner. She said to my father on this occasion, 'Have you seen my little mascot?' which he assumed was an introduction to her lover.

Hypothermia House
Burghclere
October [late 1970s]

I hope you are all well and continuing to temper your

customary hilarity with a modicum of reserve. It has been all systems go with your aged parents. Two days of Aunt Boo left us both licked to a splinter. She never stops talking, complete balls at that, and her fantasy world is even more boring than the real thing. She has no teeth and her politics combine neo-fascism with CND and Zionism, a very rum mixture indeed.

Old Cousin Camilla came down to lunch one day and though shaky was in rather good form. She was accompanied by her daughter, the one who fainted when Nidnod explained the 'facts of life' to her on the veranda at Barclay House.

My mother's Cousin Camilla or 'The Peeress from Pont Street', as my father dubbed her, was quite steely and every inch the lady, rather beautiful with creamy skin, always impeccably turned out. Camilla's husband Joss was on the smooth side, something of a club man and a gambler, who spoke with a drawl steeped in port and cigars. They had three children, John – now Lord Pender – Robin and Ann.

Budds Farm
[Late 1970s, on pig paper]

Will you please inform your highly esteemed husband that he will shortly be called to the colours? In other words he will be required to canvass for your Aunt Barbara who is the social democratic, anti-Common Market and vegetarian candidate for (I think) Chelsea. When she last stood she got 471 votes, which is itself a damning indictment of the democratic system of government.

Budds Farm
24 March 1972

I went to Mrs Webster's funeral service at Hook. Your Aunt Barbara, who hardly knew Mrs Webster, insisted on turning up looking, as she invariably does, no matter what the occasion, like a tragic widow of World War I. Plus ça change, plus c'est le même pose. In this instance the black costume was alleviated by a large white plaque denoting opposition to the Common Market, while carried by hand was a huge white plastic sack with the inscription 'Common Market – No' printed on it in letters of considerable size. Aunt Pam unkindly insisted on the removal of the plaque for the service while she seized the sack and locked it in the boot of her car.

Mrs Webster was formerly my grandfather's cook – an excellent one.

Budds Farm
Whit Monday [mid 1970s]

I have heard nothing of your Aunt Barbara recently, her energies being entirely and happily devoted to assisting Messrs Wedgwood Benn and Foot. I think it is possibly a help in the struggle for satisfaction in life to be partially insane.

Barclay House
Sunday [1965]

Cousin John Blackwell was up at the House but failed to

obtain a degree, a lapse in industry or intelligence that has not prevented him from becoming a successful schoolmaster. 'I suppose you'll be becoming a schoolmaster, sir', as the college porter observed to Paul Pennyfeather. 'That's what happens to most gentlemen that are sent down for indecent behaviour.'

Budds Farm
27 October 1969

Aunt Joan came to luncheon yesterday accompanied by a sprightly old trout of 81 who was lame, deaf and blind but in sparkling form and did not miss a trick. I filled her up with Orange Curacao and by the time she left she was thinking of tackling the Matterhorn on the difficult side. You can see we are really living it up in trendy Burghclere.

The Sunday Times
Tuesday [1969]

Uncle Reggie's brother Archie Cockburn died last week. He was a charming old boy of no small distinction in the legal profession. But then most Cockburns are cultured, whereas the Mortimers, Blackwells and Penders, with a few exceptions, are middle-class philistines with the less amiable characteristics of the Forsytes. I had lunch at White's Club last week; it is full of men with brick complexions and red carnations in their buttonholes. Ough! After five minutes there I wish to start dancing on a table waving a small red flag – and you could hardly describe me as being a member of the New Left, or the Old Left either if it comes to that.

The Old Grinder's Doss House
Burghclere
17 September [late 1970s]

Aunt Joan's visit here was a success. The weather for once was warm and sunny and Nidnod and Aunt Joan get on very well even though neither can really make head or tail of the other.

The Miller's House
23 January [mid 1980s]

I hope you are having a happy birthday and are not too depressed at taking another step down the dreaded road to old bagdom! Don't worry, though, as you are still in a good state of preservation and you may not have to worry much for about another 20 years. My grandmother more or less retired from life at 50. There was a rumour that she posted a letter when she was 52, but that is not reliably confirmed. I cannot remember her ever walking as far as the immense kitchen garden. She had six full-time gardeners. The head one, Dinsmore, had a beard, a flat-topped bowler hat and was a crusty old bugger. One never got given a few grapes or peaches to take away. Equally crusty was the chauffeur, 'Comrade Thomson', an ex coach-man who was secretary of the Hatch End Revolutionary Labour Party. He was about a furlong to the left of Vanessa Redgrave. Inside the house my grandmother's maid was a sinister Welsh woman called Morgan who was in love with Mrs Farrow, the cook. The kitchen maid was very old and known as 'Dirty Louie'. In reality, my grandmother had robust health (she did annual cures at Buxton Spa) and she was 83 when she tumbled out of bed on a chilly night and could not get back.

Best wishes and love,

xx D

Chez Gaga
[Early 1970s]

One of my few remaining relatives, Cousin Kathleen, expired last week aged 90. She always wore a collar and tie and a homburg hat like an Edwardian suffragette. A lifelong dipsomaniac, she enjoyed robust health bar the time she fell off a tallboy in the old Criterion Hotel. (How did she get there?) She was a marvel at getting hold of the hard stuff and was once brought back from Holy Communion in Stanmore in a pig cart with a net over the top.

Turf Club
24 November [1970s]

I have now got to meet a relation called Wylde (descended entail-female, as thoroughbred breeders say, from a full sister to the defunct Haliburton Stanley Mortimer). I hope he does not want to borrow money or want a job. 'Blood is thicker than water, but it is also a good deal nastier.' (Thoughts of Chairman Mao after his wife's cousins came to stay for the

Karl Marx Gala Ball at the Rosa Luxemburg People's Palace for Compulsory Democratic Recreation.) I must go and have another drink.

   xx D

Loose Chippings
Soames Forsyte
Wilts
14 June [late 1960s]

Your aunt and uncle stayed here for the night, your aunt looking more like a wire-haired terrier than usual.

Budds Farm
2 February [mid 1970s]

We flogged over to your aunt and uncle for lunch last week. A cold house, a cold lunch and a glass of cooking sherry. Your poor Great Aunt Pips who was staying looked as if she was suffering from exposure and frostbite, although she is far more like 60 than 86. She does, however, experience difficulty in picking up the drift of your mother's conversation.

The Gloomings
Sunday, February [mid 1970s]

Your Great Aunt Pips has done a Lazarus in respect of her pneumonia and left for home in her Toyota at about 95 mph.

Budds Farm
8 April [1970s]

Two people I knew and liked, both younger than me, dropped
down dead on Sunday. One of them had been lunching
recently with Aunt Pam, though I am not suggesting his death
was accelerated by malnutrition.

Sur Le Champ de Bataille
[Mid 1970s]

Relations with your uncle and aunt continue to deteriorate
and the sending of a solicitor's letter will not easily be forgiven
or forgotten. I saw them both racing at Newbury today but
my friendly greeting met with an arctic response. Words like
'monstrous' and 'disgraceful' were flung at my weary old head
and your uncle requested me to tell your dear mother to go
and jump in the lake. All very painful and perhaps the more
so as your aunt was wearing a bright pink coat of almost
unbelievable unattractiveness.

*Family trusts are common ground for family feuds. The sale
of land was at issue here. Friendly relations with Pam and
Ken were later resumed.*

Little Shiverings
Burghclere
[1970s]

Aunt Pam came racing with us in an unusually good mood
and a totally impermissible hat.

Windsor Castle
21 January [1970s]

A long day yesterday as we motored to Peterborough for the cremation of the mortal remains of Cynthia's Uncle Derek. We picked up your Aunt Pam who was very Aunt Pammish. When she saw me her first remark, as we had forecast, was 'I don't think there'll be enough lunch.' To her horror we stopped at a pub en route where three jolly commercial travellers made sheep's eyes at Aunt Pam and your mother. Even your mother did not dare to have a second drink so disapproving was her sister. The service was ruined by a chirpy vicar who, instead of reading out the moving and dignified words of the service, had the cheek to give us a scripture lesson first. Back to Chesterton where almost at gunpoint your aunt was compelled to give us a cup of tea. The General is worried as a trendy hash house, run by a Greek, is being opened at the end of their garden.

Uncle Derek was a naughty charmer. His parents had dispatched him to Kenya in his early twenties, where he fell in with the 'Happy Valley Set'. When he ran out of money and wives, both called Pat, he retired to England. He had one delightful son, Peter Fisher.

Maison des Geriatriques
27 February [1970s]

Aunt Pam is now in S. Africa. I wonder if her clothes will result in new fashions in Durban and Port Elizabeth?

Home Sweet Home
[1975, typed in red]

Aunt Pam was at Newbury races wearing a hat like an inverted wastepaper basket of magenta felt. Very fetching. Your Uncle Ken was 65 last week. Aunt Pam says she can now buy meat for him on specially reduced terms.

Chez Nidnod
27 September [early 1980s]

Why not write an article about Aunt Pam? The fact is that despite her limitations she is one of the happiest and most fulfilled women I know, very typical of her class and type.

14b Via Dolorosa
Burghclere
8 December 1983

On Sunday we lunch with Aunt Pam: whenever I enter Maison Darling I always feel a slight atmosphere of disapproval. As I am notoriously insensitive, the word 'slight' is probably inappropriate. I invariably feel goaded there to express left-wing views which I don't in fact possess (e.g. 'I think that chap Ken Livingstone is probably right, you know. By the way his father fagged for me at Eton').

Budds Farm
14 August [late 1970s]

I saw General and Lady Darling racing yesterday: if they were overjoyed to see me, they kept their feelings splendidly under control.

The Olde Lazar House
Burghclere
12 January [mid 1980s]

They say there is no such thing as a betting certainty. I believe otherwise, e.g. that if you receive a letter from Lady Pam Darling, the stamp will be second class.

Hypothermia House
16 February [1970s]

Did I tell you about the Queen and Queen Mother lunching with Cousin Tom to see his pictures? Thinks: are the Blackwells emerging from the middle class at last?

The Maudlings
Heathcote Amory
Berks
[Late 1960s]

Set off to Ireland by car – drive across Wales most enjoyable and rewarding. Dinner at Fishguard Hotel, a Victorian edifice overlooking an enchanting harbour. Midsummer Ball at hotel; wonderfully untrendy – fairy lights and a five-piece band thumping out 'Tea for Two' and 'Among my Souvenirs'. A placid night on the boat and a wonderful drive through the Wicklow Mountains the next day. Uncle Chris (78) very groggy but dead game. Aunt Star (78) in marvellous form and her sense of the ludicrous totally unimpaired. Aunt Phyl (76) lame and crusty but apt to mellow after a generous intake of Gordon's Gin. She fell yesterday and had the hell of a time getting her up again as she is so heavy. Block and tackle really needed.

Best love

xx D

When Aunt Phyl stayed with us, it was my little task to serve a fizzing glass of Epsom Salts to her before she arose from her bed in the morning. She had a generous mane of grey hair which was swept up into an unwieldy bun.

Budds Farm
[1970s]

Aunt Shirley observed the other day, 'And how is Roger? I suppose he'll soon be getting old enough to marry.' Aunt Shirley is in great form physically, eats like a horse and has a couple of keepers who hide the drink and slip her a couple of pills when the strain gets too much for them. Cousin Tom's pictures – Monets and Sisleys – are up for sale at Christie's next week. I expect they will make £250,000.

On one occasion my father had taken young Lupin to see

Aunt Shirley. She gazed at my father, saying, 'Isn't it about time you left Harrow, Roger?' – a school he never attended.

Little Crumblings
Roper Caldbeck
Bucks
3 July [1970s]

The Blackwell pictures, 2 Monets and 2 Sisleys, went for about £150,000 which will keep Cousins Tom and John off the breadline for a bit. Old Camilla Denison-Pender came here the other day; v. agreeable but I am never quite at ease with her and suspect she can be just a bit of an old B. Poor Uncle Chris had a heavy fall after dinner when we were staying at Ballynure; he is dead game and resolutely keeps on trying to get off with your mother but the flame of life flickers erratically.

Budds Farm
10 March [early 1970s]

Aunt Shirley's little quirk is to imagine every house is a hotel and when she leaves always asks, 'How much shall I tip the Hall Porter?'

Staying at a hotel in Dorset once, Aunt Shirley went into the wrong room and climbed into a bed already occupied by a honeymoon couple. My aunt was perceived as suffering from absent-mindedness, not dementia.

The Lazar House
Burghclere
4 December 1976

Aunt Shirley, 86, is now in a home. The other day she lunched
with her 94-year-old elder sister and that sister's daughter.
Aunt Shirley thought her sister was her mother, who in fact
died in 1917, and that the daughter was an insubordinate
parlour maid who refused to wear a cap and apron. The
home charges £100 per week and that does not include all
the extras. What a ghastly thing old age is!

The Old Damp Barn
Burghclere
[1970s]

Cousin Tom went to see Aunt Shirley, a robust 90, the other
day. He was getting on quite nicely when she suddenly rang
the bell. When a nurse appeared Aunt Shirley said in severe
tones: 'There's a strange man in here. Get him out of here at
once.' Her elder sister is playing good bridge at 96.

Budds Farm
25 September 1973

Thank you for your letter. I'm sorry you have taken umbrage
over something I wrote about Croydon. I am the last person
to run down the outer London suburbs. The Blackwells,
dripping with money made as wholesale grocers, swarmed
over Harrow Weald and Chipperfield. Uncle Percy Mortimer

and Cousin Flossie held court at Wimbledon. Uncle Tudor Davies went to ground somewhere near Southend. The Fishers, cousins of my father, were comfortably dug in at Streatham. My antecedents are reasonably respectable but totally devoid of social eminence. I have just had a letter from your godfather R. C. Lemprière-Robin giving me curious details about a Russian nymphomaniac who is double jointed and has come to live quite near him.

Budds Farm
20 January [mid 1970s]

Yesterday your mother and I went to Ireland for the day for your Great Aunt Star's funeral. It was no less grisly and depressing than most similar functions. Aunt Star was a remarkable woman, a very strong personality who was a kindly despot at Ballynure. Tall and handsome with a very soft and attractive voice, she had an immense zest for life. She was hard to beat on the tennis court, the golf course or the hunting field. At the same time she loved beautiful things, read a lot and was a superb gardener. Unlike most Blackwells, she was not under-sexed and had some rollicking affairs after her first, short disastrous marriage which she contracted to get away from home; easier to do now than in 1913. I have never met anyone with a better sense of fun and she was wonderfully easy to talk to and loved private jokes. When I was a rather oppressed schoolboy she gave me confidence and encouraged me in every way. I owe her an unpayable debt for many kindnesses and for many wonderful holidays at Ballynure which was once a second home to me. Courage was the virtue she admired and was luckily not short of that commodity herself. Her son was killed in the war. Her daughter, whom she adored, was carried home dead on Christmas Eve after a hunting accident. Her two sons-in-law died slowly and painfully before they were fifty. Nevertheless she never gave in, and two days before she died, riddled with cancer, she was following hounds in a car.

Best love to you all,

D

Star's elder grandson, David, became master of Ballynure.

The Old Tudor Doss House
[Mid 1970s]

I have just been up to Newmarket for several days, one of six old gents staying with Cousin Tom. There was no shortage of port and old Colonel Brownlow twice lit cigarettes in the middle, thereby burning them in half, while Colonel Poole took 25 minutes to deal a single hand at bridge. I suggested he took off his shoes and socks and tried dealing with his feet. My second cousin Pearl Lawson-Johnston won a race (or rather her horse did) worth £26,000. Pearl is the school solution of what a typical English spinster is likely to be. She dresses as if her clothes were procured at the WI autumn jumble and her honest, homely features are innocent of powder, etc. She is a JP, head of the County Nursing Association, the County St John Ambulance Association and the County Girl Guides. She is an ex MFH and was recently awarded the OBE. She is very rich as her family drum up Bovril.

Love,

x RM

Rabbit's Larder
Burghclere
[1980s]

Cousin Tom drove his new car into a tree and was lucky to evade death. He had had a bad session with his dentist and unfortunately the painkiller sent him straight into the arms of Demon Doss. Cousin Tom is a survivor, having come unscathed out of two air crashes and one other bad car crash. He wants me to go to Bali in March but I am too old for larking about with dusky beauties. Anyway I'm not absolutely sure where Bali is. Do they still have human sacrifices there? I would really prefer a fortnight in South Africa: I hate Boers but at least there would be no risk (presumably) of meeting Guardian-type feminists there.

'Eventide' Home for Distressed or Mentally Afflicted Members of the Middle Classes
[Late 1970s]

We had the Kennards to tea one day. Loopy told me that his temperament was such that it simply did not pay him to work and in any case he was perfectly content with a rich wife to support his essential needs (i.e. a regular supply of Gordon's Gin). I think that Hot Hand Henry and his bride are favouring us with their presence at Easter. It is difficult to have five minutes conversation with Louise away from HHH.

The Kennards were my sister's mother-in-law and her husband. Loopy was nothing if not a romantic. He had several marriages prior to the one to HHH's mother. His next and final wife had been the great flame of his youth, but the war had separated them and she had married someone else. When the elderly Loopy published his autobiography, he received a congratulatory letter from his old love, now a widow, inviting him to pop in when he was in London. He did pop in – but did not pop out again.

Chateau Geriatrica
Saturday [mid 1980s]

I saw Loopy Kennard at Sandown: at first I thought some elderly tramp had strayed into the members' enclosure looking for a bottle of meths. I think he is going to seed almost as fast as I am but his brain is in fact in better repair than mine. I can't remember a bloody thing nowadays except the pedigrees of long-dead horses which isn't really all that much use.

Love,

D xx

Perhaps that's enough of relations, or relations of relations. The next chapter reveals the creatures with whom my parents enjoyed unconditional love.

11

From Turpin to the Tiddlers

Chez Nidnod
Kintbury
[1970s]

Dearest Jane,
This afternoon our dogs are competing at a local Dog Show.
Three years ago dear old Cringer would have won the
Veterans Cup at Burghclere but tactlessly peed on the judge's
handbag and was demoted to second place.

Love to all,

xx D

My parents were completely English about dogs. They loved
their rumbustious presence, their humour, their unquestioning
devotion and that you could say silly things to them in a silly
voice. They didn't mind the smells, dog hair, messes or bad
breath of a good dog. Their love of dogs was something they
loved in each other, even if they did not always love each
other's dogs. When in his eighties my father was asked if he

believed in heaven, he said, 'Yes, if I could be resurrected as one of my wife's dogs.'

Their dog history included some pedigrees, but my father appreciated a good mongrel with a hotchpotch of interesting genes. Such a character came into our family life when he lolloped across the road in front of my parents' car, narrowly missing it, as they drove through Chiswick one cold and foggy night in the early 1950s. Immediately concerned, they stopped and got out to be greeted by a collarless black spaniel-type dog, wagging his tail and greeting them like long-lost friends. A stray that was not in good shape, my parents scooped him up and drove him out of London and brought him back to a welcoming home.

He was named 'Turpin' after the road – Dick Turpin's highway – on which he had nearly been annihilated. In Mortimer tradition, he had a nickname, Sir Thumpetty Bumps, in celebration of his tail, so often thumping on the ground with happiness.

On the school run, sharing a back seat packed with children, Sir Thumpetty would sit, grinning with his long pink tongue out. On hot days, the parent driving us home might stop and buy us ice lollies. On account of Turpin, we children had labelled raspberry ice lollies 'Dog's Tongues'. My mother, believing this to be a trade name, went into the confectioner's one summer's afternoon and briskly requested, 'Six dog's tongues, please.'

When Turpin's life ended in the manner in which it had so nearly been curtailed ten years previously, hit by a vehicle, our household went into quiet grief. There was no sadder mourner than my brother, who rode down to the village on his bike, returning with some stick on letters, T-U-R-P-I-N, and applied them to a little wooden cross he had fashioned to mark his beloved dog's grave at the end of the garden.

A surprise is not an experience in which everyone rejoices.

When, a few weeks after Turpin's demise, my mother produced a beautiful Dalmatian puppy as a 'surprise' for the family, the response was a memorable anti-climax. Named 'Pongo' after a dog in *101 Dalmatians*, the new puppy was handsome, happy and completely unencumbered by a brain. He was quickly known as 'Your mother's dog'. Pongo grew into a perpetual teenager, undisciplined and brimming with testosterone. 'But he's only a puppy' was my mother's refrain for sixteen years.

Owners who may address their own sex lives with discretion are perfectly happy to see their dog rogering the arm or leg of a visitor or with their nose nestled happily in the groin or up the skirt of a guest. Solomon Grundy was a bright and busy Jack Russell terrier that my father acquired for himself, and he was happy to express his sexual interests at any given opportunity. Solomon and Pongo allied themselves into a loose brotherhood, bounding off on roving parties together when chance arose. The fields and lanes around my parents' subsequent Berkshire home, Budds Farm, rang to the anxious calls of my parents summoning their two mischievous dogs and echoed to their indignant tones to each other as they exchanged accusations of negligence.

To their owners, dogs are often believed to be of a higher status than humans and unless actively aggressive – and sometimes even then – their behaviour is deemed unimpeachable. Messes in the house and peeing against the curtains are just a further celebration of their adorable animalness. In his letters, my father managed somehow to celebrate the monumental nature of the deposits of their dogs. Sell-by dates on food labels were an ignorable curiosity to my parents, a partial explanation for the curious state of both human and canine digestive systems in their household.

As he matured, Solomon was increasingly referred to as 'The Cringer'. My father had trained him to perform a little parlour trick. 'Lie down!' instructed my father, quickly followed by roars of 'Cringe! Cringe, you brute!' The Cringer happily rolled on his back with all four legs straight up in the air in humble supplication, remaining in that position until my father's smiling face indicated release.

My parents went about their different daily lives in their separate cars, their dogs on the front seat beside them, affectionate and unargumentative companions.

When Pongo's final hour came, my mother was utterly devastated, and when my mother suffered, she felt compelled to share it unreservedly. My father sympathized but he found it hard to do so on an hourly basis. He wrote to me wearily: 'At the name of Pongo, every knee shall bow.'

The Cringer, too, grew old. The sorrow of my parents was mutual when he turned up his toes. By then there was already a new canine presence in the house – Sir Peregrine van Notenpool. My mother had christened him with the name of an ancestor which even on paper nearly exceeded the size of the dog – a very camp Chihuahua, white and fluffy, with an unassailable sense of his own importance. His tail acted as a barometer – I'm uncertain what it meant when it was a fully fluffed out plume, but it meant something.

Not to be outdone, my father purchased a suitably posh chum for Sir Peregrine, a sandy-coloured little snapper named Baron Otto. These two canine pixies learnt to live alongside each other. Lashings of love were showered upon them.

The sexual antics between Otto and Perry were conjugations that could easily be overlooked, or looked over – owing to their tiddly size. I still can hear my mother chiding them indulgently for being such 'randy little dogs'.

These little yappettes thought nothing of making deposits around the house. When I tentatively mentioned the tiny dog turds which regularly lurked under a smart chair in her grandsons' bedroom there, my mother retorted, 'Damn it all, it is their house!'

Dogs can be a rewarding conduit through which the British can express emotions more readily than as human to human; in this case creating an equation where their tenderness for their individual dogs added to the sum of love between my parents.

In the last eight years of her life, as a widow, my mother was comforted by a Chihuahua of great sweetness, little nut-brown Danny, who lovingly attended my mother's every hour until he pre-deceased her by a month. At her thanksgiving service a few months later, a talented young singer gave a rendition of 'Danny Boy' which did not leave a dry eye in the house.

The dogs and their escapades scamper constantly through my father's letters.

My Dearest Jane ...

Barclay House
24 October [mid-1960s]

There was quite a nasty moment last week when the abominable Pongo sprang into a car and I thought for a moment he was going to devour a pink and succulent baby on the front seat. Fortunately he contented himself with licking the infant's features. After that traumatic experience no doubt the infant will turn out to be a second Himmler or Christine Keeler, according to sex.

Budds Farm
Tuesday [1967]

Charles's boss plus wife arrived here on Sunday on bicycles

without warning. I think they wanted to see what sort of a nuthouse Charles lived in. I liked them both. They were accompanied by a large, shaggy, elderly dog (male) whom Pongo engaged in unspeakable acts twice, once in the water trough by the tool shed. Really the modern dog is almost human in his shamelessness.

The Biological Stains Research Centre
Wedgwood Benn House
Much Dithering
Wilts
[1971]

We have the Burghclere Horticultural and Canine Show shortly. Pongo is going as Jilly Cooper, Cringer as Wedgwood Benn. I am going flat out to win the Mrs Swingthorpe Cup for Home Produce with a stuffed marrow. The local council are busy having trees felled at the top of Harts Lane. I almost admire them for their determination to make the countryside hideous in the sacred cause of motoring.

c/o Bishop of York
Ebor Castle
York
[1970s]

In the Burghclere Show dogs fancy-dress competition, Pongo is going as Mrs Whitehouse, Cringer as Margery Proops. They are both transvestites at heart. I am entering a thermos of nettle and dandelion soup for the Home Produce competition.

c/o The Official Receiver
29/31 Carey Street
London EC2
16 October [mid 1970s]

Pongo has dug a huge hole in the lawn; frankly I would like
to bury him in it. He has also been voted 'Dog of the Year' for
making, in the kitchen, the largest, most offensive mess ever
achieved by a member of the canine race.

Budds Farm
28 August 1974

On Saturday the Wrights and Pockneys came to supper. Your
dear mother had prepared an elaborate spread including a
most complicated and doubtless delectable pudding. Just
to annoy me, she released Pongo just before dinner. After
Pongo had knocked over two glasses in the drawing room,
he retired downstairs and consumed the pudding. I must say
for once your mother's admiration for Pongo showed signs
of dwindling.

The Scorchings
Burghclere
12 August 1974

Pongo collapsed after a long walk on the downs and I thought
he was a goner. However, I revived him with damp towels and
cold water, drawing the line though, at the kiss of life.

Castle Gloom
Burghclere
7 February [early 1970s]

I took Cringer for a walk this afternoon in the Palmer Memorial Park, Newbury, which is very agreeable if you are keen on discarded cigarette packets, dead shrubs, dog turds and used contraceptives.

Budds Farm
[Early 1980s]

I have just retrieved the Cringer from his canine hotel – £14 for 5 days, about the same as my honeymoon stay at Claridge's.

Chez Nidnod
Burghclere
[1979]

Your mother is in brisk form – our Welsh holiday was a great success. Solomon's name has been changed to Canute on account of his absurd conduct on the beach.

The Maudlings
Heathcote Amory
Berks
[1970s]

Cringer keeps rolling in the remains of a dead hare and comes home stinking in a very vile manner. The habits of dogs are most disgusting. No wonder people say they are 'almost human'.

Asylum View
Much Twittering
Notts
10 July 1970

Cringer has just been revolting with two young dogs; no wonder in the East the dog is the symbol for shamelessness. I always give the big Ha Ha when old ladies describe their dear doggies as 'almost human'. I reckon they must have known some curiously uninhibited humans.

The Old Dosshouse
Burghclere
[1970s]

Cringer is in disgrace following a lengthy absence. I find the concern shown for this animal by myself to be wholly discreditable but what can I do about it? Answer comes there none.

The Sunday Times
[1969]

Cringer is in love with the Bomers's dog and only looks in here for an occasional nap or meal. Faithless beast! The more I see of dogs, the more I prefer human beings and believe me I don't like them all that much!

Le Petit Bidet
Burghclere Les Deux Eglises
Sunday [1970]

Cringer is back home and apparently entertains an insatiable sexual appetite for Pongo who is permissive but bored.

Budds Farm
18 August [1970s]

Your parents pushed their rather leaky old boat out yesterday and had 20 middle-aged, middle-class locals to what Nidnod calls a 'buffet' lunch. Saturday was blazing hot: I tidied up the garden while Nidnod worked endlessly in the cook-house. As it was so hot, we decided to take a chance and base operations on the garden. During the afternoon the boiler went wrong and no one could be found to deal with it. No hot water! In the evening a girl arrived to help Nidnod with the food. She chose to bring 2 dogs with her, one of which at once made a mess an elephant would have been proud of outside the drawing room. At 8 p.m. Mr Thorn arrived to cope with the boiler but unfortunately left the door open and

Solomon bolted. I spent hours searching for him but when at last we went to bed he was still absent and your mother was in a fearful twit. At 6 a.m. the Bomers rang up; they had heard a noise in their swimming pool and on investigation had found an exhausted Solomon trying to get out with little hope of success. The pool had been covered and Solomon had gone through the plastic top! He was lucky not to be drowned.

xx D

The Crumblings
Burghclere
16 October [1970s]

I have just left poor Tiny Man (the Cringer) at Highclere kennels. The English upper and middle classes are really very weird. They feel guilt and remorse at boarding their dogs for a week at enormous expense and in luxurious surroundings: yet they have very little compunction in sending off a little boy of eight or nine to a place where the standard of living would have caused rumblings of discontent among Spartans, where they will be ill-treated by their companions, felt by the masters, and are more or less certain to be very unhappy indeed. The excuse that 'it does the boy good and makes a man of him' is just hypocritical balderdash; the real object of the exercise is to duck out of the inconveniences involved in having the boy at home; just as nannies got mothers off the fatigues of nappy changing, looking after the sick and doing all the chores involved in bringing up young children.

Chez Nidnod
15 August 1981

The Cringer was 2nd in the Veterans Class at the local dog show and was inclined to be truculent afterwards.

The Miseries
Busted
Herts
11 May [1970s]

A lot of people to supper last night including a fairly tiresome female who gave animal imitations. I was pleased when Cringer, resenting her familiarities, bit her nose quite severely.

Chez Nidnod
21 March 1982

I don't think I can face another winter in a house that is never really warm: thumping away on an ancient typewriter wearing three sweaters and with my fingers numb with cold is not all that amusing. As a matter of fact I may not have to: The Cringer and I are both deteriorating physically 'au pas gymnastique' and it is just a question of which of the two elects to give up the pointless struggle first. The poor old dog now finds difficulty in jumping into my car while arthritic joints make it hard for me to climb out of it.

The Bog Garden
[1982]

Poor Old Cringer is showing signs of wear and tear. I fear he may not see the winter through. Judging from the odd looks he gives me from time to time, I have an idea he feels the same about me!

Age Concern House
Burghclere
10 October 1982

Poor old Cringer is getting old, feeble and gaga, like his owner, but Nidnod keeps him going in a remarkable way.

The Miller's House
17 October [mid 1980s]

Just a line to say how sorry I was to hear about your well-loved dog. I remember how miserable I was when poor old Cringer's life ended. Anyway, all my sympathy to you both.

I may not be quite as dog-orientated as my parents, but I have loved several dogs dearly. Our sweet and handsome Labrador, Timber, had met his end, hit by a car.

The Miller's House
22 August [late 1980s]

We drove to Stow-on-the-Wold on Saturday to look over David Nicholson's stable. There was a big crowd there and there were constant appeals on the public address system to release dogs who had been left in cars with insufficient air. I sometimes wonder if the English are really fond of animals. I am careful not to let our little dogs stray. Baron Otto bit a cross-eyed youth delivering an order of white wine this morning, in the ankle. I hope I don't get a summons.

La Maison des Geriatriques
27 February [early 1980s]

Peregrine does not care for children.

Hypothermia House
22 February [early 1980s]

Your mother is furious with our neighbour, portly Mrs B, who has made disparaging comments on Peregrine's domestic and sexual habits. She will never be forgiven!

Budds Farm
[Late 1970s]

Nidnod's dog will sit on my head in the car which I don't fancy all that much.

Budds Farm
[Late 1970s]

Your mother is in very good form as Peregrine was judged
'Champion of the Show' at the Burghclere Flower and Dog
Show.

The Miller's House
May [mid 1980s]

I read Jilly Cooper's book 'The Common' and rather enjoyed
it though doubtless I should find her and her dogs extremely
tiresome.

The Miller's House
[Mid 1980s]

Otto has not been worse than moderately tiresome. He is
apt to hide when I am in a hurry and he plays 'hard to get'
underneath beds. His breath is not un-reminiscent of a station
lavatory in Suez.

The Miller's House
15 May 1987

Otto, who recently bit an Olympic Games gold medallist,
sends his love.
      D xx

There were a number of politicians whom my father would not have minded setting his miniature sabre-toothed Chihuahuas on. Some of Roger's funniest but fiercely felt commentaries involved the supposed great and good of British politics and they feature in the next chapter, offset by his most frivolous jests, japes and tomfoolery.

12

Stray Bats from the Belfry

Little Hangover
Great Pissups
Berks
[1970s]

Dearest Jane,
Your pig mask which you so kindly gave me is proving a great
success down here. I had an appointment with Mr Lipscombe,
manager of Lloyds Bank, Newbury, and Chairman of the
Rotary Club. I slipped on the mask just before entering his
office. On seeing me he sprang to his feet and turned quite
pale, evidently taking me for a masked robber. When I told
him I was rather concerned about a missing share certificate,
he was much relieved. Where will demon pig strike next?

> Best love,
>
> xx D

Out of Roger's bran tub came jokes, poems, quizzes, bizarre
tales – and news items. He was sometimes moved to poetry,

attributing his verse respectfully to a 'W. Wordsworth'. He taught us to recite by heart from *Ruthless Rhymes for Heartless Homes* by Harry Graham – not compulsory on any curriculum today.

> 'There's been an accident', they said,
> 'Your servant's cut in half, he's dead!'
> 'Well,' said Mr Jones. 'Then please
> Give me the half that's got my keys.'

I spent my 2/- (10p) weekly pocket money on practical jokes that hung from a board at the local post office, rarely attaining the audience glee I was banking on. Once I nearly blinded my father by spraying his nose with sneezing powder. A sobering moment. I blame him entirely – he was the leader in tomfoolery.

One day he returned home from London to find his wife and young family gathered round the tea table. 'How was your day, darling?' asked my mother. 'Well, the most extraordinary thing happened to me, in Harrods . . .' There followed with a long tale of misadventure, culminating in my father's arrest by the Harrods store detective, charged with shoplifting 'As the detective led me away,' he said gravely, 'I kept protesting my innocence.' My mother's face creased with concern. 'And then, the detective got hold of my leg and simply would not let go. He starting pulling it . . . as hard as I have been pulling yours for the past ten minutes.'

A few minutes later he let out a yelp. It seemed that he had knocked out his two front teeth on his teacup! One hand over a groaning mouth, he held his purchase from the Harrods jokes department aloft: two large bloodied fangs. My innocent mother was around the table in a flash. 'Poor Roger! Darling!' First aid was essential! Her arm round him, she steered him towards the door. My tall father, intent on hamming his part to the maximum, walked bang into the door frame, resulting in a giant bruise and twenty-four hour concussion.

Sensible in his study, his attention turned to other matters – current events and politics. His omnivorous appetite for news might incite him to letters purple with disparagement and despondency, redeemed for the reader by the pithiness of his delivery.

My father's path sometimes crossed the intelligentsia of his day. He relished encounters with those on the inner circles of power and influence. It would have been entirely out of character for him to display any degree of obsequiousness. The qualities he admired were courage, honesty, kindness, humour, a sense of duty – and intelligence well used. He was very disinclined to be impressed by money even if he might appreciate the perks it could purchase. To prick the balloon of pomposity or humbug was his regular delight. His unashamed glee in provocation often led him to adopt the opposing position in any political dialogue with a defender of convictions either to the extreme right or left. Naughty Roger – he found subversion irresistible.

The troubled 1970s – involving the stranglehold of the trade unions, at whatever cost to the country – represented what he saw as the nadir of political life in Britain. He was far from being alone in his despair on the evident decline of values and standards in society overall. That the country was being brought to its knees by intransigent union leaders and inept politicians was profoundly disillusioning to the World War II generation who had given six years of their lives to fight for their country. They felt betrayed. My father could be award-winningly gloomy and, to crown it all, there was the decline in the newspaper industry on which he depended to make his living.

The vehemence in his letters washed over this daughter

at the time. In the 1970s I was happily absorbed in looking after my family, creating a home for us in Northumberland, making friends – and running my small bookselling enterprise. Unwittingly, I left the hard realities of the world beyond to my husband who, as an industrialist on Tyneside, was at the sharp end of events.

His political and social comments – these stray bats from Roger's belfry – swoop in randomly, true to the usual style of his letters. Curious guests at a dinner party, his dog's' repellent behaviour, tycoons at Ascot, flowers in the garden, a local scandal, my mother's mood, nostalgic memories of the past and Lupin's and Lumpy's antics in the present all run together in a seamless flow with barely a paragraph break in sight. As a voracious reader, Roger's literary enthusiasms and critiques enhanced many of his letters. The following extracts veer from his gravest national concerns to his naughtiest observations on provincial life, further lightened with crackers full of treats and teases, and punctuated by his regular 'Thought for the week'.

My Dearest Jane . . .

Hypothermia House
[1980s]

I think letters, like sermons, should start with a suitable quotation. My text this week comes from G. K. Chesterton: 'A good wife stands by her husband through thick and thin, even though she realises that his head is extremely thick and his excuses extremely thin.'

Chaos Castle,
Burghclere
20 August [early 1980s]

Which well-known headmaster made himself unpopular by getting tipsy on speech day and declaring that 'Cricket should only be permitted in private by consenting adults'?

What has 22 legs and one ball? A women's hockey XI.

Thought for the week: 'Life is only made worth living by three things; to be writing a moderately good book, to be in a dinner party for six, and to be travelling south with someone whom your conscience permits you to love.' Cyril Connolly.

Chez Nidnod (Sans any bloody heating)
16 November 1978

I have just been treating myself to a course of Balzac paperbacks. I was taught to enjoy Balzac at Eton in 1927 and even won a small prize for my knowledge of his book 'Une Ténébreuse Affaire', greatly to the surprise of the master concerned. I also developed a fancy for Maupassant after translating his Franco-Prussian War stories at the age of 15. His story 'The Two Friends' still makes me blub a bit. It was at Eton that I developed a liking for the poetry of Housman, the master in question being, I am fairly sure, unaware that the author's affection for Shropshire Lads was not of an entirely innocent nature and that his deeply homosexual feelings were the mainspring of his poetical outpourings. I believe Housman, a tall bachelor with a military moustache and the foremost Cambridge classicist of his time, was a very formidable character indeed and not at all the type of man one would have expected to be in love with a corporal in the Shropshire Light Infantry.

Budds Farm
23 June [late 1960s]

I am sorry you detect fascist tendencies in me but of course 'fascist' can mean anyone to the right of Cohn-Bendit. It's just one of those words like 'democratic', 'liberty' and 'truth' that have different meanings according to the user. In my opinion students who deny freedom of speech to those whose views differ from their own and who use violence against political opponents qualify as fascists (Mark 1). They are hideously reminiscent in behaviour of Hitler's supporters in the struggle for power in Germany forty years ago. It is really sad to see young people with such closed minds. Luckily our 'protesters' are much softer physically than those ghastly Nazi thugs who really were tough and would have eaten the entire left wing of the LSE before breakfast without noticing it. I remember the shock I got when I first saw the SS Division 'Adolf Hitler'. Enormous, mindless, blond giants, dedicated to violence and very good at it too, what's more. Older generations that have had to take on Germans in two world wars find it difficult to regard even the most violent of our 'protesters' as anything but puerile and 98 per cent harmless.

Yours ever
RM

Daniel Cohn-Bendit was a German anarchist activist and the prominent front man in anti-government student riots in Paris in 1968.

Chateau Marcuse
Cohn-Bendit
Deauville
France
1960s

Over here, the dockers, who don't do all that badly on a weekly
minimum take-home of £35, are being as bloody-minded as
ever with total disregard for the precarious economic state of
the country. In greed and ignorance they almost match some
business tycoons that I know, but not quite.

The dockers' strikes affected England and France in the 1960s.

Schloss Buddestein
Worms
[1973]

I was reading yesterday of a vague and elderly Dean who went
to preach a sermon to the boys at Winchester. Unfortunately
in his usual muddled way, he embarked on a sermon destined
for a small rural community. The boys were apparently quite
surprised when he started off, 'All of you have hands horny
with toil and many of you are mothers.' On another occasion
he meant to start his sermon with the words, 'It is my half-
formed wish'. A ragged cheer went up when he intoned, 'It is
my half-warmed fish.'

Budds Farm
25 July [early 1970s]

What times we live in! A General Strike – Civil War even – is well on the way. I have started to despise my own country and to dislike most of my fellow countrymen. Odi profanum vulgus et arceo (I hate the unholy rabble and keep them away – Horace). It will be amusing, if the revolution comes, to find ourselves on opposite sides! I can picture you as Vivandière to Che Guevara Highgate Commandos while I shall be serving in a minor capacity with the Burghclere Blimps.

The 1970s was a troubled and discouraging decade in Britain and my father was in a regular state of apoplexy. I could have been up for the role of vivandière – a female supplier of military provisions.

The Old Troutery
30 January [early 1970s]

I think the decline of this once great country set in when people started to use the term 'students' in place of 'undergraduates'. Until recently I had always thought of 'students' as squalling Arabs overturning trams in Alexandria or members of a quasi secret society planning to do something unspeakable to the Minister of the Interior in Zagreb.

Chez Nidnod
Burghclere
[Late 1970s]

Do you remember Lady Knox in 'The Irish RM' saying she disapproved of gardening for young girls as 'it promoted intimacy with dowagers'?

Budds Farm
Monday [late 1960s]

It is bitterly cold and snowing hard, bringing to mind my
favourite lines from Wordsworth:

> Life has its problems for us all.
> Our dreams must go beyond recall,
> The future's chill and black.
> The girl I loved was so cross-eyed
> That every single time she cried
> The tears ran down her back.

The Sunday Times
31 October 1973

I have just received an enormous tome called (God knows
why) 'The Pearl of Days' and dealing with the history of the
Sunday Times. As an exercise in crawling up the arses of
their employers, the authors win the Nobel Peace Prize for
1973 and probably 1974 as well. If one did not know Lord
Thomson and his henchmen to be a posse of ruthless financial
cut-throats, one might regard them after reading this as next
in line for canonisation. As for H. Evans, the pinchbeck radical
who carries out the function of editor, he is made to seem the
equal of the great Delane of the Times whereas, cardwise,
he is roughly the four of clubs. I found it unattractive in the
book that the sexual eccentricities of former employees were
exposed and ridiculed. There are members of the current
hierarchy who would look fairly comic if their propensities
had been revealed in the same way. I have written a letter to
the Sunday Times thanking them for the book and giving my

opinion of it. It will not make me more unpopular with the trendy back-stabbing mob than I am already.

Best love,

xx D

Never a fan of Harold Evans, then editor of the Sunday Times, *Roger was spared working under the Rupert Murdoch regime to come! A mere reader, I enjoyed the paper under Harold Evans.*

Budds Farm
Thursday [late 1970s]

Did you ever read Harry Graham's poem on the dangers of being bright at breakfast time, featuring a row between a Rural Dean and a Bishop? As far as I can remember, the Dean was having a peaceful meal:

> Perusing as he munched his toast
> The Anglican or Churchman's Post,
> When in there walked to his distress
> The Bishop of the Diocese.

The Bishop is intolerably breezy and a row ensues, ending in blows:

> Until at last the luckless Dean
> Slipped on a pat of margarine,
> The Bishop took a careful shot
> And stunned him with a mustard pot.

14b Via Dolorosa
Burghclere
Sunday [late 1970s]

I'm sorry for the poor old boy in the Foreign Office who is accused of being a paedophile (?), a word almost unknown to me: I thought it was a form of chiropodist. Of course he's a dirty old man (aren't we all?). In a perfect world all sexual desires would fade peacefully away at 45; the trouble is that people are beset by powerful sexual desires long, long after they themselves have ceased to be sexually desirable.

Budds Farm
[Early 1970s]

Thought for the week: 'Naturally a doll who is willing to listen instead of wanting to gab herself is bound to be popular because if there is anything most citizens hate and despise it is a gabby doll.' D. Runyon.

The Bracket
Much Slumbering
Beds
[Early 1970s]

I read the Labour Party Manifesto today. I rather resent the obvious contempt the compilers feel for the intelligence of potential supporters; but no doubt they have good reason for that particular sentiment.

The Maudlings
Heathcote Amory
Berks
[1970]

The election is really very comic. The new Minister of Transport is John Peyton, once engaged to your dear mother! At the Board of Trade is my old POW friend Fred Corfield, known to all as 'Dungy Fred'. Your mother and I motored unwilling residents of Burghclere to the polling station and made them vote Tory, rather against their desires and convictions. Conservative majority in our constituency up from 3,000 to 10,000.

Edward Heath became Conservative Prime Minister.

Budds Farm
[1973]

I know you like riddles. Yes, you do and please don't argue.
    Q. What is the technical term for two rows of cabbages?
    A. A duel cabbage-way
  Good, isn't it?

Budds Farm
28 March [1970s]

This week's thought: 'Love is blind but sight is restored by marriage.'

'Bangla Desh'
Burghclere
4 December 1971

A Colonel Walker I used to know in the Army was barbarously murdered last night by IRA savages. I was at the 'Sunday Times' office today and spoke rather sharply about their soft, arse-crawling attitude to the IRA. When I said the paper was becoming known as 'The Quislings' Gazette' there was rather a nasty silence. No doubt within twelve seconds of my leaving the office, one of my lovely little liberal colleagues was off to report me to H. Evans, Middlesbrough pygmy. However, I doubt if they can sack me for my political views. I hope not, anyway.

The Geriatric Ward
Budds Farm Eventide Home for Indigent Members of the Middle Class
[Early 1970s]

I went up to London on Monday and had a superb lunch with Lanson Frères in Manchester Square. The white wine was unforgettable. When the repast drew to a close at 4 p.m. I decided to walk to my club and found myself in Carnaby St where I was sold an obscene magazine and an improbable necktie. Just for a nice sit-down I entered a cinema showing a Swedish 'love' film. It was rather less erotic than a pair of bicycling clips and I sank into a deep sleep. On emerging I met Twitch who was in good form and we had some refreshing drinks. I then went to dinner at the 'Sportsman's Club', Tottenham Court Road, this joint being owned by a character called Eric Morley and looking like a combination of a Roman Catholic Church in a backward area and one of the more expensive Neapolitan brothels. The browsing and sluicing were quite good and I had agreeable types on either side. The speeches, though, were interminable and in lamentable taste, combining the maximum obscenity with the minimum of wit.

Love,

xx D

Budds Farm
[1973]

We forgot to sing the following at dinner the other night:

> Oh that gorgonzola cheese,
> Never over-healthy I suppose,
> The old tom cat fell dead upon the mat
> When the sniff went up his nose-ose-ose-ose.
> Talking about the flavour of the crackling of the pork,
> Nothing could have been so strong
> As the terrible effluvia that filled our house
> When the gorgonzola cheese went wrong.
> (Traditional)

c/o Bishop of York
Ebor Castle
York
[1970s]

Here I am in this ancient city at present rendered vile by coach loads of elderly Americans, all with expensive cameras slung round the neck and not a sex kitten among them. The food here is typical of 'Hotel Anglais'. I hate this part of the world; all the men look like Michael Parkinson. I always have pyrophobia in places like this and can find no fire escape. I am all for cremation but not when alive, if you please.

Castle Gloom
Burghclere
7 February 1974

I hate elections and all the lies and bullshit. I don't think it matters which party gets in as this country is just about done for, rotten from top to bottom. For years we have thought the world owes us a living and now we are tottering on the edge of revolution and bankruptcy. If any tough, well-organised and determined minority group tried to seize power now it would probably succeed. The mass of British people would be too wet to leave their television sets and resist. The situation is very like 1939 – 95 per cent of the country were appeasers then and chose to take the view that if Hitler was given Danzig or Austria or Czechoslovakia, he would be quite happy and show himself to be a terribly decent chap afterwards. The attitude now is 'give way to the miners and they'll be ever so pleased. If we stand up to them it will annoy them and we might well be the subject of certain discomforts.' The plain fact is that if a constitutional government yields to a militant minority to secure short term peace, then the democratic system has had it and we are on the way to a dictatorship of the extreme left or the extreme right. I really think I would emigrate if I could think of anywhere to emigrate to! In the meantime I shall be interested to see the line taken by windy little fence-sitters like the editor of the Sunday Times. He'd rather like to go Labour but is nervous about the advertisers. If the Conservatives get in, I think we shall have general strikes and bloodshed. If Wislon gets in, we shall see a mass surrender to militancy, penal taxation for the bourgeois, and the end of this country as I've known it. Wislon's backers are far more left-wing than they were and Wedgehead Benn fancies his chances as Trotsky while Michael Foot would make a merry Robespierre.

Best love,

xx D

Here we go again! Wislon was Private Eye's *soubriquet for Labour leader Harold Wilson. Michael Foot – intellectual on the left wing of the Labour party – later became its leader (1980–83). He was famous for his informal dress – a donkey jacket.*

c/o The Official Receiver
29/31 Carey Street
London EC2
16 October 1974

I have just been writing to my local MP, upbraiding the Tories for cowardice and panic in turning on Heath immediately after an election in which the party, all things considered, did reasonably well. I agree that on TV Heath is slightly less attractive than cold boiled mutton; that women refuse to forgive his reputation for total sexual inactivity; yet in sheer ability he is far above most members of the party. He is honourable, tough and reasonably shrewd. However, in this era of hideous crisis, there are people who would apparently prefer a genial TV personality to a man of nearly first-rate ability.

Goodbye to the Conservatives and hello again to Harold Wilson. Heath's defeat paved the way for Margaret Thatcher.

Les Deux Gagas
Bonkersville
Berks
[1974]

If Barbara Castle has her way, and she will, members of the middle class will not be allowed to spend their savings (if any) on expiring in privacy, a privilege that most animals demand. There is, alas, no bolt hole left for elderly rats like myself. I think I have got out of racing just in time; in a couple of years there may not be any, at the rate things are going. The newspaper world is in a state of acute nervousness. The Daily Express may not last much longer and the Observer is just kept afloat by subsidies from the Astors. The Manchester Evening News stops the Guardian from going under. Worst of all, the stinking corrupt National Union of Journalists is trying to destroy what liberty the newspapers now possess. It will be typical of Michael Foot, who always proclaims his deep love of liberty, if he becomes the instrument that ultimately destroys a fundamental liberty. There is no place in the modern world for the reasonable man. It is the age of bloodthirsty fanatics imposing their will on an inert majority.

As the late Mr Gibbon observed, 'What is history but a catalogue of the crimes, follies and miseries of mankind.'

xx RFM

Fiery, long-serving Labour MP and minister, Barbara Castle, was just the woman to ruin my father's repose as he read the papers at the breakfast table.

14b Via Dolorosa
Burghclere
[Mid 1970s]

I wonder if we are going to have a revolution in January. I could rather fancy death at the head of a platoon of bourgeois reactionaries charging the inmates of the London School of Economics with fixed bayonets. What a mess this country is in. Of course Hitler had to be crushed, but apart from that, most of my friends who were killed in the war would reckon they had died in vain. One of the few leading statesmen I know observed the other day that we are a nation of lemmings rushing blindly towards our own destruction. He said it was quite impossible to have a conversation with union leaders like Scanlon and Gormley. They just wanted to bring the government down and did not care if the country was ruined in the process. They don't give a damn about miners' pay. The total breakdown of the established order is their true objective. I had dinner last week with Mr Ray Gunter, a former Welsh miner and ex-Minister of Labour. He is under no illusion about the aims of the more militant members of his own party.

The Gadarene swine were a thoughtful and reasonable set of individuals compared to most of our delightful fellow-countrymen. Such is the political climate that even H. Wislon seems quite nice.

The Olde Lazar House
Burghclere
12 January [1980s]

> It was evening at the factory,
> Old Gasper's work was done,
> And W. D. and H. O. Wills sat smoking in the sun.
> Before them scampered on the green,
> Their little grandchild Nicotine.

Insolvency Lodge
Burghclere
29 August 1976

As I was waiting at Newbury Station yesterday, an ambulance came roaring up and a man was removed from a 1st class non-smoker who had just cut his throat from ear to ear. I have sometimes thought of doing the same thing myself on this particular line.

Budds Farm
10 May 1977

I am writing to you less from paternal affection than a desire to try out a new typewriter ribbon. It is a perfect May evening and I am taking your mother out to supper. The blossom here is superb and it is going to be a great month for lilac. Poor old Jeremy Thorpe! I do feel sorry for him but I would not fancy him as leader of this country. I must say, if I was going to have a love affair with a male lunatic in Devonshire, I don't think

I'd pick N. Scott who looks about as physically attractive as Himmler.

The Liberal Party leader Jeremy Thorpe was accused and acquitted of plotting the murder of one N. Scott, an individual who claimed to have had an affair with him in the early 1960s.

The Turf Club
24 November [1970s]

Many thanks for your well-chosen and totally acceptable birthday present of H. M. Bateman's cartoons now located in the downstairs loo!

> The bourgeois humour
> Of H. M. Bateman
> Brings the hint of a leer
> From an old Constipateman.
> (W. Wordsworth)

Little Shiverings
Burghclere
[1979]

I have seldom seen a more villainous-looking man than the individual called Haughey who is to be Ireland's Prime Minister.
   I believe in fact he is far worse than he looks.

Budds Farm
2 February [late 1970s]

Did you know that Karl Marx hunted with the Cheshire while engaged in writing 'Das Kapital'? That Lady Zia Werner who won the Derby with Charlottown is descended from Pushkin who had black blood in him?

The Drippings
Burghclere
[Late 1970s]

I think it was the crowning humiliation for H. Wislon was to appear with Morecombe and Wise on TV. Can you picture Mr Gladstone participating with Dan Leno's balloon act or Mr Asquith butting in on Harry Tate's famous motoring sketch? I think Wislon has been ruined by La Forkbender: it was infinitely preferable when old Lloyd George stuffed a wide variety of secretaries on the table in the Cabinet Room during the lunch interval. He always kept his hair long as he thought it was a mark of his virility. Looking at his photograph, you would hardly pick him as about the randiest Welshman of his age. But then the murderer, H. H. Crippen of Hilldrop Crescent NW13 hardly looked likely to be a passionate lover, whilst another, 'Brides in the Bath' Smith, was illiterate, coarse, dirty and repellent in every respect. Yet respectable middle-class women fell for him as if he were a combination of Rudolph Valentino and Mr Onassis.

It took little for my father to find comparisons in character with legendary murderers –not least in his own family! La

Forkbender was Wislon's private secretary and personal advisor, Marcia Williams, latterly elevated to the peerage as Baroness Falkender.

Budds Farm
12 October [mid 1970s]

This week's quotation comes from the late Bishop of Bath and Wells: 'I like to get my golf over in the morning as then I am free for Bridge in the afternoon.' He also observed: 'Personally I must admit that the spiritual side of this job doesn't particularly appeal to me.'

The Old Damp Ruin
Burghclere-under-Water
3 January 1980

The revolting hypocrisy of the lefty rent-a-crowd mob has been demonstrated to the full by its action, or total lack of action to be more accurate, over the Russian invasion of Afghanistan. Not a squeak of protest from any one of them. The fact is that aggression and cruelty do not distress them at all when perpetrated by communists. However, perhaps if we keep our ears wide open we may hear a faint whimper of disapproval from that pathetic army of trendy liberal wets who comprise the bulk of the 'Guardian' readership. I have an idea that World War III is not far off. When it starts, I shall shoot the dogs, reload the guns and await the arrival of Russian parachutists in a manner I hope faintly reminiscent of Gordon awaiting the Mahdi's spearmen at Khartoum.

Your mother will certainly be in favour of a vigorous defence of her home. She is in fine bellicose trim, desires the death penalty for all strikers and is thinking seriously of doing a Charlotte Corday and knifing Arthur Scargill although not necessarily in his bath.

   Love to you all,

   D

Arthur Scargill later led the major miners' strike of 1984–5 which would be brought to an end by Margaret Thatcher, Britain's first female Prime Minister. A century earlier in the French Revolution, the radical politician Marat was assassinated in his bath by Charlotte Corday – a heroine of France.

 Budds Farm
[Early 1980s]

How do you fancy Mrs Thatcher? Quite a formidable lady, I reckon, and I would not fancy a swipe over the eardrum from her plastic shopping bag.

Detention Centre 392
Burghclere
1 February [late 1970s]

Your husband is a very well-educated man (Cries of Hear, Hear! Well spoken, Sir) so perhaps he could tell me the author of the following rather beautiful verses:

The Captain stood on his bridge alone,
With his telescope to his eye,
The ship she was sinking rapidly,
As the storm went howling by.
He saw the rush for the lifeboats,
And he noticed a peer old and grey,
Then a sailor approached and saluted
And thus to the peer did he say:

'Pray take a place in the lifeboat,
Tis a gesture I willingly make,
Since I fagged for your nephew at Repton,
It's the least I might do for his sake.
And when next, Sir, you're seeing your nephew,
Pray sing him this short refrain:
"Piddock minor went down like a Repton man,
And gladly he'd do it again."'

Chateau Geriatrica
Saturday [1980]

I wonder how old Mugabe will turn out. Probably a black
Harold Macmillan whose next objective will be to join the
Carlton club.

*Robert Mugabe became the first Prime Minister of Zimbabwe,
formerly Rhodesia, in 1980. My father was spared being a
witness to how 'old Mugabe' turned out.*

Chez Nidnod
Kintbury
3 September [mid 1980s]

The sky is dark grey like a clergyman's flannel suit, the temperature about 56 degrees F. The news is all about the hideous situation in the Gulf and the misfortunes of Dr Owen. The good Doctor went to Bradfield where he was unhappy because, according to his own account, he was very good looking and the other boys never left him alone. 'Ah, nuts alors!' as the French lady said when she was taken to see a six-day bicycle race in New York.

Dr David Owen, Labour minister, then SDP founder, now Lord Owen.

The Old Draughthouse
Much Shiverings
Berks
[Late 1970s]

I came across this rhyme yesterday in an old book:

> As for my dear one's father, he
> Was just as tactful as her mother;
> He'd always leave us, after tea,
> Alone with one another.
> Locking the door with some remark
> About how 'lovers love the dark',
> He'd turn the gas off at the main;
> And I would sit for hours with Jane
> Trying to light the stove again.

Schloss Blubberstein
Montag [early 1970s]

There have been two cases of indecent exposure in this
locality. Rather sporting, I think, considering the unfavourable
weather conditions for flashing the member virile.

> There was an old lady of Filey,
> Who esteemed her late husband so highly,
> That in spite of the scandal her umbrella handle
> Was made of his member virile.

The Shambles
Burghclere
[1980s]

Who said, and of whom: 'She was a most unsuitable wife for
Henry: she lived in Hampstead and had no clothes'?

The Bog Garden
Burghclere
[1980s]

Do you like Durham? It is one of my favourite cities. The
great Hensley Henson was once Bishop there: he spoke and
wrote superb English. He hated his Dean, a hearty muscular
Christian called Weldon who had been headmaster of Harrow.
The Bishop once observed of the Dean, 'He is a man who can
neither speak with effect or be silent with dignity.'

La Maison des Geriatriques
27 February 1982

There are some lugubrious females now camping outside
Greenham Airfield; I am inclined to doubt if any action they
take will greatly influence nuclear policy in America or Soviet
Russia.

The women's peace camp on RAF Greenham Common was
a protest against the siting of nuclear missiles there. The
'scruffy' appearance of the Greenham women and their camp
offended my father far more than their opposition to nuclear
armaments. As they were camping, they could hardly be
attired for Ascot.

Budds Farm
11 January [early 1980s]

You may recollect the remark of the Headmaster in 'Decline
and Fall' when the Welsh Silver Band turned up on Sports
Day: 'I refuse to believe the evidence of my own eyes. These
creatures simply do not exist.' Those were my sentiments
on seeing the Greenham mob. Not one in fifty knows what
'unilateral' means; they are all perfectly prepared to betray
this country at the drop of a hat and believe, mistakenly I
hope, that sucking up to the Russians will exempt them from
exile to Siberia in the event of invasion. If Nidnod had a gun,
which happily she has not, I feel sure she would give them a
peppering.

The Crumblings
Wilts
Sunday [mid 1980s]

I have just been reading about Nicholas Udall, a former headmaster of Eton. He wrote the first comedy in the English language, 'Ralph Roister Doister'. He stole all the college plate with the help of two boys, one of whom he had a passionate affair with. After a brief spell in prison, he was appointed Headmaster of Westminster. The Old Boy Network never lets you down!

The Miseries
Busted
Herts
11 May [1970s]

I am busy on various projects and may have a little business to conduct re a TV series with an actor called Robert Hardy who was the Prince Consort in the series 'Edward VII'. As he lives in the Thames Valley and hunts your mother thinks he is marvellous. He seems less oafish than most actors and at least writes to me on reasonable writing paper.

Yesterday, reading some obscure piece of military history, I came upon the name of General Sir Cameron Shute. At one stage in World War I he commanded the division my father was in. He was a fearful old sod who never shaved properly and whose chin was invariably lit up by a blaze of white stubble. He had a habit of making surprise inspections in which the latrines were invariably the first target. Hence his nickname of 'Deus ex Latrina' and the following poem:

The General inspecting the trenches
Was heard to exclaim with a shout
'I will not inspect a Division
That leaves it's excreta about.'
The Division retained its composure
And no one was heard to refute
That the presence of shit in the trenches
Was preferred to the presence of Shute.

Best love to all,
RM

The Miller's House
11 October 1983

Mrs Thatcher made a Boadicea type speech but omitted to mention (wisely) the economy. She's a terrifying old bag but she's got some guts and makes Kinnock look like a fairly agreeable but rather spotty adolescent. I managed to twist my knee climbing into my trousers this morning and am as lame as a geriatric camel.

Neil Kinnock, the Labour leader in 1983–92, never became Prime Minister. Margaret Thatcher was re-elected for a third term in the 1987 election.

The Soddens
Burghclere
[1970s]

V. wet here and local shops have run out of galoshes. It is

a fine sight to see dignified matrons hauling their shopping trolleys through eight inches of water in the municipal car park:

> Moved from the brink like some full breasted sawn,
> That, fluting a wild carol ere her death,
> Ruffles her pure gold plume, and takes the flood
> > With swarthy web. ('Morte d'Arthur'
> > – Alfred Lord Tennyson)

Alf Tennyson is my second favourite poet, No. I of course being Beachcomber's Roland Milk who always wanted 'to do something big, something clean' and was advised by Lady Cabstanleigh to go and scrub down an elephant.

From: R. Mortimer, 'Sunday Times' Correspondent for Burchglere, Wash Common and Echinswell; also assistant editor 'Swedish Teenage Love' (80p in plain envelope, inc. UK postage)
1 October 1972

I went to see a film called 'Young Winston'. It is clearly made for the American market and is bad beyond belief. The military and historical details are ludicrously inaccurate. The casting is absurd with little John Mills, who looks like a retired jockey, playing with supreme inadequacy the part of tall, purple-faced, squinting and rather terrifying Lord Kitchener.

The Sunday Times
Editor-in-Chief's Office
Midnight [1972]

I backed a horse at Ascot today because it was called de Musset. Its sire was called Alcide which was de Musset's nom de plume. I always liked the rhyme:

> Alfred de Musset
> Used to call his cat 'Pusset'.
> As was only to be expected
> His accent was rather affected.

Newbury is crammed with Asians from Uganda. Here is a reported conversation at Lloyds Bank, Newbury.

Ugandan Asian: What is the rate of exchange please?

Bank Clerk: 93p to the £.

Ugandan Asian: My friend on Tuesday obtained 95p. How do you explain that?

Bank Clerk: Fluctuations.

Ugandan Asian: You are a very rude man. Fluctueuropeans too.

The Shudderings
Burghclere
[1978]

I came across this startling piece of verse recently:

> O Moon, lovely Moon, with thy beautiful face,
> Careering throughout the boundaries of space,
> Whenever I see thee, I think in my mind,
> Shall I ever, oh ever, behold thy behind.

Bottlebanks
Burghclere
8 January 1981

I have been reading a book about the Darwin family. Old Charles Darwin used to bang on a bit about the origin of the species and one day one of his brothers observed rather sharply: 'My dear fellow, I don't give a damn for the whole kingdom of nature.'

The Miller's House
15 May 1987

I am already bored with the election. My first election was won by Mr Asquith (Liberal). He was a lazy old sod and constantly appeared in the House of Commons the worse for brandy. In the first months of the war he wrote 3 long letters a day to his girlfriend Venetia Stanley (40 years younger) confiding in her all the government secrets. His brilliant eldest son went to France with the Grenadiers and old Asquith never wrote to him once before he was killed in action.

Whenever my father mentioned Herbert Asquith, Liberal Prime Minister 1908–16, it was with deep contempt both for his inadequacy as wartime leader and, unforgivably, as an apparently unsupportive father.

The Miller's House
21 August [mid 1980s]

There is a long article in this week's 'Spectator' about Robert Byron who drowned in 1941. He was an authority on Persia

and wrote an excellent book, 'The Road to Oxiana'. I fagged
for him my first half at Eton in 1922. He was a weird character,
inclined to get cantankerous when he was tight. At Oxford he
was involved in many scenes. There was a row when he drank
too much at the Bridge House Hotel and shouted, 'All I want
is a teeny weeny little boy.' Luckily I was too scruffy and
juvenile to attract him.

*Robert Byron's biographer visited my father at home to
interview him for his research.*

The Miller's House
25 October 1987

Not a very merry month, what with the Big Storm and the
Money Crisis. I hope I shall not have slumped into pauperdom
by the time you get here. I well remember the crisis of 1931
when the Navy mutinied and there were riots in the West End
of London. I recollect the police using their truncheons without
restraint on the heads of the more aggressive unemployed. My
battalion was marched down to the Docks where there was
some tepid trouble. En route, an elderly man on the pavement
shouted out, 'Don't shoot your fellow workers, comrades!'
and Corporal Homer, an ex-miner, shouted back 'Yes I will,
Granddad!' Generally speaking, there was little ill-feeling
between the soldiers and demonstrators: the latter hated the
special constabulary and so indeed did the police who regarded
them as potential black-legs as they had helped to break the
police strike in 1919. I remember a column of marchers headed
by a fearful villain called 'Ironfoot Jack' – who had a metal
artificial foot and was a power in the world of pornography.

Best love,

xx D

Within days of each other in 1987, there was a global stock market crash – Black Monday – and fifteen million trees were blown down by gale force winds – the Great Storm.

Gloom House
Kintbury
27 October 1987

I have been reading a biography of Norman Douglas who wrote one of my favourite books, 'South Wind'. Douglas was an awful old scamp who simply could not keep off the boys and eventually had to leave England in disgrace. In Capri some nosy individual asked him if it were true he had left England under a slight cloud. 'Yes,' he replied. 'A cloud no bigger than a boy's hand.'

The Miller's House
Kintbury
[1987]

What a pity so many good English words gradually disappear from common usage. A 16th-century Warwickshire weaver advertised for sale: 'the very finest tapestry, arras, moccadoes, carolles, plonketts, grogaynes, says and sarges'.

Words I don't much care for are: bland – mellow – crisp – operation – terminal – bowels – democratic – popular – sportsman – scurf – renegade – carbuncle – manly – motherly – bosom (particularly of Abraham's) – genitals – mortgage – confidential.

14b Via Dolorosa Burghclere
[Early 1970s]

I went to Lord's for the Test Match on Thursday. The members
in the Pavilion are very democratic these days and take food
and drink to their seats. In the old days you would have been
flung out for such a flagrant breach of etiquette! I sat just
behind a very old man who alternately snored, farted and
picked his nose. Hardly the ideal mate on a hot afternoon.
Fifteen years ago I would have met 100 people I knew at a
Lord's Test Match; last week I met no friends.

Have you been reading about the Buckleberry man who
drowned his ever-loving wife in the bath? What a villain! And
yet though he was a clumsy murderer he nearly got away
with it because of the combined idleness and ineptitude of
the doctor who did the post-mortem. If the murderer had not
suddenly lost his nerve, the corpse would have been cremated
for a few more hours and he would have been safe. Well I
must stop. I hear the sound of wheels on the gravel. Can it be
the tumbrils already?

Best love,

xx D

Budds Farm
[1970s]

> Lovely big cow on the edge of the wood
> I'll give you an apple if you are good.
> I want to be kind before the chance goes;
> For Aunt Sarah told me and she always knows –
> That somebody told her (I hope he was wrong)
> You'd be put in a bottle before very long.

So lovely big cow, whose hide is all mottled,
Eat up your apple before you get bottled.

W. Wordsworth

Le Petit Nid des Deux Alcoholiques
[1980s]

Two odious characters in a van called here yesterday and said they heard I ran a caravan site (I can hardly imagine a less plausible story). When they left I made a few enquiries and discovered they were a couple of local tea-leaves just out of Winchester gaol.

Two very good jokes.

What did the male owl say to the female owl in a thunderstorm? Too wet to woo.

What did Big Ben say to the Tower of Pisa?
I have the time, you have the inclination.

Budds Farm
[1974]

I had lunch in my club last week with a howling lunatic whose company I found most enjoyable. His dissertation on the effect sago pudding had on his father's sexual appetite was most enlightening.

Budds Farm
29 August 1974

There was a hideous accident the other night at the top of the road and three youths and a girl, all locals and all on motor-bicycles, collided head-on with two cars and all were killed. They were going at a great speed, racing from a pub at Whitchurch. The funeral was macabre. All the local Hells Angels, etc. mounted their bikes, donned their best leather and 25 of them formed a cortege of honour, if that is the right word. Unfortunately a tractor came out of a side turning near the church and took them in the flank, causing four of them to be removed senseless to Battle Hospital.

Chez Nidnod
14 Rue Prinker

12 September 1973

> I asked of Heaven only a poet's boon.
> 'Fade night,' I murmured 'And of Dawn, come soon.'
> And at that moment tumbled down a hole
> Almost exclusively reserved for coal.

The Miller's House
[Mid 1980s]

In my day Eton manners were inclined to be arrogant. E.g. 1: Three boys went to see their tutor at midday and found a glass of milk and a slice of seed cake waiting for the tutor on a plate. The first boy consumed the milk, the second the cake and the third broke the plate. E.g. 2: My tutor arrived home early from a dinner party and found the captain of the house using his study and drinking his port. The miscreant's first comment was 'Sir, your port is very indifferent.' E.g. 3: My friend Ian Akers Douglas was playing cricket at Winchester and dined with a Winchester master afterwards. Offered a glass of claret, Ian accepted, took one sip and the asked the parlour maid to bring him a whisky and soda.

Love,

xx D

The Miller's House
Kintbury
2 September [early 1980s]

Thought for the week from Canon R. F. Mortimer of St Vitus's, Kintbury: P. G. Wodehouse's description of a cocktail 'that would make a week-old corpse leap lightly from the bier and enter a three day bicycle race'.

The Miller's House
Thursday 7p.m. [early 1980s]

One does read weird things in the paper. I was reading about a rape case in the 'Daily Telegraph'. The victim said she did not recognise the accused by his features but by the curious pigmentation of his penis. The judge asked for an expert on penis pigmentation to give evidence and as one was not available he acquitted the accused. Nothing exciting at

Newbury bar a few cases of indecent exposure behind the old bandstand. There has also been a shindy between two clergymen in Kingsclere.

The Miller's House
14 February [early 1980s]

There was once a Mr Deeming who married a series of women, murdered them after the honeymoon and buried them under cement in the kitchen. Sentencing him to death, the Judge said, 'Mr Deeming's motto seems to have been "Marry in haste and cement at leisure."'

Chez Nidnod
Kintbury
3 September [mid 1980s]

The great French Actress Sarah Bernhardt was once playing at Manchester and one afternoon went for a carriage drive in the country. In one village she saw some mud-plastered yokels playing football on the green. She stopped the carriage, and clad in her white furs climbed on to the seat, and observed in her delight, 'J'adore ce cricket; c'est tellement Anglais.'

The Steady Dripping
Burghclere
18 February [early 1980s]

I could bore you to the brink of extinction by telling you how good the post was when I was a dear little innocent boy: I particularly looked forward at school to the postal delivery on Sundays when I received a weekly edition of the 'Daily Sketch', in other words six numbers of the 'Daily Sketch' under a single cover. Good reading. They gave the names of the executioners at hangings.

This must be a short letter as I am due to churn out a dreary article on a boring subject for a semi bankrupt magazine. J. B. Morton – Beachcomber – was an unusual type of Harrovian, a dedicated R.C., lived till he was 94. Do you remember how he addressed his friend and fellow-scribe Bevan Wyndham-Lewis?

> Bevan, hired scribblers every day
> Must cast their choicest pearls away.
> But what a fate is yours and mine
> Who cannot even choose our swine?

Talking of swine, someone once described a Harrow master's job as 'casting sham pearls before real swine'. Cosmo Lang, a somewhat unpopular Archbishop of Canterbury, was known by his fellow bishops as 'Auld Lang Swine'.

Love to all,

xx D

The Miller's House
[Mid 1980s, typed on the back of old racing forms]

I suppose that living as you do up in the frozen north, you find it difficult to entertain your friends in the winter. I have just been reading about Tibet where the climate is similar. They have an annual beano during the cold spell. It starts off with a speech by the Public Oracle then leads on to an exhibition of sculpture in butter. The big event, though, is a competition to see who can exude the greatest amount of body heat. Competitors take off all their clothes and spend the night naked in the snow. The individual found by dawn to have melted the greatest amount of snow by the heat of their body is judged to be the winner.

There used to be a very agreeable member of Boodle's, when I was a member there, called Mr Justice Stable, more commonly known as 'Owly' on account of his features. He was a witty and humane judge and much liked. Before one case came up before him, a juror asked for leave of absence since 'My wife is going to conceive this morning.' Owly politely replied, 'It may be what you are seeking to tell me is that your wife is going to be confined this morning. Whether you are right or I am right, it would seem to be an occasion when you, personally, should be present.'

Love,

x RM

The Miller's House
[Mid 1980s]

Look forward to meeting you on May 22 for the Trooping of the Colour and I enclose two tickets. Let's hope there are no unfortunate incidents. Forty-eight years ago I was on a similar parade held in Hyde Park. A booze sodden bog-Irishman took a pot at the King. The Irishman was so pissed he missed. I knew nothing about it until I read the story in the 'Evening Standard'. Some years earlier I was on Piquet duty at the Bank of England. As usual very boring but redeemed by the Bank's free bottle of excellent port. Next day I rendered a report declaring that 'nothing unusual had happened during my tour of duty', whereupon the Adjutant produced the midday edition of the 'Evening Standard' which carried the headline 'Midnight Robbery at the Bank of England'.

Love

xx D

The Miller's House
[Mid 1980s]

What does more damage than a bull in a china shop?
A porcupine in a condom factory.

The Miller's House
April 1988

'Where every prospect pleases but only man is vile', as Bishop Heber wrote after discovering on a missionary journey that his trunks had been stolen in Ceylon.

The Miller's House
7 January 1980s

This week's quotation: 'The thing is that I am a member of that sad, ever-dwindling minority . . . the child of an unbroken home.'

'The Rachel Papers', Martin Amis

Budds Farm
7 April [mid 1970s]

SPRING in BURGHCLERE

Spring has come to bosky Burghclere; merry sunbeams
   pierce the air,
Kevin Potts is bright with pimples, Mrs Turge has died
   her hair.
Smoothly, Jackson overcharges pensioners for potted
   meat,
Major Wagstaff, pubwards hobbling, bravely bears with
   old man's feet.
In the churchyard crisp-bags, fag ends line the path to
   the Norman door,
Parson Craig trips in for matins, spots a Durex on the
   floor.
Sadly clucking disapproval, parson minces down the
   aisle,
At the organ gaunt Miss Simpson stabs him with her
   spinster's smile.
In his garden Mr Muncer views a crop of sturdy weeds
Basking in the April sunshine where last month he
   planted seeds.
Mrs Muncer, hand on Hoover, casts a love look at her
   Spouse
Through the window. Five more minutes, then it's time
   for Maxwell House!
In the schoolyard acned Eric threatens Nigel with his
   knife,
Tracey who'll be eight next birthday, ponders on the
   facts of life.
Mr Cocksedge, music teacher, casts a somewhat randy
   eye

At his pupil, Mavis Wimpole, and her pink and gleaming
    thigh.
Mrs M. proceeds to Council, plans a team in tiny head,
(sad she's left the whole agenda on the table by her bed).
Tap of typing from the Major as he writes to daughter
    Jane:
Luckes's tractor spreads manure, rich brown blobs,
    along the lane . . . to Budds Farm.

Hypothermia House
22 February [mid 1980s]

The people of this country are great survivors and I daresay
in ten years time they will still be arguing about the abolition
of public schools and the inadequacy of the railway system.
    Best love,
    D xx

*Now for a new role which lightened my father's later years
– becoming a grandfather. He relished the joys of connection
and affection unburdened by responsibility.*

13

Grandfather Roger

'You are old, Father William,' the young man said,
'And your hair has become very white;
And yet you incessantly stand on your head –
Do you think at your age it is right?'

Lewis Carroll, *Alice's Adventures in Wonderland*

By the time his first grandchild arrived, my son Piers, in April 1974, my father had accumulated plenty of parental wisdom to share. My mother immediately became a doting grandmother. My younger son Nick was born in 1976. My father absolutely understood that advice to a mother must be given sparingly and with care, whilst criticism was to be avoided in the name of self-protection. He sufficiently respected the father of his grandsons to know that he could depend on the intelligence and sense of at least one of their parents. I loved having two little boys and if my father might have on occasion questioned my maternal protectiveness, he expressed himself to me on the subject of his grandsons with interest, tenderness and as funnily as ever. My niece and nephew enjoyed equal appreciation.

Babies amused him in very small doses. He would have been amazed to witness the close involvement of modern fathers, and to see his grandson Nick, the little tearaway he knew, now a dynamic managing director of a digital marketing agency, married and a fully hands-on father of three – Ruby, Star and Laszlo. What a huge bonus and joy it is to be their grandmother.

Roger the grandfather came into his own when the babies grew into bright and merry little boys with whom he could engage in chat, games and jokes. One day he announced to his small grandsons that he and their grandmother were going to a fancy-dress party. 'Oo, what are you goings as, Grandpa?' 'I am going as a cowpat,' he replied, beaming. 'And Granny is going as a blue-bottle.'

He enjoyed each grandchild on their own terms – he was not inclined to see their future as a series of moulds into which they must fit. Highly individual himself, he responded to that quality in others, particularly enjoying it in his youngest descendants. My father's interest in sport was a well-rounded one – but by no means obsessive. He saw team games as an obvious route of pleasure for his younger grandson and a more literary future for his elder brother. His perceptions were spot on.

When they went away to school, they too became the recipients of a gentle stream of amusing and encouraging letters. I continued to receive letters of thoughtful information on their education and well-being. He lived far away, but was alive long enough for my sons to have formed a warm connection with their extraordinary grandfather. If he had lived only a further six weeks, he would have enjoyed the pride of knowing his elder grandson had been offered an unconditional place at Oxford, a thrilling moment in a family not noted for academic achievement. He would have been proud again now at the publication of Piers's first bestselling novel for young people, *The Last Wild*. Above all, he would have been delighted that both grandsons had found great personal happiness, Piers with his partner, Will, and Nick with his wife, Clare.

I've heard some say that they don't want to be called 'Grandfather' – it is too ageing. I have heard yet others say the real worry is sleeping with a grandmother. But the mellowness and sagacity of old age is so often underestimated in an era where youth must be clung to at all costs. My father did not enjoy being old. He did, however, derive real pleasure from what he could offer as Grandpa. And as some wiseacre had it: being a grandparent is the reward you get for not murdering your children.

My Dearest Jane . . .

Budds Farm
24 April 1974

Could you please send me a nice photograph of P. F. Torday that I can show to friends in the Carnarvon Arms without them actually wincing? I remember during the war an enormous gorilla-type man who was very keen on showing photographs to all and sundry of his son and heir who looked rather like Mussolini with mumps. While searching one's mind for suitable comment, the gorilla used to observe in a manner that conveyed more than a hint of a threat: 'There is nothink wrong with the kiddy.'

'Of course not,' one would reply with warm insincerity. 'He's a beautiful little fellow with a great look of you about him.'

I suppose when P. F. Torday has grown up, he will be finding himself living in an egalitarian republic with a snotty old President and a one-party government of the extreme left.

Best love to you all and not least to saucy little P. F. T.

P. F. T was eighteen days old and my father was already speculating on the future world in which he would find himself.

The Old Crumblings
Burghclere
Election night, 5 March 1974

Does Sir Denis anticipate any immediate rally in share prices?

Without an eyebrow in sight, my father had dubbed my beautiful baby son Sir Denis – after bushy-browed Denis Healey, recently appointed Chancellor of the Exchequer.

Budds Farm
15 August 1974

It was very pleasant having a surprise visit from you and Sir Denis. Does the latter wish for a year's subscription to the 'Investor's Chronicle' for Christmas?

The Crumblings
[1974]

I hope Sir Denis thrives in the heat; children, unable to grab a large gin and tonic for revival, are liable to find it trying.

Budds Farm
28 August 1974

My respects to Sir Denis. If he cries, try whispering 'Directors'
Fees' to him.

La Morgue
Burghclere
7 September 1974

Best love to Sir Denis. If he's fractious, he's probably worrying
about the wealth tax.

The Old Sludge Heap
Great Ullage
Berks
3 January 1975

I'm glad to hear you and Sir Denis are to look in shortly. How
is he reacting to the present economic crisis? I shall be pleased
to hear his views.

Budds Farm
Whit Monday 1975

How are you all? I trust my grandson is enjoying a life divided
somewhat unequally into periods for eating and repose. How
lovely it would be if only life could continue along those lines

with certain minor adjustments. Perhaps one day it will. After all, thrift has become a vice. It may follow that work will come to be regarded as mere selfish indulgence.

The Old Ice House
Shiverings
16 November [mid-1970s]

I enclose a photograph of myself at that I age I did not look totally unlike Piers. What a dear little innocent boy I was! And when I think what happened to me since.

Maisons des Demi-Morts
6 April 1976

I hope Piers relished his second birthday. What a ghastly world the poor child is growing up in! By the time he is fifteen this country will probably be occupied by the Chinese.

Budds Farm
21 May 1976

As Vice-President of the Burghclere and Newtown Population Explosion Prevention Association, I deeply deplore your current position. However as your father I must conceal my true sentiments and send you good wishes and the hope that you experience the Best of British luck. I trust the produce will turn out to be a girl; on the whole girls tend to be less tiresome than boys. What are you going to call her? How about Matilda or Martha? In Basingstoke three out of five girls are named Samantha; the boys are usually Kevin, Garth or Wayne.

Best love,

xx D

My second baby was on the way.

The Lazar House
Burghclere
4 December 1976

I hope you are not feeling too awful waiting for this infant to arrive. I really am sorry for you. If men had to produce children, the birth-rate would rapidly fall to zero. Life here is fairly dull and I am thinking of joining a punk rock group to cheer myself up. I wish you did not live so far away as we can so seldom have a laugh together. Anyway, my sincere good wishes for a happy outcome to your present condition. I am betting on a boy. Why not call him Percy after my great-uncle whose sole claim to distinction, in his nineties, was to be the oldest living Old Etonian?

Best love,

xx D

The Old Damp Barn
Burghclere
1 May [late 1970s]

I wonder what sort of life my grandsons are in for. Things can change a bit in three generations. My grandfather could have watched public executions – possibly did – lived at a time when appendicitis was usually fatal, took part in the suppression of the Indian Mutiny, attended the Great Exhibition in Hyde Park and wore black for a year after a relation died. Though never a rich man, he seldom had fewer than six servants indoors. He went to church at least once every Sunday. I think one of the biggest changes in my own life has been the decline in the power and influence of the middle and upper middle classes since the last war, and the lowering of their standard of living. The previous war destroyed the aristocracy which has now virtually ceased to exist. I expect your children are destined to live in an egalitarian society.

Love to all,

RM

Budds Farm
[Late 1970s]

Please tell Piers that Nigel Spoon Basset invariably spoons his porridge through a straw and that his favourite drink is iced goat's milk. His mother is compelled to keep a lady goat called Vanessa Redgrave.

Budds Farm
7 December [late 1970s]

I much admired the pluck of your younger son in disagreeable circumstances, while his elder brother clearly does not miss much and comes out with some telling observations.

The Crumblings
4 August [early 1980s]

How is the saucy Piers? What worries me about him is that he already possesses a sense of the ridiculous, a fearful barrier to success in life. He has wit and intelligence and his phraseology is most original for a boy of his age. I can't see him ever joining the National Front or playing football for Newcastle United.

As for Nicholas, I think he will have a very happy life, being good at games and with a sense of fun. I can see from the way he swings a golf club or kicks a ball that he will enjoy school.

Budds Farm
[Early 1980s]

Piers has a lot of charm and his success with older women is an interesting clue to the form his life will take once he has crossed the murky stream of puberty. Nicholas possesses vivacity and determination: I shall be surprised if he fails to make a success of his life. He might make an excellent soldier.

'Eventide' Home for Distressed or Mentally Afflicted Members of the Middle Classes
[1980s]

Thank you for your informative and entirely legible letter. I am glad to hear the Torday family is prospering. You will find the characteristics of your children are continually changing:

Piers will probably end up as prop forward for Gosforth and Nicholas running a successful ladies' hair-dressing establishment in SW1.

14b Via Dolorosa
Burghclere
8 December 1983

Don't worry too much about my elder grandson. I expect he's a lot tougher than you think. Of course school isn't as much pleasure as a week at the Ritz in Paris. However, most boys learn the useful lesson that life is usually uncomfortable, mostly unfair and that what you are taught is 95 per cent useless.

Budds Farm
11 January [early 1980s]

I suppose Piers is back at school. I don't think any boy likes going back to school: I'm sure I didn't although my home life was anything but a happy one. I always blubbed a bit when I said goodbye to Mabel who I suppose gave me more happiness than any other woman I have ever met. I don't suppose Piers relished going back but I am sure he is not one of those boys to whom the break with home life is almost unbearable. In his quiet way I think he has plenty of pluck. I read the following in bed this morning at 3 a.m. when in the throes of what my old friend Dermot Daly called 'that horrible insomnia':

Going to school, the cab's at the door,
Mother is waiting to kiss me once more,
Father looks sad and gives me a tip,
Poor little Mary is pouting her lip.

I can recollect Pop giving me a tip, but if my mother ever kissed me even once, the incident has eluded my memory. However 'old men forget, etc., etc.'

The Miller's House
4 July [mid 1980s]

I shall accept your invitation to stay. I shall bring boughs of freshly cut holly to flog my grandsons if they fail to grovel sufficiently.

The Miller's House
18 November [mid 1980s]

How is life up in the frozen north? I had a nice letter from Piers complaining about the cold. All schools are cold; hence chilblains. Boys from day school do much better in exams as they can swot away in the evening in nice warm houses instead of fumbling in Greek dictionaries with frozen fingers in some hideous school room, the temperature of which is about 47 degrees F. I sent Piers quite a nice diary. A fairly useless present as most boys use a diary for 3 days then never open it again.

When my parents ventured up the motorway to 'the frozen

north', they were the most delightful and appreciative guests. Christmases – often a battleground back in Berkshire – abounded in peace and goodwill. When my mother's stocking from my father consisted of two bargain bars of Lifebuoy soap and a pair of gardening gloves, she received them with exemplary graciousness. Treasured grandparents, their visits to us are amongst the happiest of my family memories.

The Ruins
Burghclere
27 October [early 1980s]

Piers is gentle and charming and possesses a lively wit for a boy of his age. I don't think you need worry too much about Nicholas being happy at school, now or in the future. I think he is a natural games player and will be able to look after himself pretty well.

Sport – football and Newcastle United in particular – remains a top pleasure for Nick.

The Miller's House
10 August [mid 1980s]

I enjoyed seeing my grandsons. I will avoid criticising them as even the limpest criticism of someone else's children can secure you a lifelong enemy. I can remember painful instances in my own family, the cause of the ill-feeling invariably being comments by my mother made with the deliberate intention of causing pain.

Piers has great charm and no lack of humour. It must be a relief to you that he is in no apparent danger of contracting athlete's heart! Nicholas is a born games-player but he is very far removed from being stupid; quite the reverse in fact. He is at any rate shrewd enough to appreciate that he has got his loving mother pretty well taped! I think he will enjoy 95 per cent of his school life and will never be short of friends.

Love to you all,

xx D

Hypothermia House
22 February [mid 1980s]

I had a letter from Piers which I much appreciated. For the young, writing a letter is a fearful fatigue. There used to be an old saying in my regiment: 'It is infinitely preferable to incur a slight reprimand than to undergo an irksome fatigue.'

The Olde Igloo
Burghclere
17 January [mid 1980s]

How are the scholar and the athlete? I expect the scholar will end up a champion wrestler, while the athlete will win a Balliol scholarship and attend intellectual parties where he will:

> 'recite in a falsetto voice
> the earlier works of Mr Joyce'.

Those lines were written by a poet, long dead, whose description of a Landseer painting at Balmoral included the lines:

'And dachshunds, of the thin and wan sort,
Retrieving grouse for the Prince Consort'.

The Olde House with No Loo Paper
29 December [mid 1980s]

Problem for Jane and Piers: punctuate the following so that it makes sense: That that is that that is not is not is not that so.

Easy quotation to remember to impress educated friends when your sons are raising hell: 'Sunt pueri pueri: pueri puerilia tractant' (children are children: (therefore) children do childish things).

Budds Farm
[Early 1980s]

Piers writes amusing letters and seems keen on gardening. An embryo Beverley Nicholls? You can't tell: boys change so quickly and he'll probably finish by being the Judo champion for N. Yorkshire. Nicholas seems the merry extrovert and with luck he may stay that way. I can't visualise him yet as an avant-garde poet winning a J. P. Sartre scholarship at Sussex University.

Beverley Nicholls was a prolific writer in many genres, including books on gardening.

The Miller's House
[Mid 1980s]

Very few children, for obvious reasons, are at their best in the presence of their parents. I think Nicholas comes into that category. He is very good fun when you are out for a walk with the dogs, less amusing when you are exuding maternal care and affection in his near vicinity. I think he is always likely to be happy and successful at school. I get the impression that au fond he is quick witted and decidedly intelligent. As long as you're not *too* nice to him, I am confident that he will turn out to be an exceptionally agreeable boy.

Chez Nidnod
3 September [late 1980s]

I hope Piers will not change too quickly at Eton. It is always a shock for a loving mother when the previously apple-cheeked loved one returns for the holidays 6ft tall, stubble on the chin and rich crop of acne rosacea on the forehead. Most boys tend to be bloody from 14 to 17, some up to 67 or even later.

The Miller's House
29 December 1987

P. F. T. continues to impress me most favourably and he has a very charming nature. Most boys of his age are beginning to develop spots and bloody-mindedness but he seems happily clear of both. N. L. T. has much to be said in his favour and is obviously very bright.

The Miller's House
26 January [late 1980s]

Thought for the week: 'Stubborn and ignorant, should make
an excellent parent', from a report on a Wellington schoolboy.
  With love to you all,
  D xx

*Happy days! Now, sadly, we move on to the last lap, but my
father's wit was as healthy as ever.*

14

El Geriatrica

'"Eventide" Home for Distressed or Mentally Afflicted
Members of the Middle Classes
[1980s]

Dearest Jane
What have I in common with Kubla Kahn, Talleyrand,
William Pitt, Bacon (F.), Wesley, Darwin, Fielding, Milton,
Newton and Ben Johnson? The answer, my dear child, is
gout. Dr H. Ellis wrote: "Gout occurs so often, in such
extreme forms, and in men of such pre-eminent intellectual
ability, that it is impossible not to regard it as having a real
association with such ability." Ellis added that typical gout
sufferers are 'eccentric and irascible'.

Love,
RFM'

Black's Medical Dictionary was the best thumbed book at the
various addresses at which my parents apparently lived:
The Old Crumblings, Chateau Geriatrica. The Old Lazar
House, 17b Via Dolorosa, The Eventide Home, Les Deux

Gagas, Bonkersville and, most frequently, Chez Nidnod are just a handful.

Not only my father but my mother and brother dipped deep into the sinister pages of this medical bible, combing them urgently for symptoms. My mother was keen on self diagnosis; my brother Lupin, with very challenging health problems of his own, became a fount of extraordinary medical information, maintaining a personal drug pharmacy from which he prescribed for others in extreme circumstances; my father, ever fearful that he was well within reach of the grim reaper, anticipated any new pain or discomfort to be the signal towards the departure gate.

The prospect of Christmas could bring on a whole new inventory of near fatal maladies.

Pronouncements on his death peppered my father's conversation for as far back as I can remember. The effect could be lowering but his robust presence happily prevented me from taking them too seriously. My mother did – of course. To these ruminations my father would add further caustic comment: 'No one is indispensable', to which my mother would retort, 'Your trouble is you are just a cynic.' Cynicism was an armour my father wore well – appreciated the most by those who were least near to him.

From my father's letters I learnt of the lives – and deaths – of many people of whom I had never heard, let alone known. At the time, in the natural self absorption of youth and the consuming preoccupations of the present, these vignettes and obituaries were rather wasted on me. Nowadays, I understand full well the gentle solace it brings to commit these reflections to paper – I do it myself.

Memories of childhood and youth become sharper in old age; what happened yesterday morning is forgotten but the distant past can be recalled in effortless detail. My father's nearly photographic memory enabled him to paint vivid period pictures of his childhood and youth in his letters.

I never asked my father where his epistolary obsession with skin conditions had erupted from – all those little rashes, spots, warts and growths which he liked to attribute to many an innocent individual who crossed his path. It was an immediate way of debunking just about anyone from a millionaire racehorse owner to a café waitress. There was a large ration of carbuncles amongst the bill of blemishes described in his letters. The fact that my father was scarcely squeamish on paper was not equalled by an ability, in the flesh, to cope with even the smallest wound, ache or pain in any practical manner – that he left to my mother.

Roger had a few problems with God. In his book, the Almighty was sorely lacking in a sense of humour. My father had spent too many hours on his knees in school chapels without any noticeably helpful answers to his prayers manifesting themselves. As for the mercy of the Almighty in the trials of war, God, in his omnipotence, had not seemed prepared to intervene in any discernible manner.

If he did not turn to God in his later years, my father could still be moved by a good hymn, or carol – particularly if it was his own version:

> Hark the herald angels sing,
> Beecham's pills are just the thing.
> Peace on Earth and mercy mild,
> Two for a man and one for a child.

The hymn with the line 'Let me to thy bosom fly' convinced him as a child that there was a weird little insect – the bosom fly – buzzing about somewhere.

As old age gripped him and his health declined, he was

increasingly wont to quote: 'Oh death where is thy sting – Grave where is thy victory?'

Shortly after his eighty-second birthday in late November 1991, this plea was answered.

'I don't want a memorial service, just a quick fry-up', my father had written as a postscript in one of his letters to me.

As she carefully organized his memorial service, my mother said to me, classically: 'If your father was here he would never let me do this.'

In contradiction to his oft-expressed edict, my father was not in any respect 'dispensable'. He was of a quality that was irreplaceable.

For all his intelligence and talent, my father was a deeply modest man who never applauded himself for his achievements. If he did not believe in the possibility of resurrection, he has been reincarnated through his inimitable letters, bringing laughter and pleasure to many.

My Dearest Jane . . .

Budds Farm
10 February [late 1960s]

I did a lot of gardening today and nearly had a little stroke; it is always dangerous when your ears start popping and you think you hear the Luton Girl's Choir singing 'Jesus Wants You for a Sunbeam'. I knew an elderly woman who had a minor stroke when packing her suitcase to go and stay near Ipswich for the weekend. The stroke was down her right side but she pluckily went on packing with her left.

Budds Farm
October [late 1960s]

A very old friend of mine died last week; he had a coronary
and fell off a bar stool clutching his glass to the end. Not an
ignoble finish for a man whose failing was too much charm
and too many friends.

Budds Farm
9 March [early 1970s]

I am now off to order a new suit . . . something that will
proclaim my inherently reactionary nature and reluctance to
compromise with this piddling era in which my declining years
have to be spent. I'm thinking of leaving all my money, which
isn't much, to the newly formed Ashford Hill Community
Centre run by drop-outs from the meteorological department
of Bracknell University.

Budds Farm
28 August 1974

I have bought two new pairs of spectacles at reckless expense.
One pair I can't see through at all. The other was made for an
individual with a head like a giant pumpkin and falls off at
the slightest movement.

Les Deux Gagas
Bonkersville
Berks
[1974]

I am now a retired man, almost at the end of the road. One more river and that old river is Jordan, one more river, just one more river to cross. I hope you saw me in a longish TV interview last Friday. I think it was quite good. Needless to say no one at Budds Farm could bother to watch! Perhaps morbid self-interest to the exclusion of everything else is a family failing. I become an OAP this week. As Anthony Powell wrote, 'Getting old is like being increasingly punished for a crime you have never committed.'

Love
xx D

The Ministry of White Fish
[Mid 1970s]

I saw an orthopaedic surgeon from Oxford about my knee last week. I rather liked him (Dr Spivey) as he is young, not given to bullshit and keen on racing and gardening. He said an operation would be painful and possibly unsuccessful; the joints are worn out and cannot be replaced. I have just got to put up with an infirmity which may get progressively worse. I must not kneel in the garden or walk more than 2 miles. The danger is that the leg will get crooked and I shall end up looking like a retired jockey.

How grisly prospects were for knackered knees back then.

Budds Farm
[1974]

After 2 glasses of Cyprus sherry these days I am apt to think
I am Halfdene the Dane; and behave accordingly.

Chez Nidnod
Monday [early 1970s]

I went to the funeral of a good friend of mine last week. The
vicar, who looked like a well-worn lavatory brush, started
the service by appealing for money for the church. This
annoyed me. The address was entrusted to a grandson, a
priggish youth of 19 who chose to give a pompous sermon
advising the older members of the congregation to study
the Bible as they would be 'for it' themselves before long
themselves and it would be foolish to leave things too late!
I could have kicked him down the aisle! Finally a Royal
Artillery trumpeter played 'Lights Out' but unfortunately this
did not deter the organist from blasting away at Bach on his
instrument. The resulting din was horrific!
  Love,
  RFM

Budds Farm
2 February 1975

Death came as a relief to the poor old Duke of Norfolk whose
arteries had ceased to function and no petrol was reaching
the carburettor.

Bernard, Duke of Norfolk, had a racing stable at Arundel.

My parents used to stay with him and his wife Lavinia, sister of my father's notorious chum, Lord Belper.

Budds Farm
14 October 1978

We are all much saddened by John Pope's death. I have known him since 1922 and he was a loyal and generous friend to your mother and myself. Behind all the jokes, the stories and the ragging, he was a man of high principles, immensely public spirited, and devoted to his faith and his Church. He set high standards for himself and never fell below them.

The House of a Thousand Draughts
Burghclere
17 November [mid 1970s]

Most people I know are either dying or getting married (the latter the worse misfortune) and in either case I am faced with unwanted expense. This week's boring quotation: 'Le bonheur consiste simplement à se fermer les yeux' (Happiness consists simply in shutting your eyes) – Baudelaire.

The Many Leakings
Burghclere
31 October 1981

A sad week for me as Gerry Feilden, a good friend for 52 years, died very suddenly. Two days previously he had asked Nidnod and me to join him in Bali for a holiday! Last

Tuesday he lunched with friends at White's, drove home and died reading the evening paper. Not a bad way to end the long journey. He was 77 and his life had been happy and successful.

A fellow Coldstreamer, my father had been second-in-command to Gerry Feilden in the BEF in France in 1940. Ultimately he became a major-general and senior steward at the Jockey Club. An annual race at Newmarket – the Feilden Stakes – commemorates him.

Budds Farm
19 February 1978

Don't let your husband work too hard. After all, youth passes fairly swiftly and it is very seldom in later life that one regrets memories of self-indulgence and extravagance. After all, what on earth is the point of temptation if no one ever yields to it? I don't regret periods of indolence etc. in my twenties; only time wasting, lack of enterprise and allowing myself to be bored when there was so much for me to do.
    Best love,
    xx D

The Old Slagheap
Burghclere
17 December [early 1980s]

The late H. Balzac wrote in 'La Femme de Trente Ans': 'La jeune fille n'a qu'une coquetterie, et croit avoir tout dit quand elle a quitté son vêtement; mais la femme en a d'innombrables et se cache sous mille voiles; enfin elle caresse toutes les vanités, et la novice n'en flatte qu'une.' I thought that might cheer you up now that you are over thirty and on the road to the dreaded kingdom of Old Bagdom from which no woman ever returns. Men over thirty head swiftly for Old Bufferdom which is rather worse. Another quotation from Balzac: 'Il est facile de nier ce que l'on ne comprend pas.' I feel about 97. I have just been reading about a man who is convinced he will live to 300 because he has never washed his face in hot water.

    Love,

    xx D

'Cheering' thoughts for the over thirties? More of an exercise in French comprehension.

The Crumblings
Burghclere
[Early 1980s]

I have to have the wound on my leg dressed daily by the district nurse. Nurse Simcox went on holiday and told me that Nurse Leech would call here instead at the usual time. At 9.30 a.m. sharp the doorbell rang and there was a charming little blonde creature, quite saucy but a teeny bit dirty, I thought. I ushered her into the sitting room and began to remove my trousers. This seemed to surprise her, even alarm her, and she said 'There must be a mistake, I am here from the farm with a tractor to harrow your field.' Thus as distressing and humiliating scene was narrowly averted. Nurse Leech arrived shortly afterwards.

Chateau Geriatrica
Saturday [mid 1980s]

My blood pressure has been a bit high lately and the other day someone reminded me (unkindly) of the old blood pressure song which starts off:

> Singing in the brain, I've got that singing in the brain,
> It's a horrible feeling, blood pressure again.

I believe there is an alcoholics hymn that begins:

> Lead blindly tight, amid the revolving room.

The Old Crumblings
[Mid 1980s]

Where did you leave those pills you picked up at the surgery for me? I can't find them, not even in the deep freeze. If I am without them for 48 hours, I run the risk of cardiac arrest, impetigo and a rare disease called 'curates clap' caused by eating green rhubarb.

Maison des Gagas Kintbury
[Mid 1980s]

A lot of lunch and dinner parties lately. Mostly jolly young people, barely a day over 68. Your godfather Brig. Robin has been very poorly with a poisoned toe. Possibly a love bite from the redhead in a local shoe shop. Lucky it was only his toe, I say!

The Miller's House
[Mid 1980s]

I went to the surgery for a chat with Doc Yates: we get on pretty well together and he is certainly nicer than the average GP. He thinks I may last out till Christmas but some days I'm as weak as a vole.

The Miller's House
17 March [mid 1980s]

People are dying like flies round here. Our charming friend Dame Ann Parker Bowles dropped dead without warning two days ago. I first knew her fifty years ago when she was a real 'Tatler' girl of that era, pretty, lively and more intelligent than most. Her father won the Derby with Parthia. Pre-war, you could not have pictured her as Girl Guide yet she became a most efficient head of that body. She was mad on racing and was a fellow committee member of mine on the Berkshire Animal Health Trust. Her very amusing husband died quietly one morning while reading the 'Sporting Life' after breakfast. I knew her father, Sir Humphrey de Trafford, pretty well.

Dame Ann Parker Bowles was the mother-in-law to Camilla, now the Duchess of Cornwall. Her Coldstreamer father, Sir Humphrey de Trafford MC, was a prominent racehorse owner.

The Miller's House
15 May 1987

Nidnod is now all set for her stay in hospital. Though not,

413

happily, a dangerous operation, it is not a pleasant one and she is being calm and courageous. How lucky that women are far braver over health than men are! The dogs are going to be very unhappy without her and I myself will be completely lost.

My mother was soon home and up and about again.

The Miller's House
16 January 1987

I enclose a small birthday present which will just about cover the cost of a couple of bottles of tonic water. Oh, for by-gone happier days when a new novel by a leading author could be obtained for 7/6d! Happy birthday and best of luck! Looking back 78 years, my life seems to be an extraordinary mixture of hideous misfortune and quite unmerited good luck. Perhaps they cancel out, but I don't really think so. I don't actually regret much except appalling ingratitude, odious snobbishness, moral cowardice and a few other things I won't mention!
    Best love,
    xx D

My father's lifelong advice was: 'My dear child, life is essentially unfair and the sooner you realise it the better.' I have had more than my fair share of good luck.

The Miller's House
17 January [late 1980s]

Very many happy returns for your birthday. When I think

of what has happened in my lifetime, I wonder what sort of world it will be when you reach 80! I imagine the population of this country will be composed largely of incontinent geriatrics who can be cured of everything bar the ghastly frailties of old age. Enjoy yourself while you still can.

Very best love and come and see me before Demon Moss uproots my middle stump.

xx D

The Miller's House
16 June [late 1980s]

Just back from London. I watched the Queen's Birthday Parade on TV. I rode in the parade in 1947 but of course we had a king then! My horse was called Virile (a gelding!) and was frequently ridden by senior policemen at race meetings in the suburbs. He used to pee when the National Anthem was played. We went to a huge drinks party at the Guards Club. Purgatory! Nidnod has given me an eye lotion which has virtually robbed me of my sight. I've had to buy a new electric pad – no warmth, it's like being kissed by an Eskimo. I shan't go to Ascot. I first went in 1958. I think I've had my ration.

The Miller's House
3 May 1990

I recently paid my first visit to London this year and went to a lunch at Boodle's for Coldstream officers who served in Egypt and Palestine between 1937 and 1945. There were 24 acceptors among the survivors and two I remembered as spry young officers turned out to be the Bishop of Lincoln and the Regius Professor of Modern History at Oxford. The Duke of Devonshire said my strong language made him nervous!

The Many Leakings
Burghclere
31 October [early 1980s]

I am a great admirer of Gertrude Bell, one of the outstanding Englishwomen of this century. She was born in Co. Durham and I think there is a memorial to her in a church not far from you. It consists of a translation she made of a verse in Persian:

> Thus said the Poet: When death comes to you
> All ye whose life-sand through the hour glass slips,
> He lays two fingers on your ears, and two
> Upon your eyes he lays, one on your lips,
> Whispering: Silence!

I'd rather like to see it.
Best love,
xx D

I wish we had managed to visit Gertrude Bell's memorial at the church at East Porton, in North Yorkshire. These beautiful lines were from her translation of the works of the Persian poet, Hafez, and were later inscribed on the card for my father's thanksgiving service.

Budds Farm
Sunday [late 1980s]

I enjoyed most of this summer but frankly I do not anticipate seeing another. If you can only remember some of the old jokes, that is as much immortality as I expect.

xxxx D

My Dearest Father – We have. xxxx